# Queer Multicultural Social Justice Education: Curriculum (and Identity) Development Through Performance

A Volume in:
Research for Social Justice:
Personal~Passionate~Participatory Inquiry

*Series Editors:*
Ming Fang He
JoAnn Phillion

# Research for Social Justice:
# Personal~Passionate~Participatory Inquiry

*Series Editors*
Ming Fang He
*Georgia Southern University*

JoAnn Phillion
*Purdue University*

**Books in This Series:**

*The Blab of the Paved: "Bad Kids" and the School They Called Family* (2020)
Jeff Spanke

*Culturally Responsive Pedagogy:*
*Promising Practices for African American Male Students* (2020)
Dennisha Murff

*(Un)Learning to Teach Through Intercultural Professional Development* (2017)
Candace Schlein

*A Reader of Narrative and Critical Lenses on*
*Intercultural Teaching and Learning* (2016)
Candace Schlein & Barbara Garii

*Internationalizing Teaching and Teacher Education for Equity*
*Engaging Alternative Knowledges Across Ideological Borders* (2016)
Jubin Rahatzad, Hannah Dockrill, Suniti Sharma, & JoAnn Phillion

*Beyond Retention: Cultivating Spaces of Equity, Justice, and*
*Fairness for Women of Color in U.S. Higher Education* (2016)
Brenda L. H. Marina & Sabrina N. Ross

*Are You Mixed? A War Bride's Granddaughter's Narrative of Lives*
*In-Between Contested Race, Gender, Class, and, Power* (2016)
Sonia E. Janis

*Internationalizing Teacher Education for Social Justice:*
*Theory, Research, and Practice* (2014)
Suniti Sharma, JoAnn Phillion, Jubin Rahatzad, & Hannah L. Sasser

*Canaries Reflect on the Mine: Dropouts' Stories of Schooling* (2012)
Jeanne Cameron

*Esperanza School: A Grassroots Community School in Honduras* (2012)
Eloisa Rodriguez

*Dreams Deferred: Dropping Out and Struggling Forward* (2009)
Chris Liska Carger

*Personal ~ Passionate ~ Participatory: Inquiry into Social Justice in Education* (2008)
Ming Fang He & JoAnn Phillion

# Queer Multicultural Social Justice Education: Curriculum (and Identity) Development Through Performance

Michelle Lynn Knaier

INFORMATION AGE PUBLISHING, INC.
Charlotte, NC • www.infoagepub.com

**Library of Congress Cataloging-In-Publication Data**

The CIP data for this book can be found on the Library of Congress website (loc.gov).

Paperback: 978-1-64802-443-6
Hardcover: 978-1-64802-444-3
E-Book: 978-1-64802-445-0

# CONTENTS

## PART I

### AWARENESS OF SELF (AND OTHERS): A COMMON THREAD

# ABSTRACT

*Keywords:* autoethnography, identity awareness, multicultural education, queer curriculum development, queer multicultural social justice teacher education, queer theory

In this book I examine how performing (and sharing our) autoethnographic explorations as curriculum development strategies, and using autoethnographic modes (e.g., storytelling) as curriculum, may provide education curriculum workers, and explorers, with opportunities to explore their own multicultural identities (e.g., race/ethnicity, socioeconomic status, exceptionality, religion, sexual orientation, and gender), how their identities may intersect with curriculum development, and their stories alongside those of others. In Part One, I tell three (hi)stories highlighting how multicultural education, queer theory, and autoethnography support the practice of identity awareness (of self and others). In Part Two, I share nine explorations developed for this project of creating a queer multicultural social justice education curriculum, along with my performances of and reflections on each exploration, which include how *performing* the explorations impacted their development. Finally, in Part Three, I apply these ideas to my practice of becoming a queer educator. I reflect on some of the tensions I wrestled with, on becoming aware of myself as a teacher and a student *simultaneously*, and on my use of language and curriculum development practices. In sum, I advocate for queering

*Queer Multicultural Social Justice Education: Curriculum (and Identity) Development Through Performance,* pages vii–viii.

autoethnography and using it for curriculum development—thus, simultaneously queering the act of curriculum development—for the purposes of developing identity awareness (of self and others) and honing queer multicultural social justice education curriculum development practices. During your engagement with this text, I invite you—the reader—to reflect on these practices, perform the explorations, and ponder how these explorations may impact your curriculum development practices. *I also encourage you to share your stories.*

# DEDICATION PAGE

*Black Lives Matter.*

# RESEARCH FOR SOCIAL JUSTICE

## Personal~Passionate~Participatory Inquiry

### Ming Fang He and JoAnn Phillion

*Research for Social Justice: Personal~Passionate~Participatory Inquiry* is a book series which features social justice research on life in schools, families, and communities. This work connects the personal with the political, the theoretical with the practical, and research with social and educational change. The inquiries demonstrate three distinct and interconnected qualities. Each is personal, compelled by values and experiences researchers bring to the work. Each is passionate, grounded in a commitment to social justice concerns of people and places under consideration. Each is participatory, built on long-term, heart-felt engagement, and shared efforts. The principle aspects of the inquiries that distinguish them from others are that researchers are not detached observers, nor putatively objective recorders, but active participants in schools, families, and communities. Researchers engaged in this form of inquiry have explicit research agendas that focus on equity, equality, and social justice. Rather than aiming solely at traditional educational research outcomes, positive social and educational change is the focal outcome of inquiry.

*Queer Multicultural Social Justice Education: Curriculum (and Identity) Development Through Performance,* pages xi–xiv.
Copyright © 2021 by Information Age Publishing

Researchers engaged in personal~passionate~participatory inquiry in this series are diverse and their inquiries are far ranging in terms of content, people, and geographic locations studied. Their studies reflect new and exciting ways of researching and representing experiences of disenfranchised, underrepresented, and invisible groups, and challenge stereotypical or deficit perspectives on these groups. It is our hope that this book series will inspire preservice and in-service teachers, educators, educational researchers, administrators, and educational policy makers to commit to the enactment of educational and social change that fosters equity, equality, and social justice.

The work in this book series draws on diverse research traditions which promote social justice (Ayers et al., 2009) and the "Democratic Ideal" (Dewey, 1916, pp. 86–88) in education and life. The work of Du Bois (1903/1994), Cooper (1892/1988), Woodson (1933/1977), Freire (1970), and Ayers (2006) has also influenced social justice work in terms of its emphasis on the emancipatory, participatory, and social activist aspects of research. This work builds upon narrative inquiry (Clandinin & Connelly, 2000; Schubert & Ayers, 1999), particularly cross-cultural and multicultural narrative inquiry (He, 2003; He & Phillion, 2008; Phillion, 2002; Phillion & He, 2008; Phillion et al., 2005) in response to recognition of the complexity of human experience in increasingly diversified societies. These researchers incorporate narrative, story, autobiography, memoir, fiction, oral history, documentary film, painting, and poetry into inquiries. One special quality of their inquiries that distinguish them from other forms of educational research lies in understanding experience in its own terms rather than categorizing experience according to predetermined structures and theories (Phillion, 1999). Their inquiries are "peopled" with characters, rather than filled with categories and labels. In some forms of traditional educational research, experience is seen, shaped, and written about by the researcher using theoretically derived forms; in effect the experience is determined by the theory. Experience is the starting point of these inquiries and is in the forefront at every stage of research. Their inquiries arise from experiences of researchers and participants, rather than being formulated as abstract research questions, and they proceed by continual reference to experience as field texts are collected, analyzed, and interpreted, and as meanings are crafted.

Researchers engaged in this form of inquiry also draw on critical race theory (Gutierrez-Jones, 2001; hooks, 1991; Ladson-Billings, 1998, 2003; Parker et al., 1999; Stovall, 2005, 2016) and use stories to disclose hidden and silenced narratives of suppressed and underrepresented groups to counter metanarratives that portray these groups as deficient and inferior. They ask themselves questions about what is missing from the *official story* that will make the problems of the oppressed more understandable. By telling counter stories, researchers recognize the importance of commitment to equity and social justice and their obligation to link inquiry to social and educational change. The explicit aim of democratic and social justice work is to engage with oppressed groups and individuals and empower them to take effective action toward more just and humane conditions.

Three distinct and interconnected qualities, *personal~passionate~participato ry*, permeate the process of these social justice inquiries. Researchers not only collect, but often live in the stories of people with whom they engage in inquiry. They position stories collected in historical, socio-political, economic, linguistic, and cultural contexts, and contextualize their inquiries within struggles of under-represented individuals and groups. Stories are presented in life-like ways; readers vicariously experience complexities, contradictions and dilemmas of people's lives. There is a sense of "being there" and a sense of urgency for change. The stories told challenge orthodoxy, awaken critical consciousness, and create possibilities for change.

The work featured in this book series, embedded in life in schools, communities, and societies on the one hand, and powerful ideas of being human with strong commitment to a just society on the other, are at the heart of social justice work. Researchers begin with conscious reflection on experience to challenge assumptions, "to raise embarrassing questions," and "to confront orthodoxy and dogma" (Ayers, 2006, p. 85). They listen to "issues that marginalized or disadvantaged people speak of with excitement, anger, fear, or hope..." (Ayers, 2006, p. 88). They learn directly from individuals and communities about problems and obstacles they face and explore possible solutions by drawing upon the experience and knowledge of participants. Researchers demonstrate strong commitment to the plight of their participants and the injustice embedded in the larger society. This commitment permeates every aspect of life, begins with small changes, and expands to larger contexts.

Personal~passionate~participatory inquiry thrives on the researcher's passionate involvement, strong commitment, and unfaltering advocacy for disenfranchised, underrepresented, and invisible individuals and groups. This passion, commitment, and advocacy can not be cultivated in isolation. Rather, it calls for researchers to work with allies in schools and communities, to take to heart the shared concerns of individuals and groups, to build a community to develop strategies for the enactment of educational and social change that fosters equity, equality, social justice, freedom, and human possibility. Such a community can only flourish when the efforts of researchers join with the efforts of all educational stakeholders—pre-service and in-service teachers, educators, administrators, educational policy makers, students, parents, and community members. We hope that the inquiries featured in this series will help social justice researchers and workers of this community move beyond boundaries, transgress orthodoxies, and build a participatory movement to promote a more balanced, fair, and equitable human condition. An expanded community, such as this, embodies possibilities and creates hope for more fulfilling, more equitable, more humane lives in an increasingly diversifying world.

## REFERENCES

Ayers, W. C. (2006). Trudge toward freedom: Educational research in the public interest. In G. Ladson-Billings & W. F. Tate (Eds.), *Education research in the public interest: Social justice, action and policy* (pp. 81–97). Teachers College Press.

Ayers, W., Quinn, T., & Stovall, D. (2009). *Handbook of social justice in education.* Routledge.

Clandinin, D. J., & Connelly, F. M. (2000). *Narrative inquiry.* Jossey-Bass.

Cooper, A. (1892/1988). *A voice from the South.* Oxford University Press.

Dewey, J. (1916). *Democracy and education: An introduction to the philosophy of education.* Free Press.

Du Bois, W. E. B. (1903/1994). *The souls of Black folks.* Fine Creative Media.

Freire, P. (1970). *A pedagogy of the oppressed.* Seabury.

Gutierrez-Jones, C. (2001). *Critical race narratives: A study of race, rhetoric, and injury.* New York University Press.

He, M. F. (2003). *A river forever flowing: Cross-cultural lives and identities in the multi-cultural landscape.* Information Age.

He, M. F., & Phillion, J. (2008). *Personal~passionate~participatory inquiry into social justice in education.* In M. F. He & J. Phillion (Eds.), *Research for social justice: Personal~passionate~participatory inquiry.* Information Age Publishing.

hooks, b. (1991). Narratives of struggle. In P. Mariani (Ed.), *Critical fictions: The politics of imaginative writing* (pp. 53–61). Bay.

Ladson-Billings, G. (1998). Just what is critical race theory and what's it doing in a nice field like education? *International Journal of Qualitative Studies in Education, 11*(1), 7–24.

Ladson-Billings, G. (Ed.). (2003). *Critical race theory perspectives on the social studies: The profession, policies, and curriculum.* IAP.

Parker, L., Deyhle, D., & Villenas, S. (1999). *Critical race theory and qualitative studies in education.* Westview.

Phillion, J. (1999). Narrative and formalistic approaches to the study of multiculturalism. *Curriculum Inquiry, 29*(1), 129–141.

Phillion, J. (2002). *Narrative inquiry in a multicultural landscape: Multicultural teaching and learning.* Ablex.

Phillion, J., & He, M. F. (2009). Multicultural and cross-cultural narrative inquiry in educational research. *Thresholds in Education, 34*(1&2), 2–12.

Phillion, J., He, M. F., & Connelly, F. M. (Eds.). (2005). *Narrative and experience in multicultural education.* Sage.

Schubert, W. H., & Ayers, W. C. (Eds.) (1999). *Teacher lore: Learning from our own experience.* Educators International Press.

Stovall, D. (2005). A challenge to traditional theory: Critical race theory, African-American community organizers, and education. *Discourse: Studies in the Cultural Politics of Education, 26*(1), 95–108.

Stovall, D. (2016). *Born out of struggle: Critical race theory, school creation, and the politics of interruption.* State University of New York.

Woodson, C. G. (1933/1977). *The mis-education of the Negro.* Africa World Press.

# FOREWORD

### Kathryn M. Obenchain

Early in my graduate school career, and later than it should have been in my life, I was introduced to the term "multicultural education." One of my professors even labeled it as a "current trend" in education, possibly as an expectation that it would fade away. In many ways, my discovery of the early 1990s work of James Banks, Christine Bennett, Geneva Gay, Christine Sleeter, and others was a welcome validation of multiple unsettling sexist experiences, and their subsequent dismissal (by others), as real and relevant. While I found comfort from these well-respected scholars, I also experienced a crucial component of learning. Understanding multicultural education, its breadth, purposes, and its promises, was uncomfortable for me as a white, Protestant, cisgender, heterosexual woman from a rural, and predominately white, midwestern community. While I had individually experienced sexism and saw the structures of systemic sexism all around me, I now had to ask how I participated in, promoted, and benefited from other identities I claimed or that were assigned to me—including my identities as white, cisgender, and heterosexual, among others. As a former high school social studies teacher, I found myself questioning all those lessons about Manifest Destiny, Thomas Jefferson, the US Constitution, the World Wars, and the Cold War that I had taught. I was questioning my omission of so much US history like the women's movements, the Progressive Movement, the Harlem Renaissance, the Stonewall uprising, and so much more. As an educator and college graduate, why

*Queer Multicultural Social Justice Education: Curriculum (and Identity) Development Through Performance,* pages xv–xviii.

was a multicultural lens so new and unfamiliar to me? What damage had I done to my students through my teaching, given my assumptions of what was *normal* and my accompanying behavior as the teacher, the person in power? And what did all of this mean to me as someone studying to become a teacher educator?

These were, and are, questions that I continue to ask of myself. These questions require deliberate and focused examination because of another one of my evolving identities—that of a teacher educator. Thirty years into this career, the learning continues, and it remains uncomfortable, as it should. Learning is difficult intellectual work. This is precisely the space for Michelle Knaier's book. She has written a theoretically grounded, well-conceptualized, innovative, and accessible text, a curriculum, that has the potential to affect how all educators— pre-service, in-service, administrators, teacher educators—do their work in more socially just ways.

In this book, Michelle Knaier continues her mission to transform education by transforming teacher education into a socially just endeavor. This requires that teachers teach toward social justice. Michelle lays a strong theoretical and methodological foundation for queer multicultural social justice education in the early chapters of her book. The tenets of multicultural education which focus on identity examination provide a solid grounding for the need for self-awareness as a crucial early and sustainable practice. Michelle uses queer theory to undergird a disruptive process for examining identity, deconstructing and challenging normative beliefs, and resisting boundaries and labels, particularly as they relate to gender and sexuality in challenging heteronormativity, and all socially constructed identities. In this process of queering, Michelle's scholarship goes beyond an examination of personal identities and into our enacted identities as teachers and teacher educators. Using critical autoethnography, a methodology complementary to queer theory, Michelle describes and models a curriculum to facilitate the reader's critical self-examination. This masterful integration effectively makes the case for the relationship between theory and method with particular emphasis on the need to first, and then consistently, study their own lived experiences, beliefs, and assumptions.

From this theoretical and methodological work, in Part Two of Michelle's book, she models a queer curriculum development process through a series of nine lessons that she calls explorations, reminding us that language is important, having the power to position individuals and groups of individuals in destructive ways. Each exploration includes a description with suggested learning objectives as guidance and suggested readings. In addition to developing these explorations, Michelle shares her own exploration through each one, and I encourage each of you to spend time both with the structures of the explorations as well as the self-awareness process that Michelle shares. She lays bare her thinking, past and present pain, grief and joy, evolving questions, and some answers to those questions.

This process continues into Chapters Four and Five. Both of these chapters illustrate the recursive, critical, and continual reflection required to learn. She looks back into the first three chapters and her explorations, taking note of where she has changed and what she must do differently. She also looks forward to continued learning and the opportunities that it will bring, and to the necessity of this work. Michelle's book ends. There is a last page. However, the last two chapters make it clear that Michelle's explorations will continue, and she invites each of us, her readers, to join her. It is a worthwhile endeavor for each of us.

I am writing this foreword in the summer of 2020 during another divisive presidential campaign season and months into a pandemic that has killed tens of thousands of Americans, as well as hundreds of thousands around the globe. COVID-19 has disproportionally affected American communities of color and communities who continue to be systematically deprived of quality nutrition and health care, and limited economic opportunities, among other injustices. The abuses of unjust policing and legal systems are exposed to light in numbers and ways that are undeniable. The names of Breonna Taylor, George Floyd, and Ahmaud Arbery, are now a part of our collective conscience. Whether this exposure and accompanying protests propel the US forward into systemic changes that support a more just society remains unknown. However, I believe—I must believe—that education holds great power. Our work as educators, and specifically teacher educators, is essential. Our actions in creating a just, safe, welcoming, and rigorous learning environment for all students will create spaces for students to thrive individually and collectively. As teacher educators, we must do the same as we work and learn alongside pre-service teachers. As Michelle writes at the end of Chapter Two, her work facilitates

> the kind of education that provides opportunities for and encourages educators to examine and (de)construct identity and its espoused privileges; the kind of education that may increase my success as a teacher educator; and, certainly, the kind of education that would have provided the much needed support my young self deserved.

Michelle deserved, as do all students, to learn from teachers who are justice-oriented in their commitments and their actions.

Perhaps, as I continue to learn from Michelle, there is a better term than *student*. What if we unpack all of the assumptions that come with *student* and instead use the term *explorer*, as Michelle suggests or another term? As a teacher educator, my role, as is that of my colleagues, is to work and learn alongside pre-service teachers to critically, mindfully, and deliberately continue our work in becoming social justice-oriented teachers. As Michelle shares her journey and critical reflections with her readers, she provides each of us one way to continue our learning. A critical autoethnographic analysis requires that we examine and challenge our beliefs, identities, and assumptions, to become more just and to create socially just learning environments for our students.

Delving into Michelle's book, using the curriculum she provides to advance our learning and help us be better teacher educators is valuable. Her guidance, scholarship, questions, and insight push me to be better. As teachers and teacher educators, the subject matter content we choose to include matters, as does the content we choose to exclude. The instructional methods we choose matter. The ways in which we interact with our students matter. The United States in 2020 will eventually become a part of history, and at some point, there will be a high school social studies teacher whose identities are similar to mine. What histories will she choose to teach and how will those choices contribute to improving the world?

—*Kathryn M. Obenchain*

# ACKNOWLEDGMENTS

As a queer educator who incorporates critical theories, such as queer theory, into my research on queer(ing) curriculum and creating queer multicultural social justice education curriculum (Knaier, 2020), I am grateful for the opportunity to publish my work. Throughout my academic career, I have been fortunate to have had accepting and affirming teachers and mentors. Here, I want to extend a special thanks to my doctoral committee: Dr. Jake Burdick, Dr. Will Letts, Dr. Kathryn Obenchain, and Dr. JoAnn Phillion; and my teacher education program mentors: Dr. Beth Shiner-Klein and Professor Karl Klein for guiding me on this journey and encouraging me to find and use my voice. I appreciate you for your work, your support, and your dedication to social justice.

I must also acknowledge that my journey to becoming a queer scholar would not have been possible if not for the strength and courage modeled by my mother, Rose. She served as an inspirational icon throughout my life. Her desire to provide, protect, and persevere was unwavering until the day she died. To my mom, I owe my courage and ability to take risks (both personally and professionally). This includes the risks every queer author may face when publishing their work.

Further, I could not navigate through life's trials and tribulations without the consistent support of my family. My sister, Sherry, is a strong, courageous woman in her own right. She is the one person to whom I can say truly what I am feeling. Moreover, I could not pursue my passions, or my dreams, without the un-

*Queer Multicultural Social Justice Education: Curriculum (and Identity) Development Through Performance,* pages xix–xx.

conditional support of my partner, Bob. He is an inspiration and an adventurous life-partner. I am grateful for him and his love. Finally, I am appreciative of the emotional support provided by my feline colleagues, Brody, Weston, and Zack. To paraphrase Dickens, there is no greater gift than the love of a cat.

# PREFACE

I knew my book had found its home once I was introduced to the *Research for social justice: Personal~passionate~partcipatory inquiry* book series. Upon reading the Series Foreword, which introduces work that "connects the personal with the political, the theoretical with the practical, and research with social and educational change," I easily envisioned how my work is represented in this statement. Subsequently, I realized that this series and this project were inspired by many of the same scholars, theories, and methodologies.

Having realized this, I (re)visited and reflected on some of the foundational literature upon which personal~passionate~participatory inquiry (PPP), and thus, this series, are built. Through this exercise, I recognized how my work captures the qualities highlighted in each. For example, this book is filled with (hi)stories, innovated inquiries, and storytelling, which are infused with pragmatic explorations and practices for (in)formal multicultural social justice educators. These critical elements capture the essence of the inquiries featured in this series as described by He and Phillion (see, Series Foreword):

> Researchers not only collect, but often live in the stories . . .. They position stories collected in historical, socio-political, . . . and cultural contexts, and contextualize their inquiries within struggles of understanding individuals and groups. Stories are presented in life-like ways; readers vicariously experience complexities, contradictions and dilemmas of people's lives.

In sum, this book, set with in the frameworks of multicultural social justice educa-tion, queer theory, and autoethnography, is the story of my journey through the performance and development of queer curriculum, seeking to question assump-tions with the purpose of promoting equity, equality, and social justice.

To further center my work within this series, I reflected on my experiences as a graduate student, mentee, and colleague of Series Editor Dr. JoAnn Phillion. I was (and continue to be) influenced by her social justice philosophies, caring teaching methods, and personal stories. Her approach to multicultural social jus-tice education, which includes mindful publishing practices and empathetic learn-ing strategies, embraces "narrative imagination," which is "the ability to reflect on experience, question assumptions, and actively empathize with others" (Phil-lion & He, 2004, p. 3). These are characteristics that I, too, promote through the development of *queer multicultural social justice curriculum* (Knaier, 2020), as presented in this book.

Indeed, as the influence of our shared foundational (hi)stories is evident, I con-cur with the vision put forth by Phillion and He (2004). They write, "[t]he goal is to enable our students to learn to listen to and hear the stories of others, not through abstract reasoning, but through developing emotions and empathic under-standing, through examining hearts and minds" (p. 3). Here, I not only prescribe such practices, I model them by engaging in self-examination (Nussbaum, 1997) and by sharing personal stories through autoethnographic methods (e.g., storytell-ing, photographs, poetry) (Chang, 2008; Ellis, 2004). Alongside my multicultural social justice education scaffolding, queer perspectives, and autoethnographic methodology (see, Chapters One, Two, and Three, respectively), I concurrent-ly engage in personal~passionate~participatory inquiry "by questioning whose knowledge should be considered valid and how experience should be interpreted, theorized, and represented"; and I "confront[] issues of equity, equality, social jus-tice, and societal change through both research and action" (He & Phillion, 2008, pp. 11–12). These actions are incorporated in the curriculum I developed for this project and in the queered curriculum development process I present.

As a way of explicitly situating my work within this book series, I offer below a truncated analysis of this body of work through a personal~passionate~particip atory inquiry framework. I peer at my work—as an incomplete whole—through the prism of the three "distinct and interconnected qualities" of PPP: personal, passionate, and participatory (see, Series Foreword). I then conclude as a means of bringing the fractured light back together as a whole.

## PERSONAL

*Each is personal, compelled by values and experiences*
*researchers bring to the work.*

I note in Chapter One that this book maps my epistemological path to de-veloping a queer multicultural social justice teacher education curriculum. Included throughout these pages are personal, reflective, and critical stories about my experiences, for example, as a child, teacher, and genderqueer-woman, set in the context of multicultural social justice education and its values. This includes examining my white privilege, my assumptions of others, and my actions toward racial and other social injustices as curriculum development practices.

## PASSIONATE

Each is passionate, grounded in a commitment to social justice
concerns of people and places under consideration.

One of the mantras repeated throughout the book is: One must know themselves before they can know others (Banks, 2006b; Gollnick & Chinn, 2004; Grant & Sleeter, 2011a; Howard, 2006; Nieto & Bode, 2012). This objective is particularly important when "teaching ~ ~ learning" (see, Chapter Four, A break to ponder) multicultural social justice practices, which is why I focused on it for this project. This study models what such an exploration of self as a means of knowing others may look like. It is my hope that by sharing my stories, you will be inspired to share yours as a means of promoting social justice and awareness of social injustice within ourselves and in society—performances that are desperately needed in today's hostile social climate.

## PARTICIPATORY

Each is participatory, built on long-term, heart-felt engaging, and shared efforts.

I relay in the following introduction that there appears to be relatively little *use* of queer autoethnography as a tool to *advance* education in the form of curriculum development—and that by using autoethnography to explore the experience of, and enhance, curriculum development, I am applying the method in a different, and possibly new, manner. This meant I did not have a tour guide for this journey. I advanced through uncharted territory, trusting myself and looking to past experiences to guide me through unharmed. This project was mentally, emotionally, and physiologically challenging. I had to actively relive and reflect on harmful parts of my past, and my ideologies of the present, while creating new, proactive curriculum for future use. Indeed, my study does "reflect new and exciting ways of researching and representing experiences of disenfranchised, underrepresented, and invisible groups, and challenge stereotypical or deficit perspectives on these groups" (see Series Foreword).

## CONCLUSION

In sum, this book encompasses these three PPP qualities. I take a pragmatic approach by sharing my intimate journey, my stories, and myself with you—the reader—as I actively perform and model the development of queer explorations (i.e., lessons) and curriculum (*Personal*). I begin this journey with three accessible (hi)stories of multicultural education, queer perspectives, and autoethnography (see, Chapters One, Two, and Three, respectively). These easy-to-navigate stories provide you with important background knowledge, highlighting the evolution of, commonalities between, and need for each discipline, along with their connection to identity and identity awareness as a form of social justice practice and advancement (*Passionate*). Then, I share and perform the nine explorations developed for this project, collectively titled *Queer Explorations of Identity Awareness*. Modeling for you in practical terms how to *queer* curriculum and its development, I openly examine my raw performances, discuss my personal and analytical reflections, and embrace my own personal experiences and revelations that occurred throughout this project (*Participatory*).

Finally, I close with a creative, reflective, and story-like analysis of the process that includes a call to action from you to share your stories as a way of knowing yourself—and others—as a form of social justice education and advancement. This book is intended for all formal and informal educators interested in performing and developing queer multicultural social justice curriculum and practices alongside personal~passionate~participatory inquiry. Inspired by Ayers (2006), I invite you on this "voyage" with "hope and urgency" (p. 83). *It is time we share our stories as a form of curriculum, activism, and coming together.*

# INTRODUCTION

I am an educator. I am a former middle and high school science and computer applications teacher. I have also served as a Multiculturalism & Education Instructor and a Multicultural Education Lecturer. As an academic, I incorporate critical theories, such as queer theory, into my research on queer(ing) curriculum and creating queer multicultural social justice teacher education curriculum (Knaier, 2020)—a critical approach that breaks down, and may reach beyond, rigid identity labels by implementing methods, such as critical autoethnography,[1] which provide learners with opportunities to investigate ways to dismantle heteronormativity, rethink binary systems of identification, and deconstruct socially constructed identities through personal investigation and story-sharing.

I am also a photographer, a homeowner, a partner, and a cat mama. All of these characteristics are components of my Michelleness: "It's a verb. It's a conjunction. A preposition. It's a philosophy. A way of life. It's your name with 'ness' attached to it" (Stuber et al., 2006). I find these components, or identities, easy to explore, describe, and share. But what about some of my other identities? Those not-so-easy to determine and/or explain. Identities such as socioeconomic status, religion, sexual orientation, gender, race/ethnicity, and exceptionality—col-

---

[1] Although Pinar (1994a, 1994b) and his work on including autobiography in curriculum studies had an early influence on my academic approach, I am not applying that, or his theory of "currere," in this project. I have taken a critical, queer autoethnographic path for this project.

---

*Queer Multicultural Social Justice Education: Curriculum (and Identity) Development Through Performance,* pages xxv–xxx.

lectively, my "multicultural identities" (Banks, 2016). Indeed, my Michelleness is much more complicated—and queerer—than the make-up of these six, rather broad categories. Categories such as these may carry multiple meanings—or, in some cases, no meaning. But, adhering to current multicultural literature (Banks & McGee Banks, 2016), I am choosing to stay within the realm of these six categories for this project.

This venture allowed me to explore these identities—an opportunity not given (or taken) by many, but one that is essential to be an effective multicultural social justice educator (Banks, 2006b; Gollnick & Chinn, 2004; Grant & Sleeter, 2011a; Howard, 2006; Nieto & Bode, 2012). I explore my multicultural identities, and their intersectionality, as part of performing and developing queer multicultural social justice teacher education curriculum. Ultimately, I analyzed my experience of implementing these queer curriculum development methods.

## MY EN[QUEER]Y

My intent was to conjure questions about identity awareness (of self and others) within myself and the reader through the curriculum developed for this project. Indeed, through this project, I hope to advance the kind of multicultural education that provides opportunities for, and encourages, educators (e.g., K–12 classroom teachers, caregivers, artists) to examine and explore their identities and the way they teach (e.g., develop curriculum, nurture relationships with students, and learn from others) in conjunction with their identities. My data collection is set within the experience of developing a queer multicultural social justice teacher education curriculum. Further, this project addressed many queries I had (and may still have) about myself as an individual, a queer multicultural social justice educator, and a curriculum worker (i.e., one who develops, analyzes, and/or delivers curricula). *I am a queer educator.*

### Guiding Question

The question guiding this study is: How may queering critical autoethnography and using it as a queer curriculum development method provide an opportunity for becoming more aware of, and working toward, an understanding of identities (e.g., socioeconomic status, religion, sexual orientation, gender, race/ethnicity, and exceptionality), as well as impact curriculum development? Though, as I stated, this project addressed many questions. Indeed, it provoked me to ask several questions I could not possibly explore within the timeframe or scope of this project—or, possibly, even in my lifetime. This exploration is a beginning of a lifelong, fluid exercise in identity self-awareness, queer curriculum development, and storytelling.

## Significance of Study: Promoting Identity Awareness Within Multicultural Curricula

Grant and Sleeter (2011a) assert that it is impossible "to understand other people without first understanding yourself and how your perspective shapes how you interpret others" (p. 10). As an educator (e.g., teacher educator, photographer, sister), I should actively explore ways to understand my multicultural identities (e.g., socioeconomic status, religion, sexual orientation, gender, race/ethnicity, and exceptionality) and comprehend why I hold certain perspectives to better understand, develop, and deliver multicultural content in ways that relate to others (e.g., students, family members). Though it is a personal choice to partake in these types of exploration, educators—including teacher educators—should be encouraged to practice such methods and, furthermore, incorporate some of these techniques into multicultural education practices. Doing so can provide tools that may guide others—including K–12 classroom teachers—in the processes of achieving their own identity awareness (of self and others).

Following the advice of many multicultural education experts, I conducted an autoethnographic study of my experience developing a queer multicultural social justice teacher education curriculum as a means of knowing myself, and thus being able to better respond to, and teach, my students (Banks, 2006b; Gollnick & Chinn, 2004; Grant & Sleeter, 2011a; Howard, 2006; Nieto & Bode, 2012). In this study, I worked within the framework of queer theory (Britzman, 1995; Letts & Sears, 1999; Kissen, 2002; Mayo, 2007; Murray, 2015)—which allows me to explore my identity and the understanding of others' identities without strict rules. I not only apply queer theory to the way I think about gender and sexuality in relation to power, but I infuse it into the ways I develop curricula and share and analyze my experiences. To complement my framework, I chose a queer method, autoethnography (Adams & Holman Jones, 2008; Bochner & Ellis, 2016). This method allows me to convey and analyze my research in various ways (e.g., poetry, storytelling, social science prose). Through these processes, I devised a queer curriculum development method that may encourage (in)formal teachers (current and prospective) to become more aware of, and work toward an understanding of, their own multicultural identities within the process of developing queer multicultural social justice teacher education curriculum.

## Application of Framework to this Study

By launching queer theory, de Lauretis (1991) encouraged us to move away from "the hegemony of white, male, middle-class models of analysis" (Halperin, 2003, p. 340), thus offering an "escape" from these dominant viewpoints. In this manner, I concur with Meyer (2007) who asserts that queer theory calls on "educators to question and reformulate through a queer pedagogical lens . . . how they teach and reinforce gendered practices in schools," "how they support traditional notions of heterosexuality," and "how they present culturally specific information in the classroom" (p. 28). In short, queer theory works against the norm—not only disrupting heteronormativity, binaries, and socially constructed identities, but also in other areas such as (de)constructing curriculum, research, personal identities, and critical analysis standards—as demonstrated throughout this project.

### Queering Critical Autoethnography as the Method for this Study

Over the years, Banks' approach to multicultural education has evolved to fit the needs and realities of the field and of society (see, Banks, 1988, 1993, 1994, 1996, 1999, 2004, 2006a, 2006b, 2010, 2013). Learning from Banks, I understand that my work must evolve as society and culture change. Frameworks, such as queer theory, and methods, such as autoethnography, allow for flexibility in these inquiries, reflecting changes in my identities, perspectives, and self, as well as the ways I perceive and interact with others. Further, as Banks (2006b) realizes, "the biographical journeys of researchers greatly influence their values, their research questions, and the knowledge they construct." And, "[t]he knowledge they construct mirrors their life experiences and their values" (p. 2). However, the journeys represented in this project are more than biographical (an account of one's life), they are autoethnographical (which connects autobiographical stories to wider cultural, political, and social meanings and understandings). Autoethnography serves to engage and affect the reader. It is the engagement between the researcher and the audience, and the actions taken by both parties, that make autoethnography a powerful method (Ellis, 2004).

While critical autoethnography is already a queer method (Adams & Holman Jones, 2008; Bochner & Ellis, 2016), in this study I queer how one *uses* this method—as a curriculum development tool. Scholars within education, such as Adams (2011), Miller and Rodriguez (2016), and Pillay et al. (2016), *show* the connection between autoethnography and queer theory. Many educators and scholars use autobiographical and other narrative approaches to write *about* their experiences of teaching multicultural education and of interacting with students (Bochner & Ellis, 2016; Chang, 2008; Ellis, 2004; Feuerverger, 2005). However, there appears to be relatively little *use* of queer autoethnography as a tool to *advance* education in the form of curriculum development. Indeed, I could not find any literature on using autoethnography as a curriculum development method. Thus, by using autoethnography to explore the experience of, and enhance, curriculum development, I am applying the method in a different, and possibly new, manner.

## A BOOK OF (HI)STORIES

This book is a book of (hi)stories. Overall, it is a story of how my research evolved and culminated in this project. And within that story, I share many personal stories based on my life experiences, my reflective and reflexive practices, and my research. *But I don't just tell my story—I encourage you to tell your stories.* In Part One, *Awareness of Self (and Others): A Common Thread*, I tell three stories.

Each story, or chapter, delves into historical origins of multicultural education, queer theory, and autoethnography, respectively. Along with evolutionary details, I highlight how the significance of identity exploration and awareness for educators is a common theme found in each discipline, framework, or method.

In Chapter One, I explore the (hi)story of multicultural education within the United States. I tell a story of how multicultural education has changed since its inception; and I specifically address why and when gender, sexual orientation, and other LGBTQ (lesbian, gay, bisexual, trans*, queer) issues were incorporated into the multicultural education movement. Finally, I discuss how multicultural education has been integrated into teacher education curriculum, with a special emphasis on the importance of identity awareness (of self and others).

In Chapter Two, I provide an account of queer origins and principles of queer theory—specifically, how it interrupts heteronormativity; fractures binary systems, such as gender; and deconstructs the socially constructed aspects of identity. Further, I explore "queering" as cultural analysis and how these theoretical perspectives may be applied to multicultural teacher education, including the exploration of identities (of self and others).

In Chapter Three, which closes Part One, I recount my methodology literature review. Set within the framework of queer theory, I show how queering critical autoethnography, and using it for curriculum development, may help educators obtain a greater understanding of oneself and one's perspectives and identities, to better relate to students. This chapter is riddled with personal accounts shared by educators who use and praise autoethnography as a method to question and explore identity awareness (of self and others). I close Part One with *Stories as Curriculum*, which describes how I perceive "curriculum" and argues that curriculum includes all aspects of our experiences—including our stories. I also offer some possible benefits and risks to sharing our stories; and I concede that we should be given the choice of when and how to share them.

In Part Two, *Explorations of Identity Awareness: Queer Curriculum (Development and Performance)*, I build on the foundation presented in Part One. I introduce the curriculum developed for this project: *Queer Explorations of Identity Awareness* (see, Appendix). I share the aim for this curriculum, the targeted participants, the intended outcomes of the explorations, and some adaptations and suggestions for implementing the curriculum. Next in *Elements of the Explorations*, I define the features of the explorations. Finally, Part Two consists of nine *Explorations* in lieu of chapters. Each exploration consists of a set of directives; my presentation or performance of the exploration; and my reflection of the exploration including how performing the exploration impacted its development. It should be noted that the content presented in Part Two serves as my data for this study.

In Part Three, *Reflective Analysis and Discussion*, I return to chapters. Chapter Four offers a reflective, autoethnographic analysis of the project. I present this analysis in four sections: *Queer Multicultural Social Justice Teacher Education*, where I reflect on the objectives and need for such curriculum; *Breaking the Norm*, where I reflect on some of the tensions I wrestled with during the development of the (un)structured nature of the curriculum; *Breaking a Binary*, where I identify myself as a teacher and a student simultaneously (Freire, 1970) and reflect on this extraordinary experience; and *Breaking Down (De)constructions*, where I reflect on realizing, adopting, and practicing queer language and curriculum development practices. Then, I conclude with a section titled *(Non)conclusion*, where I reflect on the fluid, never-ending endeavors of practicing identity awareness and curriculum development (Banks, 2006b; Grant & Sleeter, 2011a; Loutzenheiser, 2001; Nieto, 2010; Nieto & Bode, 2012; Oliva & Gordon, 2013).

Finally, in *Chapter 5: Our Stories Continue*, I discuss how I plan to further this research, as well as conduct other explorations, through autoethnographic methods (Chang, 2008; Ellis, 2004), purposeful storytelling (Phillion, 2002), and engaging with others—thus, moving closer to answering my guiding question. However, I also leave you with some unfinished thoughts, and I challenge you to continue the work we have started here together. *Our work as explorers, learners and teachers, and queer educators has only just begun.*

## MY HOPE

This project is not merely about me or my Michelleness. It is about how educators (e.g., teacher educators, classroom teachers, parents, young people) should and may practice identity awareness (of self and others) as a means of teaching toward social justice. And it was through the analysis and synthesis of these (hi)stories that I found my path to—and awareness of—queer multicultural social justice teacher education. Ellis (2004) confides: "Awareness was what I hoped would result for readers and myself" (p. 22). Adhering to Ellis' approach to autoethnography—an approach that includes the researcher—I, too, hope for such awareness—*a self-awareness as a means of becoming an effective multicultural teacher educator*. Further, I hope my story, and the (hi)stories presented in this book, spark a desire for you, the reader, to reflect on what makes up you and your *you-ness*.

# PART I

AWARENESS OF SELF (AND OTHERS):
A COMMON THREAD

# CHAPTER 1

# MULTICULTURAL EDUCATION

My teacher education included, and incorporated, multiculturalism, inclusiveness, tolerance, and acceptance based on social justice and democratic teaching practices and methods. I took my education seriously, and, as a science teacher working toward social justice, tried to be inclusive and cognizant of students' needs. Though I do not speak Spanish, I offered worksheets and notes in Spanish whenever I could. I worked with the English Language Learner (ELL) staff as best I could. I stressed to my students that "We are all scientists, and we perform science everyday"—hoping to make personal, relevant connections. I offered extra credit in the form of mini science projects done at home with families. I had an "open door" policy and invited parents and caregivers into my classroom whenever they wanted to visit. I highlighted the work of women scientists and scientists of color. And, I vehemently addressed anti-gay or homophobic behavior. I say "tried to be inclusive" because as I reflect on that time, I realize I did not do enough.

My graduate work reminded me that new teachers tend to "forget" what they learned throughout their teacher education program—and that *saying* you are a multicultural teacher is not enough. My experiences as a classroom teacher and an instructor to preservice teachers—and in-depth exposure to the foundational works of multicultural education pioneers presented in this chapter—influenced my working toward becoming a queer multicultural social justice educator. Part One of this book maps my epistemological path to developing a queer multicul-

*Queer Multicultural Social Justice Education: Curriculum (and Identity) Development Through Performance*, pages 3–21.
Copyright © 2021 by Information Age Publishing

tural social justice teacher education curriculum. Part Two builds on this foundation and outlines the characteristics and intended outcomes of such curricula as I applied them to this project. And Part Three offers a reflective analysis of my experience.

In this chapter, I often refer to the foundational work of James A. Banks as I explore the history of multicultural education within the United States. I tell a story, or a (hi)story, of how multicultural education mirrors civil rights movements and how it has changed since its inception. In this (hi)story I include why and when gender, sexual orientation, and other LGBTQ issues were incorporated into the multicultural education movement. At the close of the chapter, I discuss how multicultural education has historically been integrated into teacher education curriculum and emphasize the importance of identity awareness (of self and others) by educators.

## A BRIEF (HI)STORY

"Education" is a theme that appears throughout civil rights histories. People are *taught* to be racist. Children *learn* how to treat others. Therefore, we must *teach* our citizens to embrace multicultural diversity (Zinn, 2001). The American civil rights movements create environments in which that educational effort may grow. Take a moment to remember the many people who lost or gave their lives to pursue civil rights and other liberties for themselves and others. Indeed, the struggle for civil liberties continues today in the United States. *Black lives matter.*

### Civil Rights Movements

In the mid-twentieth century, racial justice began to be addressed in the United States. In 1954, in *Brown v. Board of Education*, the United States Supreme Court ruled against "separate but equal" in relation to segregated schools. In 1955, as part of her fight toward justice, Rosa Parks refused to give up her seat in the "white" section of a bus. These actions, and the actions of many others, sparked a bus boycott in Montgomery, Alabama. Blacks were ready to demand social justice. In the words of Martin Luther King, Jr.:

> We have known humiliation, we have known abusive language, we have been plunged into the abyss of oppression. And we decided to rise up only with the weapon of protest. It is one of the greatest glories of America that we have the right of protest....We must use the weapon of love. We must have compassion and understanding for those who hate us. We must realize so many people are taught to hate us that they are not totally responsible for their hate. (as cited in Phillips, 1956)

Unfortunately, given the ongoing oppressive political and social climate, and the elevated tensions of recent years, King's words are just as relevant today—and "the weapon of protest" continues to be deployed in the service of equal rights and civil liberties.

As the civil rights movement began to gain the support of blacks and some whites, peaceful acts of protest, like sit-ins, the travels of the Freedom Riders, and demonstrative marches provided a platform for activists. Mass demonstrations swept across the South. Even "little black children participated—a new generation was learning to act" (Zinn, 2001, p. 454). Though not all protesters practiced peaceful tactics, the overwhelming message from King was "love and peace." This message then spread to other non-dominant groups. The Black Civil Rights Movement "gradually became a movement for recognition of the rights of all minority groups, including Mexican-Americans, Native Americans, Asian-Americans, and Puerto Ricans" (Gay, 1983, p. 561). Moreover, the "women rights movement, the movement for the rights of people with disabilities, and, later, the movement for gay rights adopted some of the goals, strategies, and language of the Black Civil Rights Movement" (Banks, 2006b, p. 9).

Indeed, women also started to organize. Feminists, people who work for the political, social, and economic equality of the sexes, wanted women's work and contributions to society, along with their minds and bodies, to be valued. "The leaders of this movement, such as Betty Freidan and Gloria Steinem, demanded that political, social, economic, and educational institutions act to eliminate sex discrimination and provide opportunities for women to actualize their talents and realize their ambitions" (Banks, 2013, p. 4). Goals for the movement included: equal pay for equal work; eliminating laws that discriminated against women; hiring more women in lead positions; and increasing the participation of men in household chores and child rearing (Banks, 2013). Within educational institutions, supporters wanted to see an equal representation of women in textbooks and more women in administration. Books like *The Feminine Mystique* (Freidan, 1963), *Sisterhood Is Powerful* (Morgan, 1970), and *Against Our Will* (Brownmiller, 1975) brought feminist issues into the hands and conversations of women across the country. And with the 1973 decision in *Roe v. Wade* and other important victories, women's civil rights began to be protected.

Additionally, during this time, "people with disabilities, senior citizens, and gays and lesbians formed groups that organized politically ... and made significant inroads in changing institutions and laws" (Banks, 2013, p. 5). In 1951, the first gay rights organization in the United States—the Mattachine Society—was founded (Grant & Sleeter, 2011a). Although many consider the 1969 Stonewall riots the beginning of the LGBT civil rights movement (Grant & Sleeter, 2011a), there were many battles fought prior to this historical event (Rupp & Freeman, 2014). Nevertheless, "it was not until the Compton Cafeteria riot in San Francisco and the Stonewall Inn riots in New York City that LGBT-identified people would boldly and collectively assert their right to exist and assemble in the public sphere" (Tremmel, 2014, p. 164). Today, the struggle for LGBTQ civil rights remains. It was only recently that the United States Supreme Court invalidated the Defense of Marriage Act in *United States v. Windsor* (2013), and lifted bans on same-sex marriage in *Obergefell v. Hodges* (2015). The LGBTQ community continues to fight for federal non-discrimination laws in the workplace and regarding medical treatments, and the battle for LGBTQ equality—and civil rights generally—is far from over. In addition to civil rights, "[t]hese groups, like ethnic groups of color, also demanded that schools, colleges, and universities respond to their cultural needs, hopes, and dreams" (Banks, 2006b, p. 10). Progress has been slow.

### Strife Within Civil Rights Movements

Although many non-dominant groups have worked toward equal rights and civil liberties for their respective members, and while activists have adopted actions and language from others' causes, these groups have not always worked together. In fact, many minority groups *reject* members of their *own* group based on other characteristics or identities that such individual members might express. For example, gay black men were, and some continue to be, outcasts in the African American community (Conerly, 2000); bisexual individuals are often not recognized within the LGBTQ community (Rupp & Freeman, 2014); and there has been a long-standing tension between lesbians and gays (McGarry, 1998). But we need to realize that a person is not just black; is not just gay; or is not just a man. By acknowledging that the intersectionality (Lorde, 1984) of identities has an "impact on individuals' experiences as well as others' perceptions of them" (Pollard, 2013, p. 153), groups could begin to work together to secure social justice for all.

Indeed, some civil rights activists realized that solidarity between and among groups could benefit each individual group. For example, "the civil rights and Black power movements [continued to] set the standard for activism during the 1960s" (Mayo, 2014, p. 27). And in 1970, the founder of the Black Panthers, Huey Newton, "declared his support for the gay liberation movement and exhorted his comrades to reject their antigay attitudes and eliminate words such as *faggot* and *punk* from their everyday vocabularies" (Lekus, 2014, p. 231, emphasis original). Newton (1973) instructed:

> Whatever your personal opinions and your insecurities about homosexuality and the various liberation movements among homosexuals and women (and I speak of the homosexuals and women as oppressed groups), we should try to unite with them in a revolutionary fashion.... And I know through reading, and through life experience and observations, that homosexuals are not given freedom and liberty by anyone in the society. They might be the most oppressed people in the society. (p. 143)

This recognition and acceptance of the oppression of others, especially "others" *within* the same racial or ethnic group strengthened the efforts of each oppressed group. It is this understanding of the intersectionality of identities—within us and others—that resonates in the goals of multicultural education.

## THE EVOLUTION OF MULTICULTURAL EDUCATION

The evolution of multicultural education mirrors the development and progress of civil rights movements in the United States. First, ethnic, or mono-ethnic studies were developed for respective populations. This approach then bifurcated into multiethnic studies. These courses were attended by those of various ethnicities who wanted to learn about different cultures. And eventually, multicultural education was established. Multicultural education addresses issues concerning not just race and ethnicity, but also socioeconomic status, gender, sexual orientation, exceptionality, and other cultural differences, and can be integrated into a range of curricula—including teacher education.

### Ethnic Studies

In the mid-1960s, during the emergence of the Civil Rights Movement, "African Americans and other ethnic groups demanded that the schools and other institutions establish ethnic studies courses that focused on their specific ethnic groups and hire more teachers of color" (Banks, 2006b, p. 7). This was considered "the first phase of the school response to the ethnic revitalization movement of the 1960s and 1970s," and according to Banks, the *mono-ethnic courses* phase (p. 7). It comprised of "courses and units that focused on the histories and cultures of specific ethnic groups" (p. 7). These are race- or ethnic-centered classes taught primarily to those of the featured ethnicity.

However, it became clear that those of other ethnicities also would benefit from enrolling in these classes. Indeed, ethnic studies courses began to attract students of varied ethnic and racial backgrounds from a wide range of disciplines—including teacher education. These courses offered an opportunity for white students to "learn to respond to non-Whites positively and sensitively," by bringing awareness "of the perceptions of their culture that are held by other ethnic groups and of the ways in which the dominant culture evolved and attained the power to shape the United States in its image" (p. 76).

Such ethnic studies courses still exist today (e.g., Black Studies, Chicano Studies). They continue to "challenge the knowledge normally taught in schools, arguing that that knowledge reinforces control by wealthy White men over everyone else" (Grant & Sleeter, 2013, p. 49). Further, "this approach offers an in-depth study of oppressed groups for the purpose of empowering group members, developing in them a sense of pride and group consciousness, and helping members of dominant groups understand where others are coming from" (p. 49). These courses also address the complexity and intersectionality of identities and how these attributes affect the quality of education for those who identify with multiple labels—a shift toward an inclusive, transformative multicultural curriculum.

## Multiethnic Studies

Though the need for ethnic studies courses continues, multiethnic studies—curriculum that reflects a holistic and pluralistic ideology by incorporating the interactions among ethnic cultures—filled a niche, specifically in teacher education. "Its aim was to bring about structural and systemic changes in the total school that were designed to increase educational equality" (Banks, 2004, p. 13). Given that teachers were predominately white, Banks (2006b) realized:

> it might be harmful for ethnic content to be taught by teachers who had negative racial and ethnic attitudes, [therefore he] constructed a concept of *multiethnic education* that included not only curriculum reform but also the attitudes, perceptions, and beliefs of the school staff, school policy and politics, teaching styles and strategies, assessment and testing procedures, and the language and dialects sanctioned in the school. (p. 8)

In other words, given the lack of diversity in teacher populations, multiethnic studies provided a learning environment where white, middle-class preservice teachers could gain knowledge about other cultures, and therefore possibly offer a more empathic teaching approach to their students.

Multiethnic studies, however, did not initially capture the complexities of cultural education. According to Gay (1983), as multiethnic education progressed its mission was

> no longer seen simply as the transmission to minority students only of cultural information about ethnic minority students [but] it has moved from the correction of errors of omission and commission in portrayals of ethnic experiences to the promotion of ethnic pluralism as a social value at all grade levels. (p. 560)

This reform is the basis for multicultural education.

## Multicultural Education

When the term *multicultural education* was adopted, some scholars felt that the focus on racial and ethnic issues would diminish as other identities (e.g., socioeconomic status, religion, gender, sexual orientation, and exceptionality) were brought under the umbrella term (Banks, 2006b; Gay, 1983). Here, I introduce various approaches to multicultural education that highlight some of the differences and commonalities that developed within the discipline (Banks, 2006b; Nieto & Bode, 2012). These include anti-racist education, culturally sustaining pedagogy (which emerged from culturally relevant and culturally responsive education), and multicultural social justice education, which includes anti-racist, culturally sustaining education, and other elements. These approaches consist of overlapping ideas and are largely used at once within multicultural learning environments (e.g., K–12 and teacher education) as a means of teaching toward social justice.

### *Anti-Racist Education*

Events, such as the killings of Breonna Taylor, Sandra Bland, Michelle Cusseaux, Natasha McKenna, George Floyd, Ahmaud Arbery, Trayvon Martin, Michael Brown, Eric Garner, Tamir Rice, Walter Scott, and Freddie Grey (to name just a few of the victims), highlight the brutal injustices to which Black women and men are subjected in the United States. And aside from the possibility of being shot and killed by the police, Black citizens and other citizens of color endure race-related prejudices, inequalities, discriminations, and other racist practices. Taibbi (2015), in describing horrific and wide-spread law enforcement abuses, explains:

> Most Americans have never experienced this kind of policing. They haven't had to stare down the barrel of a service revolver drawn for no reason at a routine stop. They haven't had their wife and kids put on an ice-cold sidewalk curb while cops ran their license plate. They haven't ever been told to get the fuck back in their car right now, ... had their dog shot and their kids handcuffed near its body during a wrong-door raid, ... or dealt with any of a thousand other positively crazy things non-White America has come to expect from an interaction with law enforcement. (p. 42)

Indeed, racism continues to be a powerful social force in the United States.

An important aspect of anti-racist education is teaching citizens that everyone, regardless of race or ethnicity, may experience prejudice and discrimination; however, not everyone may experience racism. For racism to occur, there must be an imbalance of power between the parties (e.g., individuals or institutions) (Banks & McGee Banks, 2016). It is because of this imbalance of power that racist behavior can and does continue to occur in our society—and not just within the legal system (McLaren, 1994). This unjust behavior makes multicultural education, specifically the element of anti-racist education, necessary within educational institutions and their curricula.

In the realm of education, schools, and classrooms, Pollock (2008) defines "racism" as "any act that, even unwittingly, tolerates, accepts, or reinforces unequal opportunities for children to learn and thrive; allows racial inequalities in opportunity as if they are normal and acceptable; or treats people of color as less worthy or less complex than 'white' people" (p. xvii). Because racism can be systemic, or institutional, in nature, Banks and McGee Banks (2013) maintain that implementing anti-racist reform includes examining "curriculum materials, grouping practices, hiring policies, teacher attitudes and expectations, and school policy and practices"; after which "steps are taken to eliminate racism from these school variables" (p. 353). The goal is to omit racism from all parts of the school, not just within a single practice or classroom.

Teachers must understand that simply integrating superficial lessons incorporating people of color is not enough. Teachers may incorporate materials or stories about Rosa Parks or Martin Luther King Jr., but unless these portrayals are accurate and not perpetuating racist beliefs and ideas, they may do more harm than good. Kozol (1975) addressed this weak approach in an article which "graphically documents how schools bleed the life and soul out of even the most impassioned and courageous heroes, such as Helen Keller and Martin Luther King Jr., in the process making them boring and less-than-believable caricatures" (Nieto & Bode, 2013, p. 317). Integrating meaningful conversations about civil rights movements, historical persons of color (and those of other diverse identities), and other relevant topics regarding race and racial tensions into the curriculum, will not only inform students but allow safe, constructive discussions about race to take place—an experience that is often not available to students, especially white students (Luttrell, 2008).

Unfortunately, in some instances, educators adopt a "colorblind" approach when it comes to their students. These teachers assert that they want "all of their students" (even those of color and of lower ability) to succeed (Pollock, 2008). However, "many White teachers [nevertheless] feel great discomfort when racism is discussed in the classroom" (Nieto & Bode, 2013, p. 318); and according to Pollock (2004), "this discourse is in fact highly racialized because the deletion of race in both classroom practice and policy talk is a deliberate and race-conscious act" (Nieto & Bode, 2013, p. 318). Moreover, there are reasons for this omission. Luttrell (2008) explains that because "there is typically no vehicle in white people's lives for actively discussing and interpreting racism with people of color, white teachers are unpracticed and at times fearful of what they will learn about their own racism" (p. 277; Berlak & Moyenda, 2001; Nieto & Bode, 2012; Sleeter, 1996). The opportunity for such critical dialogue, however, is in itself a strong argument for anti-racist, multicultural teacher education.

Ultimately, teachers must include accurate representations of Black History and important people of color—all while seeing, understanding, and identifying with their students. Creating an anti-racist learning atmosphere allows students the opportunity not only to express their identities, but to explore those identities. Such a space is possible only when educators are aware of and accepting of multicultural identities—including their own. Not only must teachers hold affirmative beliefs about racial diversity, they must infuse these beliefs into their teaching and classrooms to create anti-racist learning spaces.

In sum, "[m]ulticultural education without an explicit antiracist focus may perpetuate the worst kind of stereotypes if it focuses only on superficial aspects of culture and the addition of ethnic tidbits to the curriculum" (Nieto & Bode, 2013, p. 316). Gillborn (2008) concludes: "We know that racial inequalities in education and in society at large may well outlive us, but we commit ourselves to opposing these injustices and mitigating their reach" (p. 246). Through knowing and understanding our racial (and other) identities—and those of our students—we can begin to respond to the needs of our students and offer the tools they need to succeed.

### Culturally Sustaining Pedagogy

Because teachers today are faced with more diverse (racially and otherwise) classrooms, a trend that will continue to grow (Nieto & Bode, 2012; U.S. Census Bureau, 2010), they must ask: Who are my students? Which cultures are represented in my classroom? What other diversities exist? How can I personalize the learning atmosphere and curriculum content to meet each student's needs? Culturally sustaining pedagogy (Ladson-Billings, 2014; Paris, 2012; Paris & Alim, 2014), an approach that emerged from culturally relevant teaching/pedagogy (Ladson-Billings, 1995) and culturally responsive teaching (Gay, 2002), incorporates *responsiveness*—or, "our capacity as teachers to know and connect with the actual lived experience, personhood, and learning modalities of the students who are in our classrooms" (Howard, 2006, p. 131)—into our curriculum for the purpose of fostering "linguistic, literate, and cultural pluralism as part of the democratic project of schooling" (p. 95).

Culturally relevant teaching connects curriculum to students' lives and proficiencies, gives students a voice within the classroom and a chance to apply learned knowledge to their personal experiences, and offers students an opportunity to learn from each other's experiences—which are often culturally diverse. Further, creating learning spaces "in which all feel a sense of belonging," and may allow all students "to experience the affirmation of their identities," may cultivate "the dispositions, provide the knowledge, and develop the skills children and adults need in order to work together in diverse and inclusive schools and communities" (Derman-Sparks, 2004, p. 19). According to Ladson-Billings (1995), culturally relevant pedagogical practices "produce students who can achieve academically, produce students who demonstrate cultural competence, and develop students who can both understand and critique the existing social order" (p. 474). Ultimately, being responsive to what students are sharing in the classroom, while adjusting curriculum to make it relevant to students' lives, helps teachers make solid connections with their students' understanding of concepts—including those that impact their lifestyles, traditions, and beliefs.

According to Gay (2002), culturally responsive teaching is defined as "using the cultural characteristics, experiences, and perspectives of ethnically diverse students as conduits for teaching them more effectively" (p. 106). The elements of culturally responsive teaching include developing a knowledge base about cultural diversity; including ethnic and cultural diversity content in the curriculum; demonstrating caring and building learning communities; communicating with ethnically diverse students; and responding to ethnic diversity in the delivery of instruction (Gay, 2002, 2010). And although the original application of this approach was focused on ethnicity, it may be applied in multicultural classrooms to include the major multicultural identities: ethnicity; socioeconomic status; exceptionality; religion; sexual orientation; and gender.

Banks (2010) sums up the responsiveness approach by stating that the academic achievement of students from diverse racial, ethnic, cultural, linguistic, and social-class groups will increase if schools and teachers reflect and draw on students' cultural and language strengths. Gay (2010) confirms that "[t]eachers must learn to recognize, honor, and incorporate the personal abilities of students into their teaching strategies" (p. 1). Ultimately, teachers are encouraged to survey and evaluate their students' current knowledge, experiences, and abilities to create a learning atmosphere that includes and enhances learning practices. They must "understand different cultural intersections and incompatibilities, minimize the tensions, and bridge the gaps among different cultural systems [including the systems in school and at home]" (Gay, 2010, p. 12). In doing so, "the teacher of culturally diverse students becomes a cultural liaison and has the responsibility for developing a connection between the culture of the students and the culture of the school" (Shade et al., 1997, p. 19).

However, while "responsive" and "relevant" teaching have their place in the (hi)story of multicultural education, these approaches may eventually be replaced by, or at least incorporated into, culturally sustaining pedagogy. Paris (2012) argues that this innovative approach "is interested not in relevance or responsiveness, but in sustaining and extending the richness of our pluralist society. Such richness includes all of the languages, literacies, and cultural ways of being that our students and communities embody—both those marginalized and dominant" (p. 96). Further, it "requires that our pedagogies be more than responsive or relevant to the cultural experiences and practices of young people—it requires that they support young people in sustaining the cultural and linguistic competence of their communities while simultaneously offering access to dominant cultural competence" (p. 95). We have much work to do to reach this goal—including improving teacher education and recruitment.

Indeed, culturally sustaining, -responsive, and -relevant teaching will be implemented within our K–12 classrooms only if these practices are first incorporated into teacher education programs. Moreover, not only must teacher education change, but the type of prospective teacher must change. "Teacher educators (Grant, 1989; Haberman, 1991, King, 1991; King & Ladson-Billings, 1990; Zeichner, 1989) have demonstrated that many prospective teachers not only lack [the ability to recognize social inequities and their causes] but reject information regarding social inequity" (Ladson-Billings, 1995, p. 477). Perhaps implementing culturally sustaining, culturally responsive, and culturally relevant practices throughout teacher education will nurture identity awareness of future teachers, consequently opening their eyes to the harsh, unfair reality of our society.

Ladson-Billings (1995) explains that culturally relevant pedagogy is "a theoretical model that not only addresses student achievement but also helps students [including future teachers] to accept and affirm their cultural identity while developing critical perspectives that challenge inequities that schools (and other institutions) perpetuate" (p. 469). Therefore, we must offer teacher education programs that prominently incorporate multicultural education perspectives, methods, and ideologies. For our teachers to teach toward social justice—an intended outcome of multicultural education—they must recognize social injustice, and they must be willing to take on the role of social activist within their classrooms (Sleeter, 1996).

### *Multicultural Social Justice Education*

Nieto and Bode (2012) define social justice as "a philosophy, an approach, and actions that embody treating all people with fairness, respect, dignity, and generosity" (p. 12). This notion of social justice is embedded in multicultural education. However, social justice education also addresses *injustice*. According to Grant and Sleeter (2013), it "deals more directly than the other approaches with oppression and social structural inequality based on race, social class, gender, [or] disability" (p. 50). Indeed, the "goals are to reduce prejudice and discrimination against oppressed groups, to work toward equal opportunity and social justice for all groups, and to affect an equitable distribution of power among members of different cultural groups" (Grant & Sleeter, 2013, p. 49). This transformative approach to multicultural education seems to address Banks' (2006a) concern with the broken system.

Though theorists do not exactly agree on the characteristics of multicultural social justice education, the notion of sociotransformative action and change on the part of those engaged is similar. For example, Grant and Sleeter (2013) propose that there are four practices unique to multicultural social justice education: 1) democracy is actively practiced in the schools; 2) students learn how to analyze institutional inequality in their own life circumstances; 3) students learn to engage in social action so they can change unfair social processes; and 4) bridges are built between various oppressed people (e.g., people who are poor, people of color, and white women) so they can work together to advance their common interests. Similarly, Nieto (2012), who approaches multicultural education from a sociopolitical perspective, lists seven characteristics of multicultural education: anti-racist education; basic education; important for all students; pervasive; education for social justice; a process; and critical pedagogy.

Gay (2004) further explains that multicultural education "teaches content about culturally pluralistic contributions to humankind and U.S. society; engages students actively and interactively with their own and others' cultural identity; and develops the kind of social consciousness, civic responsibility, and political activism needed to reconstruct society for greater pluralistic equality, truth, inclusion, and justice" (p. 32). Multicultural education is thus more than debunking stereotypes and utilizing various teaching techniques—it is about empowering students with the belief that they may make change within society.

Furthermore, it is "because [multicultural education] uses critical pedagogy as its underlying philosophy and focuses on knowledge, reflection, and action (praxis) as the basis for social change, [that it] promotes democratic principles of social justice" (Nieto, 2012, p. 42). Although the academic discourse about multicultural education is important, the multicultural reform movement will not advance unless we—educators and other stakeholders—connect these approaches to social movements (e.g., civil rights movements). We must put them into practice. Without action on the part of educators—and teaching children how to act—social justice will not prevail (Sleeter, 1996).

### LGBTQ-Inclusion

Though the early approaches of multicultural education focused solely on race and ethnicity, as women's rights, gay liberation, and the intersectionality of these identities became predominant concerns, the field of multicultural education and the issues it addresses broadened to envelop gender and sexual orientation—both of which fall under LGBTQ identities and issues. Banks and McGee Banks (2013) define multicultural education as:

> an educational reform movement, ... whose major goal is to change the structure of educational institutions so that male and female students, exceptional students, and students who are members of diverse racial, ethnic, language, and cultural groups will have an equal chance to achieve academically in school. (p. 1)

This well-intentioned definition, however, may exclude members of the LGBTQ community. The categorization of gender (or sex if the case may be) as "male and female" erases those who identify outside of this prescribed binary. For example, I identify as *genderqueer-woman*, which means I do not subscribe to the socially constructed gender binary system or to masculine and feminine gender labels—and thus am excluded from the definition above. Others may identify as a third gender or as no gender at all (Bornstein, 1994; Butler, 1990, 2004). Thus, our language and concepts can be improved upon when defining multicultural education—an education that is supposed to be *all-inclusive*.

Indeed, there have been advancements in multicultural education—for example, "preservice programs have begun to teach teachers how to create classrooms free of racism, sexism, able-ism, and classism" (Kissen, 2002, p. 2). However, "little has been done to integrate sexual diversity into the teacher education curriculum" (p. 2). Sexual orientation and gender identity are topics educators are hesitant to embrace (Murray, 2015), especially at the K–12 level. There are many reasons for this. For instance, those in charge of public education sometimes obstruct LGBTQ-inclusiveness under the misconception that the classroom—and the curriculum—will become sexualized. The fact is, the curriculum is already sexualized—it favors heterosexual, cisgender (i.e., those whose gender matches their assigned birth sex) individuals, and celebrates heteronormativity (i.e., the notion that heterosexuality is the norm) (Letts & Sears, 1999; McLaren, 1994; Pinar, 1998). Further, the literature regarding the LGBTQ Civil Rights Movement, LGBTQ issues, and LGBTQ-inclusiveness is relatively sparse in current multicultural education texts. Letts (2002) affirms: "It would not be an overstatement to characterize texts that deal with multicultural education as 'thin,' if not emaciated, in their treatment of sexual diversity and minoritized sexualities" (p. 120). Can we really consider this inclusion?

Even though groundbreaking scholars, such as Letts and Sears (1999), editors of *Queering Elementary Education: Advancing the Dialogue about Sexualities and Schooling* and Kissen (2002), editor of *Getting Ready for Benjamin: Preparing Teachers for Sexual Diversity in the Classroom*, advocated for the inclusion of gender identities and sexual orientation—outside of gender binary norms and heteronormativity—within teacher education decades ago, LGBTQ issues have been shallowly incorporated into multicultural education. This may change however, as the demand for LGBTQ civil rights (e.g., marriage equality, transgender rights [medical and otherwise], LGBTQ-inclusive curriculum, and banning discrimination based on sexual orientation and gender) becomes more prominent.

Thus, although LGBTQ-inclusiveness has made its way into multicultural education, the progress of its incorporation has been slow. To illustrate this point, Lipkin (2002) acknowledged, "when it comes to readying educators to deal effectively with LGBT[Q] students, there is virtual silence—few public demands and little reform of undergraduate and graduate curricula" (p. 13). And, over a decade later, Murray (2015) points out that "teacher preparation programs rarely acknowledge queer aspects of multiculturalism." Thus, "[a]s a result a majority of K–12 educators enter the field of teaching unprepared and/or unwilling to discuss queer issues as they relate to students and families, curriculum, and instruction" (p. 5). It seems that LGBTQ-inclusive education is on the same, slow trajectory as anti-racist education.

Indeed, LGBTQ-inclusive curriculum shares some of the obstacles of other attempts at inclusiveness. Like those who argue for anti-racist curriculum (Aronson & Steele, 2005; Banks & McGee Banks, 2013; Kozol, 1975; Nieto & Bode, 2013; Pollock, 2008), and touching on the notion of teacher "colorblindness," Nieto and Bode (2012) state:

> if used to mean nondiscriminatory in attitude and behavior, color blindness is not a bad thing. On the other hand, color blindness may result in refusing to accept differences and therefore accepting the dominant culture as the norm. In the case of lesbian, gay, bisexual, and transgender (LGBT) students, this attitude may be expressed as "I don't care what they do in their private lives; I just don't want them to broadcast it." This may be touted as accepting and nondiscriminatory, but the same statement is not generally made about heterosexual students. (p. 156)

Furthermore, many teachers, including teacher educators, may have personal and professional reasons to avoid LGBTQ-inclusiveness. Just as white teachers may not want to discuss race or racism for fear of learning about their own biases, Murray (2015) explains that "[t]eacher educators often exclude queer topics because the issues are beyond their consciousness, they are unsure of whether and how to approach such subject matter, and/or because of personal homophobic beliefs" (p. xiii; Lipkin, 2002; Sears, 1992).

Others conclude that "[p]reservice teachers, perhaps because they simply do not know about LGBTQ youth and culture or because they are resistant to thinking about sexual and gender diversity, are especially in need of more concerted education about their own effects on students and the pressures of institutionalized heteronormativity" (Mayo, 2014, p.14; DePalma & Atkinson, 2006; Ferfolja & Robinson, 2004; Wyatt et al., 2008). Murray (2015) continues, stating:

> Beyond a lack of awareness, many educators don't even know if they are allowed to discuss queer topics in their schools…. The fact that teacher preparation programs rarely address these issues only exacerbates fearful unknowns and perpetuates risk factors for queer youth. (p. 15)

These sentiments make clear that teacher education programs are failing preservice teachers.

Thus, actively incorporating LGBTQ issues into multicultural education will require addressing them not only in the K–12 curriculum, but also in preservice teacher education. Lipkin (2002) argues that "[e]ducation students need both extensive information on LGBT[Q] topics and practical methods for dealing with homosexuality in schools" (p. 18). He asserts that college courses should teach preservice teachers to: "understand the significance of LGBT[Q] issues in education"; "reduce bigotry, self-hatred, and violence by increasing tolerance for sexuality differences"; "facilitate the integration of LGBT[Q] families into the school community"; and "collaborate with the greater community in achieving these ends" (p. 18).

It is obvious that these scholars are echoing the pleas of Banks (1988, 1999, 2004, 2010, 2013, 2016) and his work in developing multicultural education, its purpose, and how it should be implemented. They share Banks' concern to integrate multicultural education practices into all aspects of schooling. They also suggest that there is much more work to be done. Indeed, just as earlier forms of multicultural education have advanced civil right movements, LGBTQ-inclusive multicultural curriculum in K–12 classrooms, teacher education, and across higher education may help members of our society better understand, and eventually accept, LGBTQ people as productive and contributing citizens. While I reflect on this (hi)story of LGBTQ-inclusiveness within multicultural education, I want to reiterate the importance of recognizing identity intersectionality—including gender identity and sexual orientation—as an element of including LGBTQ concerns and (hi)stories into multicultural education.

### Intersectionality

In 1983, Apple and Weis argued that ideologies—beliefs, principles, and thoughts—are not only in one's head, they are "social processes" (p. 24)—processes that "sometimes overlap, compete … and clash with each other" (p. 24). "It is actually out of the articulation with, clash among, or contradictions among and within, say, class, race, and sex that ideologies are lived in one's day-to-day life" (p. 24). Indeed, beliefs and perspectives are not formed by only one aspect of one's identity but are formed when the "intersectionality" of one's identities is acknowledged.

Intersectionality applies not only to beliefs—but to the many personal and cultural variables that constitute an individual. The idea of intersectionality of identities (Apple & Weiss, 1983; Gay, 2010; Grant & Sleeter, 1985; Lorde, 1984; Truth, 1851; Pollard, 2013) is a common thread through the progression of civil rights movements and the evolution of multicultural education. For that reason, LGBTQ-inclusive curriculum and multicultural education converge in their need to address intersectionality.

There is, however, an historical struggle within multicultural education between focusing on one identity versus the intersectionality of many identities. For example, "[v]ictims of racism and ethnic discrimination and violence worry that attention to other forms of human diversity dilutes multicultural education's ability to address their concerns" (Ladson-Billings, 2004, p. 57). Some argue that the "complexity of identities that individuals experience makes it difficult to craft a multicultural mission that speaks to the specificity of identity" (p. 57). And, "attempts to be all things to all people seem to minimize the effective impact of multicultural education as a vehicle for school and social change" (p. 57). Ladson-Billings (2004) continues, noting that the incorporation of queer studies (Fuss, 1991; Sedgwick, 1990) and gender issues into multicultural education added to the complexity of identities in a way that might distract from instances in which discrimination is aimed at just *one* aspect of identity. Thus, identity awareness requires a balancing of concerns for intersectionality and those instances in which discrete aspects of identity are salient.

Building on Lorde's (1984, 1988) work, queer scholar Mayo (2014) takes an "intersectional approach" (Lekus, 2014, p. 232) when it comes to thinking about LGBTQ students and LGBTQ-inclusivity. She examines "how sexual orientation and gender identity are one aspect of students' identities that also intersect with their other identities" (Mayo, 2014, p. 14). Consequently, an important goal of multicultural education—as learned from civil rights movements—is to teach the idea of intersectionality of race, ethnicity, socioeconomic status, sexual orientation, gender, and ability. "By taking account of the intersections of categories of identity, it becomes clear that the identities of all people are multiple" (p. 28). Indeed, "[b]y examining the critiques of the various rights and liberation movements, we can further understand that all communities are made up of diverse people, not all of whom are adequately served by the community norms or political groups that claim to represent them" (p. 28). It is within these complexities that real advancements—such as LGBTQ-inclusiveness—can be made within multicultural education. Ultimately, one must recognize the "interlocking ways race, gender, and sexuality shape meanings, lives, and possibilities" as a "necessity of fighting for justice" (Mayo, 2014, p. 22; Combahee River Collective, 1982;

Lorde, 1984, 1988). The key to eliminating oppressive behavior is by taking an "intersectional approach" to discussing identities and ideologies—an approach that should be incorporated into every teacher preparation program.

## MULTICULTURAL TEACHER EDUCATION

Presently, multicultural education represents six categories of identification: race, ethnicity, socioeconomic status, sexual orientation, gender, and ability. However, the attention given to these identities is not evenly balanced (Banks, 2016; Grant et al., 2004). And though multicultural education reform started over forty years ago, non-dominant groups still struggle for recognition. This lack of recognition offers citizens—including students—a false representation of our society, culture, and history. In addition, misleading or false representation offers false hope. The mantra "if you just work hard you will succeed," often repeated in schools, is largely a myth. Millions of children in this country are not given the same opportunities as their white, middle-class peers (Kozol, 1991). Indeed, even with civil rights movements and campaigns, laws and policies that are supposed to protect "equal education for all" in the United States are often not applied equally.

Furthermore, equal application of law and policy does not ensure equitable outcomes. This is evident in the "disproportionate number of students who are African American, Mexican American, Puerto Rican, American Indian, and some Asian American groups [who] score below European American students on national standardized tests." Further, "the number of females, students of color, and low-income students participating in advanced science and mathematics classes is not proportionate to their representation in schools." Sadly, these students "are offered little or no encouragement to enroll in advanced courses that are necessary to be successful in college" (Gollnick & Chinn, 2004, p. 29). Thus, educators should consciously consider the intent and spirit of law and policy, to increase the likelihood that those whom the system may be failing receive equitable treatment.

To accomplish this, however, educators need to *understand* the struggles of non-dominant groups. While multicultural education has come a long way in providing new teachers with this knowledge, through teacher education curriculum, much *still* needs to be done. This is particularly true about LGBTQ issues. Indeed, the invisibility of LGBTQ people is still rampant in K–12 and teacher education curriculum (Murray, 2015). We do not need to look much further than the quotations above to note the acceptance of a gender binary and the absence of transgender and intersex people. But "a multicultural approach values diversity and encourages critical thinking, reflection, and action," and "through this process, students are empowered both individually and collectively to become active learners" (Nieto, 2012, p. 54). This approach can and should be used at all levels of education—from preschool to teacher education—and should include the struggles of the LGBTQ community.

## *Multicultural Social Justice Teacher Education*

Controversial topics and critical thinking are not widely taught in K–12 education. They must nevertheless be incorporated into *teacher education*. Nieto (2012) critically points out that "as institutions, schools are charged with maintaining the status quo, and discussing such issues might seem to threaten the status quo" (p. 52). Therefore, teacher educators need to persuade future teachers to break free from "domesticating education" (Freire, 1970) and perpetuating the status quo, and encourage them to design curriculum that promotes critical literacy. Comber (2001) asserts that "when teachers and students are engaged in critical literacy, they will begin asking complicated questions about language and power, about people and lifestyle, about morality and ethics, about who is advantaged and who is disadvantaged" (p. 271). They will be engaged in multicultural social justice education.

The need for multicultural teacher education developed when educators realized that the attention that people of color, women, LGBTQ people, and those of other non-dominant groups received within the classroom was negative or minimal. Baker (1973, 1994) noticed the need for and developed one of the first multicultural teacher education programs. Her objectives included: providing "experiences that would help student teachers develop an educational philosophy consistent with multicultural reality," exposing "students to the historical and cultural dimensions of ethnic groups" and, encouraging "the planning of classroom learning experiences that would reflect various cultural perspectives" (Baker, 1973, p. 306). Moreover, current goals of multicultural teacher education include informing prospective teachers of the reality of diversity within society; what to expect in classrooms; and how to implement, or at the very least start thinking about, multicultural education and its importance.

The minimalization, or absence, of multicultural teacher education has practical consequences. Grant and Sleeter (2013) emphasize that "a teacher's failure to consider the integration of race (including national origin), social class, and gender can lead to an oversimplified or inaccurate understanding of what occurs in schools and, therefore, to an inappropriate or simplistic prescription of educational equity and excellence" (p. 45). Ultimately:

> schools should be model communities that mirror the kind of democratic society and multicultural citizenship we envision. In democratic schools, the following occurs: curriculum reflects the cultures of the diverse groups within society; the languages and dialects that students speak remain respected and valued; cooperation rather than competition is fostered among students; and students from diverse racial, ethnic, and social-class groups experience equal-status in the school. (Banks, 1999, p. 58)

For this to occur, "teachers must obtain a more liberal education, greater familiarity with ethnic cultures, and a more acute awareness of the racist assumptions on which much social science research is based if they are to become effective change agents in minority education" (Banks, 2006b, p. 113).

It is important to acknowledge that the need for multicultural social justice teacher education stems, in part, from often innocent limitations that preservice teachers bring to the field. Nieto and Bode (2012) point out that:

> most teachers are sincerely concerned about their students and want very much to provide them with the best education possible. Nonetheless, because of their own limited experiences and education, they may know very little about the students they teach. As a result, their beliefs about students of diverse backgrounds may be based on spurious assumptions and stereotypes. (p. 6)

These limitations, however, can be overcome. As Baker (1973) explains, "the purpose of multicultural education is to make individuals aware of the diversity reflected by individuals, groups, and communities. It encourages an understanding and appreciation of similarities and differences among cultures" (p. 306).

But it is not enough to be aware of the juxtapositions between cultures. The real tension lies within us. We need to struggle to understand our own identities, how they intersect, and how they affect or impact our behavior and perspectives. To be sure, each of the elements of multicultural education (e.g., anti-racist, responsiveness, and social justice), along with an understanding of intersectionality, should be prominent within a multicultural social justice teacher education classroom. Each of these elements compliments and reinforces the other. But further, *identity awareness*—a practice that most people, including teachers, do not nurture—must also be cultivated. The first step in employing a multicultural social justice education is recognizing societal injustices and how our own personal beliefs and identities contribute to maintaining or challenging the status quo. Awareness is an important step, but it is merely the beginning toward real change.

### Identity Awareness

Even during the preliminary stages of multicultural education, one of the goals of ethnic studies was that "an individual must clarify his or her own sense of ethnic and personal identity before he or she can positively relate to individuals who belong to other ethnic and racial groups" (Banks, 2006b, p. 75). Indeed, many scholars agree that teachers must know who *they* are *and* who their students are—while understanding the changing nature of and fluidity of identity—if they are going to be successful (Banks, 2006b; Gollnick & Chinn, 2004; Grant & Sleeter, 2011a; Howard, 2006; Nieto, 2010; Nieto & Bode, 2012). Moreover, teacher preparation education should emphasize practices in self-awareness and the importance of being aware of, and teaching in connection to, student identities. By understanding and accepting how you identify and appreciating the intersectionality of these identities, as a teacher you will understand yourself and your perspectives and will have a greater chance to understand the perspectives of your students—thus developing effective multicultural social justice curricula.

Ultimately, identity awareness is the first step toward teaching multicultural education that promotes social justice.

## CONCLUSION

The (hi)story of multicultural education continues as scholars explore new perspectives, ways of knowing, and influences of identity. Indeed, my work may add to this (hi)story. With a focus on identify awareness (of self and others), a queer theory framework, and autoethnographic methods, I propose and explore *queer multicultural social justice teacher education*—a critical approach that breaks down, and may reach beyond, rigid identity labels that may provide learners with opportunities to investigate ways to dismantle heteronormativity, rethink binary systems of identification, and deconstruct socially constructed identities in personal and meaningful ways. The next two chapters provide foundational, practical, and personal (hi)stories of queer theory and autoethnography, respectively, as major components of this project.

# CHAPTER 2

# QUEER PERSPECTIVES

We all look at the world through theoretical frameworks, lenses, or perspectives. We may utilize more than one lens at a time or strictly adhere to one framework as we analyze our world. We may not know how to identify this framework or even be aware that it exists. Our perspectives are formed through our experiences, knowledge, and identities. Even before I heard the term "queer theory" I practiced it as my worldview. And the more I learned about queer theory, the more it seemed to "fit" me.

I, like queer theory, buck against the norm. I started questioning the quintessential gender norm at a very young age. As a young girl, I questioned why I had to, and in fact refused to, wear dresses—they made me so unhappy. They did not reflect me or my young Michelleness. But the norm was for little girls to wear pretty dresses on Easter Sunday, for example. Indeed, I did not (and still do not) have an affinity for stereotypical *girl* (or *woman*) things, like dolls (and babies). I share part of my story of gender aversion in "What makes *girls* and *boys* so desirable?: STEM education beyond gender binaries" (Knaier, 2019b):

> As a child, I did not play with dolls. Instead, I played tackle football with the boys from the neighborhood. I created zoos with blocks and little plastic animals. I designed racetracks in the sandbox for my matchbox cars. During my adolescent years, I recognized that, unlike my sister, I did not have an affinity toward babies. I never had the desire to become a mother, and so many times my mom and aunts would say

to me, "Wait until you're older. You'll change your mind." Then they would laugh. This always upset me. I felt like they were not listening to me. (p. 209)

I felt like I did not fit in or belong. The reality is: I did not, and still do not, fit in with my biological family. I am a genderqueer atheist who hails from a heteronormative, Catholic family. Luckily, I was able to find my queer, chosen family—a family that "fits" me.

But what about those students who do not fit in at home or at school? Generally, young people (like my young self) do not get to choose their family or the school they attend. These schools are often secure in their heteronormative ways and are thus a breeding ground for bullying behavior (Kosciw et al., 2018). One way of combating heteronormativity within K–12 classrooms is through LGBTQ-inclusiveness and queer teacher education, as discussed in Chapter One. For this to occur, however, queer multicultural social justice teacher education must be implemented. Sadly, lesbian, gay, bisexual, transgender, and queer (LGBTQ)-inclusiveness within multicultural education is "thin" (Letts, 2002, p. 120), if not non-existent. However, developing multicultural social justice education (one that serves to "prepare future citizens to take action to make society better serve the interests of all groups of people" (Grant & Sleeter, 2013, p. 50)) through the lens of queer theory (a framework that supports the exploration of gender and sexuality in relation to power) may result in a more inclusive education by breaking down barriers created and supported by the heteronormative status quo. Ultimately, by implementing queer theory doctrines within all aspects of education (e.g., curriculum, policy, and environment), we may "create more equitable, relatable, safe and socially just environments in which [all] students can learn" (Zacko-Smith & Smith, 2010, p. 7). By uniting these disciplines—queer theory and multicultural social justice education—and implementing them within teacher education, queer multicultural social justice teacher education may be developed.

In this chapter, I relay an origin story of queer theory. Beginning briefly with critical theory and the works of Derrida and Foucault, I introduce some of the main underpinnings (e.g., deconstruction of identity categories and power in relation to identity labels) that inspired Butler (1990, 1993)—whose works, in turn, gave rise to queer theory. Next, building on the work of Snyder and Broadway (2004), who applied queer theory as a means for interrupting heteronormativity, fracturing binary systems, and deconstructing socially constructed aspects of identity within biology textbooks, I explore how these three principles are broadly represented within queer theory. Although queer theory is more complex than these three principles, these are the features I focus on in this study. Then, I attempt to define *queer* and the act of *queering*; all the while knowing that these terms may be inherently undefinable. Finally, I discuss how queer theory may be applied to multicultural social justice teacher education by briefly describing the need for LGBTQ-inclusive education; discussing how to queer multicultural social justice teacher education; and exploring identities (of self and others) within queer multicultural social justice teacher education.

## QUEER ORIGINS

Recognizing the "interlocking ways race, gender, and sexuality shape meanings, lives, and possibilities" is a "necessity of fighting for justice" (Mayo, 2014, p. 22; Combahee River Collective, 1982; Lorde, 1984, 1988). This notion echoes the words of critical theorists. Marcuse (1965, 1991a, 1991b), for example, asserted that the intersectionality of identities (i.e., race, ethnicity, sexual orientation, gender, and ability) within the working class must be recognized and that these groups had to come together as members of the working class to revolt and create change. As one commentator explained, "[p]eople of color, women, gays, and intellectuals sought to make sense of the world and gain a measure of existential meaning and purpose for themselves" (Bronner, 2011, p. 91). The idea that people with different or intersectional identities must work together to promote change and demand justice is not only pertinent to civil rights movements (as discussed in Chapter One), but also a foundation upon which queer scholars built.

"Critical theory insists that thought must respond to the new problems and the new possibilities for liberation that arise from changing historical circumstances" (Bronner, 2011, p. 1). This responsive-evolution of critical theory permitted the emergence of queer theory "from feminist paradigms and post-structuralist/post-modernist theory" (Johnson & Lugg, 2011, p. 236). Inspired by the works of Derrida (e.g., deconstruction, (de)centering) and Foucault (e.g., dichotomous logic, normalizing discourses), and born from the works of Butler (1990, 1993), Sedgwick (1990) and others, "queer theory" thus "implies a radical politics approach to deconstructing gender and sexuality" (Johnson & Lugg, 2011, p. 236)—an approach that would, ultimately, impact multicultural teacher education.

## PRINCIPLES OF QUEER THEORY

The phrase "queer theory" was coined by Teresa de Lauretis (1991) (Giffney, 2009; Halperin, 2003; Johnson & Lugg, 2011; Plummer, 2011; Turner, 2000). As Halperin (2003) recounts:

> [de Lauretis] had heard the word "queer" being tossed about in a gay-affirmative sense [...] in New York during the late 1980s. She had the courage, and the conviction, to pair that scurrilous term with the academic holy word, "theory." The intent of her intentional provocation was "to unsettle the complacency of 'lesbian and gay studies,'" to "open a wider space" within the field of empirical social sciences "for reflections of a theoretical order, to introduce a problematic of multiple differences into what had tended to be a monolithic, homogenizing discourse of (homo)sexual difference, and to offer a possible escape from the hegemony of white, male, middle-class models of analysis." (pp. 339–340)

Thus, de Lauretis encapsulated a way of conducting academic analyses that may support inclusive, intersectional, or decentered ways of thought. Ultimately, through the advent and implementing of queer theory, one tries to dismantle or deconstruct "the center" of identities, or categories of people, which allows for marginalization against binary opposites (e.g., man-woman, straight-gay, good-evil), thus eliminating such marginalization of and categories of "others" (see, Derrida & Spivak, 2016).

Consistent with this approach, featured within queer theory are three principles: interrupting heteronormativity; fracturing binary systems; and deconstructing socially constructed aspects of identity (Snyder & Broadway, 2004). Admittedly, queer theory is more multifaceted than these three categories, as it engages with and interrupts these ideals, and others, simultaneously. In this chapter, however, I focus on these three ideas to provide a lens through which educators may engage with queer theory. Additionally, included in this summary are examples of how each of these features may influence or intersect with education, thus supporting the need for *queer(ing)* multicultural teacher education.

### Interrupting Heteronormativity

"Queer theory is at heart about politics—things like power and identity, language, and difference" (Wilchins, 2014, p. 9). These are the complexities Foucault explored and analyzed, providing a basis for other theorists who continue the difficult task of studying, questioning, and combating harmful societal norms, such as heteronormativity. These widely accepted norms deeply affect our culture and our behaviors. Sumara and Davis (1999) explain that "[l]iving within heteronormative culture means learning to 'see' straight, to 'read' straight, [and] to 'think' straight" (p. 202). Moreover, heteronormativity not only dictates our language regarding gender, sex, and sexual orientation, and our aesthetic and behavioral expressions of them—it also claims that human life is *dependent* on its existence. Warner (1993) affirms:

> Het[erosexual] culture thinks of itself as the elemental form of human association, as the very model of intergender relations, as the indivisible basis of all community, and as the means of reproduction without which society wouldn't exist. (p. xxi)

These harmful heteronormative beliefs and fallacies are (re)enforced in schools, workplaces, homes, and the media via made-up gender stereotypes, unlawful segregated spaces, and discriminatory policies.

The popular acceptance of the "superiority of heterosexuality" and the "deep-seated hatred or fear of those who love the same gender (homophobia)" (Sears, 1999, p. 7) reinforces a powerful heteronormative status quo—effectively denying the existence of other ways of being. Foucault explored the normalization of heterosexuality and other societal norms, inspiring Butler (1990, 1993) and Wittig (1992) to argue

> that heterosexuality is a complex matrix of discourses, institutions, and so on, that has become normalized in our culture, thus making particular relationships, lifestyles, and identities, seem natural, ahistorical, and universal. (Sullivan, 2003, p. 39)

Concurrently, these cultural assumptions demonize and ridicule "other" relationships, lifestyles, and identities outside of the assumed norm—which is evidenced by bullying behaviors and anti-LGBTQ policies within schools and in society at large.

Heterosexuality, and thus, heteronormativity, are social constructs designed to keep power and control over "others." Because of this, "heterosexuality, as it is currently understood and experienced, is a (historically and culturally specific) truth-effect system of power/knowledge." And thus, "its dominant position and current configuration are contestable and open to change" (p. 39). Queer theory implemented within educational settings may be a catalyst for such change. Britzman (1995) asserts that through the application of queer pedagogy (an academic discipline devoted to exploring the intersection between queer theory and critical pedagogy), we can

> attempt to move away from psychologic explanations like homophobia, which individualizes heterosexual fear and loathing toward gay and lesbian subjects at the expense of examining how heterosexuality becomes normalized as natural. (p. 153)

Through this examination of "normalization," and by engaging in critical discourse, queer theory may disrupt heteronormativity. For example, Snyder and Broadway (2004) offer that by implementing queer theory in a classroom setting, educators may "interrupt heteronormative thinking to eliminate the destructive homophobia and heterosexism and create more interesting forms of thinking" (p. 621). Further, these practices may work toward deconstructing and combating the acceptance of normalized binary systems, such as sexuality (e.g., straight or gay), biological sex (e.g., male and female), and gender (e.g., masculine and feminine).

### Fracturing Binary Systems

Foucault was critical of dichotomous logic, for example, of "the (humanist) distinction between rulers and ruled [and] power and powerless" (Sullivan, 2003, p. 42). His foundational analysis allowed for the expansion of these critical ideas in relation to binary systems generally. Though cultural norms, particularly in the West, continue to categorize people into binary groups (e.g., male/female, masculine/feminine, gay/straight), not all of us fit into these socially-defined boxes—and some of us do not fit into any (Butler, 1993; Fausto-Sterling, 2000). For example, biological sex identities occur on a spectrum (Butler, 1990, 2004; Fausto-Sterling, 2000; Killermann, 2013) and are not captured by a male-female binary system (e.g., intersex).

Moreover, the socially accepted gender binary (as well as other binary systems) eliminates and ignores the nuances of gender identity and its relationship with biological sex and sexuality (as well as other identities, such as ethnicity and ability). Indeed, as Butler (1990) presents:

> If one "is" a woman, that is surely not all one is: the term fails to be exhaustive, not because a pregendered "person" transcends the specific paraphernalia of its gender, but because gender is not always constituted coherently or consistently in different historical contexts, and because gender intersects with racial, class, ethnic, sexual, and regional modalities of discursively constituted identities. As a result, it becomes impossible to separate out "gender" from political and cultural intersections in which it is invariably produced and maintained. (pp. 4–5)

Further, "[b]y taking account of the intersections of categories of identity, it becomes clear that the identities of all people are multiple" (Mayo, 2014, p. 14), non-binary, and complicated. Sullivan (2003) assures that "[an intersectional] approach [to identity] would undermine dichotomies such as heterosexual/queer in that it would demonstrate that heterosexuals have multiple subject positions and thus not all heterosexuals are situated socially, politically, economically, in the same way" (p. 49).

Additionally, queer theory acknowledges and critically analyzes the relationship between sexuality, sex, and gender, for the terms are not synonymous or prescriptive. As Sedgwick (2008) explains:

> [G]ender is *definitionally* built into determinations of sexuality, in a way that neither of them is definitionally intertwined with, for instance, determinations of class or race. It is certainly true that without a concept of gender there could be, quite simply, no concept of homo- or heterosexuality. (p. 31, emphasis original)

Thus, these identities, and their complexities, should be recognized and examined. By deconstructing binary systems, we understand that sex, gender, and, thus, *sexuality* are much more complex than the oppositional binaries generally accepted.

Once more, gender is a powerful example of how rethinking a binary yields compelling insights. Building upon Foucault's analysis of how dichotomous logic is construed and enacted through power, knowledge, and language as practiced in culture, and upon Derrida's concept of deconstruction, Butler (1990) asserts that gender is performed and regulated through societal norms. Jagose (1996) claims that:

> one of [Butler's] most influential achievements is to specify how gender operates as a regulatory construct that privileges heterosexuality and, furthermore, how the deconstruction of normative models of gender legitimates lesbian and gay subject-positions. (p. 83)

Moreover, in *Gender Trouble*, a work considered to be an early development and application of queer theory, Butler (1990) "sought to undermine any and all efforts to wield a discourse of truth to delegitimate minority gendered and sexual practices" (p. viii). Additionally, Butler's work attempts "to destabilize the entire system of sex regulation," and "binary oppositions such as gay/straight" (Sim & Van Loon, 2004, p. 158).

Butler also expands on "Foucault's (1978/1990) argument about the operations of power and resistance in order to demonstrate the ways in which marginalized identities are complicit with those identificatory regimes they seek to counter" (Jagose, 1996, p. 83). An excerpt from *Gender Trouble* supports this assertion:

> To expose the foundational categories of sex, gender, and desire as effects of a specific formation of power requires a form of critical inquiry that Foucault [...] designates as "genealogy." A genealogical critique refuses to search for the origins of gender, the inner truth of female desire, a genuine or authentic sexual identity that repression has kept from view; rather, genealogy investigates the political stakes in designating as an *origin* and *cause* those identity categories that are in fact the *effects* of institutions, practices, discourses with multiple and diffuse points of origin. The task of this inquiry is to center on—and decenter—such defining institutions: phallogocentrism and compulsory heterosexuality. (Butler, 1990, p. xxxi, emphasis original)

Indeed, gender performance is "politically shaped" (Butler, 1990, p. 175).

Butler asserts that "gender is a performance with clearly punitive consequences. Discrete genders are part of what 'humanizes' individuals within contemporary culture," and "we regularly punish those who fail to do their gender right" (p. 190). Such punishments are witnessed daily within schools, are broadcasted within the media, and are reflected in anti-transgender policies. But, by interrupting heteronormativity and rethinking and deregulating sexuality, biological sex, and gender categories, queer theory attempts to legitimize each of us as individuals—thus, recognizing the need for deconstructing not only these categories, but other socially constructed identities as well.

### Deconstructing Socially Constructed Identity

Disrupting heteronormativity, dissolving binary systems, and deconstructing socially constructed identities are difficult to untangle—for each is defined by the other. By offering opportunities within classrooms, particularly within teacher education programs, to discuss, deconstruct, and construct personal identities in relation to other identities represented in our culture, we can begin to not only break down binaries, but also dismantle the socially constructed language used and understand the power given to certain labels.

In practice, queer theory examines and deconstructs language while recognizing the effects of its use. Zacko-Smith and Smith (2010) explain:

> Language fashions our understanding, positions us to take action, and exerts an influence on our day-to-day lived realities; using it carelessly can certainly lead to oppression, injustice, and violence. In particular, theorists such as Foucault (1980) demonstrated how language can be used to dominate and control, [...] and requires that educators pay attention to the ways words, both written and spoken, impact the lives of students and the greater community. (p. 7)

Further, without the opportunity to examine the cultural and historical aspects of language and behavioral norms, we continue to support the status quo. Meyer (2007) concludes:

> By continuing to live within prescribed linguistic and behavioral matrices, the hierarchical binaries of male-female and gay-straight remain unchallenged. This work of dismantling socially invented categories is necessary to create educational spaces that liberate and create opportunities as opposed to limiting and closing down the diversity of human experiences. (p. 23)

To be certain, "queer theory does not intend to flip the [socially constructed heterosexual/queer binary] hierarchy, but to rupture the boundaries to see that they are not polar opposites but a part of each other, and that the implied value and order are not rigid (Angelides, 1994; Derrida, 1997)" (Snyder & Broadway, 2004, pp. 620–621). Moreover, by applying queer theory to education, we offer opportunities for, the encouragement of, and the practice of analyzing our language and its power, as it is applied to self and others—a practice necessary to promote multicultural social justice education, a sociotransformative approach to realizing and combating injustices and inequities within society.

Again, queer theory is more complex than each of these elements: interrupting heteronormativity, fracturing binary systems, and deconstructing socially constructed aspects of identity. However, "combined, these principles *queer* by deviating from normalized and rigid identities, challenging the status quo, rejecting assimilation, and questioning the notion that the social order of sexuality is the natural order" (Snyder & Broadway, 2004, p. 619; italics added). But what does it mean *to* queer?

## QUEER(ING)

Since de Lauretis (1991) coined the term "queer theory," there has been much discourse within the fields of education, gay and lesbian studies, and in other contexts about what *queer*, and thus *queer theory*, actually is. Originally an anti-gay epithet, *queer* is a term "rescued from its history" and is "now embraced by [some] people who eschew rigid sexuality and gender categories" (Petrow & Chew, 2011, p. 19)[1]. And, although "it has been criticized for referring to nothing in particular yet entertaining the possibility of encompassing everything, queer is the term that now defines an entire body of academic thought: queer theory" (Johnson & Lugg, 2011, p. 236; Turner, 2000). Here, de Lauretis (1991) clarifies her intent:

> In sense, the term "Queer Theory" was arrived at in the effort to avoid all of these fine distinctions in our discursive protocols, not to adhere to any one of the given

---

[1] Not all those who "eschew rigid sexuality and gender categories" embrace the term *queer*.

terms, not to assume their ideological liabilities, but to both transgress and transcend them—or at the very least problematize them. (p. v)

It is this intent to "problematize" societal assumptions, constructions, and attributes of sex, gender, and sexuality that drives queer theory.

Queer theory is a performative, academic pursuit. It indicates action. It is a *verb*. To clarify Britzman (1995) expounds:

Those who seem uncomfortable think the term queer is a noun or an identity. But the queer and the theory in Queer Theory signify *actions*, not actors. It can be thought of as a verb, or as a citational relation that signifies more than the signifier. (p. 153, emphasis original)

*Queering*, or *to queer*, is to take action against the heteronormative status quo. Here, Mayo (2007) describes its complexities:

Queer theory works the verb "to queer" to centralize the constant need for critical attention to the processes of subjectification, whereby particular meanings of identity come to form potentially limiting understandings of identities, practices, and communities. (p. 80)

Further, supporting this notion of *action*, "Doty [(2000)] suggests that 'queer' may be a particular form of cultural readership and textual coding that creates spaces not contained within conventional categories such as gay, straight, and transgender[ ]" (Plummer, 2011, p. 201)[2].

It is thus through the queering of analyses, conversations, and learning spaces that educators and students are encouraged to queer their own thinking and perceptions of themselves, others, and their environment. Furthermore, implementing queer curriculum may bolster learners to explore their identities and the ways in which these identities intersect and impact each other. In Chapter Three, I illustrate how queer theory as a cultural analysis, or framework, may be applied to multicultural social justice teacher education.

## QUEER MULTICULTURAL SOCIAL JUSTICE TEACHER EDUCATION

In Chapter One, I explored the historical beginnings and evolution of multicultural education within the United States, which included the incorporation of LGBTQ issues within multicultural education and the integration of multicultural education into teacher education curriculum. There, I focused on *LGBTQ-inclusive multicultural education*. Although some scholars may not use the terms *LGBTQ-inclusive* and *queer* education synonymously, if done correctly they may be coextensive. To be certain, LGBTQ-inclusive curriculum is not produced by

---

[2] Here the brackets ([ ]) represent my omission of the term *transgendered*, as I choose not to use the politically-incorrect term in my writing.

simply adding one or two accomplished LGBTQ people or monumental LGBTQ civil rights events to pre-packaged curriculum—though some educators are content to go only so far. In fact, LGBTQ-inclusive curriculum should reflect the principles of queer theory as I have presented them in this chapter.

Indeed, multicultural education is an appropriate means for interrupting heteronormativity, rethinking binary systems, and deconstructing socially constructed aspects of identity. As defined by Gay (2004), *multicultural education* is "a set of beliefs and explanations that recognize and value the importance of ethnic and cultural diversity in shaping lifestyles; social experiences; personal identities; and educational opportunities of individuals, groups, and nations" (p. 33). Similarly, as a critical theory, queer theory is used "to criticize and analyze society to promote human emancipation and to expose ideas and systems that impede them and focus on issues of power and justice and the ways that the economy, matters of race, class, and gender, ideologies, discourses, education, religion, and other social institutions and cultural dynamics interact to connect a social system" (Kincheloe & McLaren, 2000, p. 281). Thus, a critical application of queer theory within multicultural teacher education may encourage educators to examine and (de)construct various socially constructed identities (their own and others) and how these identities are influenced by power and justice within our society, with the goals of interrupting heteronormativity, rethinking binary systems, and dismantling socially constructed aspects of identity—thus moving us toward an equitable and more just society.

## The Need

Queer theory has pragmatic relevance to education. Hardships, inequities, and injustices largely unique to LGBTQ student populations (e.g., antigay name-calling, retarded social development, and lack of support of LGBTQ youth) in school settings can be curbed through implementing LGBTQ-inclusive curriculum (Knaier, 2017). Evidence to support this claim is reported by the Gay, Lesbian & Straight Education Network (GLSEN) (Kosciw et al., 2018), which found that when schools have gay-straight alliances, outward support from teachers, and LGBTQ-inclusive curriculum, antigay name-calling decreases, LGBTQ students are better supported and mentored, and the overall policing of sex, gender, and sexuality declines. But a simple inclusive curriculum may not be enough.

The *policing* of identity, or perceived identity, that occurs in school settings can escalate into violent forms of aggression or *bullying* (a form of aggression that seeks to police and enforce societal norms). Importantly, "bullying needs to be understood in terms which acknowledge the regime of normalizing practices in which sex/gender boundaries are policed" (Martino & Pallotta-Chiarolli, 2003, p. 54). Statistics show that students with characteristics inconsistent with heteronormative ideals or that push the boundari er (and other) binaries (e.g., boys that are feminine) are at a higher risk for bullying (Kosciw et al., 2018).

Given its grounding in rigid notions of identity, the problem of bullying may be best addressed through queer theory. Zacko-Smith and Smith (2010) assert:

> The true innovation that the use of Queer Theory provides educators is that it changes the focus from understanding LGBTQ students as an "other," prompting a reexamination of what it means to view sexuality without the use of the strict labels and "organizing terms" that have become all too easy to associate with it, and which ultimately serve as a mechanism for harassment, discrimination and, occasionally, violence. (p. 6)

Through this "reexamination," and the deconstruction of harmful "organizing terms," students might move past these damaging labels—thus eliminating the senseless shaming and bullying associated with such labels.

### Queer(ing) Multicultural Social Justice Teacher Education

Sedgwick (1990) and Butler (1990, 1993) established a solid foundation for the development, growth, and application of queer theory. In turn, the work of these pioneers encouraged scholars within the field of education, such as Pinar (1998), Letts and Sears (1999), Kissen (2002), and Murray (2015), to utilize queer theory to transform multicultural education, teacher preparation education, and K–12 education. They did so not only through theoretical advancement but through practical advice regarding curricula, policies, and physical learning environments—elements needed to create cohesive learning atmospheres that support educational equality (Banks, 2004). Scholars such as these provide the foundation for my understanding of the history of queer theory and its attributes, as well as how this fluid, yet powerful, framework may be used to analyze and queer multicultural social justice teacher education.

As introduced above, *inclusivity* is part of queering education. There are many effective ways to introduce and include LGBTQ histories, accomplishments, and stories into already developed multicultural teacher education curricula, such as reading literature written by queer authors, studying LGBTQ Civil Rights Movements, and discussing the varying attributes of families (e.g., having two moms or a grandparent serving as parent). Coupling these ideas with "making sure that the language used and the resources (books, videos, workbooks, etc.) chosen for classes do not support the sexual orientation and gender identity status quo" may make a big difference toward *queering* education (Zacko-Smith & Smith, 2010, p. 7). In addition to inclusive language and resources, educators should consciously avoid making assumptions regarding the sex, gender, and sexuality of their students, including stereotypes that intersect, for example, with race, ethnicity, and socioeconomic status. By modeling critical approaches to identity, such as by asking students' their preferred names and pronouns, teacher educators may set an example of a queer approach to education.

Moreover, not only must future teachers be given an opportunity to examine and acknowledge their heteronormative beliefs and practices, they must recognize the many seemingly harmless, yet incredibly harmful practices that occur every day within classrooms (Murray, 2015). "Practices such as lining up, playing games, desk placement, and dress codes tend to be organized around (binary) gender and teachers can often reinforce gender stereotypes in their response to children's atypical behaviors and preferences in well-meaning attempts to save them from peer pressure (Slesaransky-Poe & Garcia, 2009)" (Carrera et al., 2012, p. 1008). But, when these actions are analyzed through the lens of queer theory in a multicultural teacher education setting, future teachers can begin to identify the potential harm these everyday practices may inflict on their students.

Still, *queering* multicultural teacher education is more than simply implementing LGBTQ-inclusivity. While inserting LGBTQ histories, accomplishments, and stories into the daily curriculum is beneficial (Kosciw et al., 2018), and recognizing heteronormative beliefs and practices is vital, queering multicultural curriculum is much more nuanced than that. Queer multicultural social justice teacher education is a critical approach that breaks down, and may reach beyond, rigid identity labels. By implementing methods, such as autoethnographic exercises, students are given opportunities to investigate ways to dismantle heteronormativity, rethink binary systems of identification, and deconstruct socially constructed identities in personal and meaningful ways.

Further, by engaging in queer multiculturalism we are "examining one's beliefs about sex, gender, and sexuality and coming to terms with one's comfort and knowledge (or lack thereof) about these topics and the epistemological implications that all of this has for each of us" (Letts, 2002, p. 124). By encouraging such explorations through the application of queer theory, students may question assumptions of and (de)construct identities while combating heteronormativity (Britzman, 1995). Indeed, when queer theory is applied to curriculum, learning communities, and policies, the beliefs, ideals, and norms attending to gender and sexuality may be deconstructed allowing for the "opening [of] new social imaginaries" (Carrera et al., 2012, p. 1009).

Moreover, if this approach to multicultural social justice teacher education is not implemented, the heteronormative status quo will continue. Taylor (2002) points out that "[t]he omission [of anti-heterosexism education] matters because we need future teachers to confront and unlearn their own homophobia (or apathy about others' homophobia) before they assume their influential places in the public school system (Baker & Fishbein, 1998; McCaskell, 1999)" (p. 220). However, to achieve such an understanding, one must become self-aware. Murray (2015) asserts that "[a] self-awareness of their own disposition can help teacher candidates confront queer issues in school even in the presence of self-conflicting ideological beliefs" (p. 35). The practice of analyzing and (de)constructing our perspectives and identities is a queer approach to learning.

Further, modeling such explorations within multicultural social justice teacher education may allow these practices to trickle down into K–12 classrooms and other levels of education. Meyer (2007) concludes that "[i]n order to move in this direction, it is important to apply the lenses offered by Queer Theory to creatively work through the current obstacles that prevent teachers from teaching passionately and connecting with their students and communities in meaningful ways" (p. 29). By queering multicultural social justice teacher education, we may encourage future teachers to critically examine their "dispositions toward queerness" in addition to their multicultural identities (e.g., race, ethnicity, socioeconomic status, sexual orientation, gender, and ability) in relation to power—an important element in pursuing social justice and promoting social justice education.

### Exploring Identities (of Self and Others)

As presented in Chapter One, multicultural education scholars note the importance of exploring and knowing one's own identity. Moreover, many agree that teachers must know who they are and who their students are—while understanding the changing nature and fluidity of identity—if they are going to be successful (Banks, 2006b; Gollnick & Chinn, 2004; Grant & Sleeter, 2011a; Howard, 2006; Nieto & Bode, 2012). Similarly, identity plays a role in queer theory. Johnson and Lugg (2011) assert that "the primary concern for queer theorists is identity and identity construction" (p. 236). They argue that the "principal inquiries [of queer theory] are the meanings of queer identities, the practices that are involved in shaping categories of identification, and the differences among those with similar identities (Turner, 2000, pp. 8–9)" (p. 236).

However, exploring identity does not necessarily mean finding appropriate *labels*. Rather, it may mean finding that identities are much more complex than descriptive language allows. Accordingly, educators may be "freed to envision and teach about culture as something that far exceeds tidy boundaries, something that flows. […] This is often quite at odds with the intent (whether tacit or enacted) of multiculturalism to bound and essentialize cultures or identity categories" (Letts, 2002, p. 122). Indeed, queer theory not only explores identity construction, but also "questions the notion of identity and its value for political practice because it recognizes that identity determined by national heritage, or derived from oppositional systems such as race, sex, gender, and sexuality, are inadequate (Greene, 1996)" (Snyder & Broadway, 2004, p. 620). Thus, merely knowing the identification categories in which students "fit" is not the secret ingredient to successful teaching (Fifield & Letts, 2014; Letts & Fifield, 2000).

While examining one's identity is an important reflective practice, it may not be enough for educators to be successful. Ultimately, the key to the connection of queer theory and identity may rest in exploring, but not *essentializing*, identity. Letts (2002) explains that "multicultural education as queer curriculum practice *exceeds* a focus on identities, individuals, or collectivities. It must move beyond the very important issues of [LGBTQ] people to also consider knowledge construction and validation, the allure of heteronormativity, the power of dichoto-mies, and critical textual practices" (p. 130, italics added). Examining and developing identity awareness may be consistent with an ultimate desire to move past identity labels and identity politics. The former may lead to the latter.

## CONCLUSION

Jagose (1996) warns that "[t]o attempt an overview of queer theory and to identify it as a significant school of thought [...] is to risk domesticating it, and fixing it in ways that queer theory resists fixing itself" (pp. 1–2). Likewise, Halberstam (1997) warns that *queer* "is in danger of stabilizing into an identity rather than remaining a radical category of identity" (p. 260). Educators can employ queer theory and yet counter this stabilization through "examining the complications that race, class, gender, and ethnicity bring to what is defined as ... LGBTQ," while also "insist[ing] on queer presence and being careful that one version of queer does not itself become another form of normal" (Mayo, 2014, p. 77).

Heteronormative beliefs and the policing of gender roles and other socially constructed identities are intertwined and supported within our culture. It is this entanglement of normalizing some identities while regulating other, marginal identities that is problematic. Indeed, the unfortunate acceptance of heteronorma-tive power within our culture allows socially constructed labels to define us and influences how we define each other. I propose to queer multicultural teacher education in a way that supports LGBTQ students and the LGBTQ community—and that encourages learners (including heterosexual and cisgender people) to consider, question, and analyze the role gender, sex, and sexuality interact with, influence, and maintain social power and control.

*Queer* multicultural social justice teacher education is a critical approach that breaks down, and reaches beyond, rigid identity labels—thus allowing students, in part, to investigate ways to dismantle heteronormativity, rethink binary systems of identification, and deconstruct socially constructed identities. This is the sort of multicultural education that I am interested in advancing through my research and work: the kind of education that provides opportunities for and encourages educators to examine and (de)construct identity and its espoused privileges; the kind of education that may increase my success as a teacher educator; and, certainly, the kind of education that would have provided the much needed support my young self deserved.

CHAPTER 3

# QUEER(ING) CRITICAL AUTOETHNOGRAPHY

Phillion (2002) asserts that narrative research, including purposeful storytelling, begins "with people's experiences and their lives rather than with theory" (p. 553). By "thinking narratively" (p. 553), we immerse ourselves in, and therefore enhance, our research. Arguably, I cannot separate my multicultural beliefs and practices from my everyday life; nor can I separate *myself* from analyzing academic research. It is because of this inability to separate my personal self from my professional self (and all my other selves) (Whitlock, 2010), that I recognize why my identities matter when I create curriculum, and why curriculum development is an appropriate experience to examine. As the autoethnographer of this study (and as a queer multicultural educator), I developed *Queer explorations of identity awareness*; performed and developed the curriculum and analyzed the process and data and shared my findings (i.e., my story) using autoethnographic methods. Based on my literature review and personal engagement with this process, I argue that educators should perform and practice such exercises.

As a writer, my perspectives, personal beliefs, and foundational frameworks are always reflected in my work (see, Knaier 2017, 2019a, 2019b, 2020). I analyze the world, including readings, photographs, and experiences, based on my present knowledge and past experiences—just as a reader of my work would do. More-

*Queer Multicultural Social Justice Education: Curriculum (and Identity) Development Through Performance*, pages 37–47.

over, I combine my story with new knowledge as I am learning it; I reflect on past experiences as I read the world; and I negotiate an understanding of how I fit into the larger narrative. In other words, I "think narratively."

As mentioned in Chapter One, as I explore the history of multicultural education within the United States and how multicultural education has been integrated into teacher education, I find the importance of identity awareness (of self and others) to be a consistent thread throughout the literature (Banks, 2006b; Gollnick & Chinn, 2004; Grant & Sleeter, 2011a; Howard, 2006; Nieto & Bode, 2012). Indeed, as Banks (2006b) asserts that we must explore and attempt to understand our personal identities before we constructively and effectively relate to others. In his scholarship, he critically analyzes and shares personal stories and anecdotes from his lived experiences. Throughout his career, Banks (2006b) wrote about his experiences with racism, his participation in Black Civil Rights Movements, and his first-hand accounts of school desegregation. In fact, Banks' catalog of work reads like an autoethnography—one that consists of critical reflection, investigation, and portrayal of entwined personal and cultural experiences. Further, "autoethnography benefits greatly from the thought that self is an extension of a community rather than that it is an independent, self-sufficient being, because the possibility of cultural self-analysis rests on an understanding that self is part of a cultural community" (Chang, 2008, p. 26). It is this juxtaposition and the integration of self and community that verifies that we can only know ourselves in relation to others (Jagose, 1996).

Scholars of queer theory also highlight the importance of identity awareness, as well as identity (de)construction. For example, Murray (2015), a scholar of queer multicultural teacher education, explains that teacher candidates who examine "their own disposition" may address "queer issues in school even in the presence of self-conflicting ideological beliefs" (p. 35). Therefore, by applying queer theory to multicultural teacher education future teachers may practice self-awareness. In this chapter, I introduce critical autoethnography—a narrative method that educators may use to work toward such awareness. I propose that by engaging in autoethnographic methods, both writers and readers of the work may engage in reflexive and transformative experiences—which may ultimately impact others (e.g., students). The aim is that through engaging in autoethnography, educators may become more aware of, and work toward an understanding of, their own identities (e.g., race/ethnicity, socioeconomic status, exceptionality, religion, sexual orientation, and gender) within the process of developing effective queer multicultural teacher education curriculum.

Further, I acknowledge that critical autoethnography is a *queer* method (Adams & Holman Jones, 2008; Bochner & Ellis, 2016), as it includes characteristics of critical theory—more specifically queer theory. For example, autoethnography boosts critical awareness and supports the analyzing of the normative ideas of self and others. Finally, I propose to queer this method further by *using* it for curriculum development—thus, queering the act of curriculum development. Indeed, documenting and critically reflecting upon the process of developing multicultural curricula that encourages critical self-reflection (Mezirow, 2009; Nieto, 2003), promotes social justice (Grant & Sleeter, 2013), and nurtures creativity and self-expression (Ellis, 2004), may enhance self-awareness and curriculum development (Knaier, 2020). I conclude that queer critical autoethnography as a method for curriculum development moves beyond theory and pragmatically applies queer research methods and frameworks. This may provide educators the opportunity to better understand themselves and others—including their students—thereby *becoming* more effective and just multicultural educators.

## CRITICAL AUTOETHNOGRAPHY

Autoethnography is a method that *includes* the researcher in the research. Some social scientists believe that the researcher cannot and should not be removed from ethnographic studies (Chang, 2008; Ellis et al., 2010). They reason that including the researcher as a participant allows for dynamic data and analysis, which contribute to and further social science research. Moreover, Ellis, Adams, and Bochner (2010) explain that "autoethnography is one of the approaches that acknowledges and accommodates subjectivity, emotionality, and the researcher's influence on research, rather than hiding from these matters or assuming they don't exist" (paragraph 3). Indeed, through autoethnography the writer "engages in extensive self-examination and self-reflection, and purposively thinks about and includes extensive cultural and contextual description of his or her life" (Burke Johnson & Christensen, 2014, p. 453). Hence, researchers cannot remove themselves from reporting or experiencing the effects of their research—nor should they (Chang, 2008; Ellis et al., 2010).

Autoethnography is "research, writing, story, and method that connects the autobiographical and personal to cultural, social, and political" (Ellis, 2004, p. xix). Further, autoethnographic forms of storytelling "feature self-consciousness and introspection portrayed in dialogue, scenes, characterization, and plot" (p. xix). Typically written in first-person voice, autoethnographic texts may appear in a variety of forms, including short stories, fiction, photography, personal essays, journals, fragmented and layered writing, and social science prose (Ellis, 2004, p. 38). In these ways, autoethnographic methods give researchers freedom, not only in the way they present their work, but also in the way they analyze it. Moreover, writing autoethnography is more than simply telling a story—it consists of sharing intimate details, making cultural connections, and practicing critical analysis. In this project, I am also using autoethnography as my analysis and reporting method (see, Chapter Four).

However, there are different schools of thought regarding the way analysis and interpretation of data occur in autoethnographic research (Chang, 2008; Ellis, 2004). Chang (2008) contends autoethnography "combines cultural analysis and interpretation with narrative details," and that it "follows the anthropological and social scientific inquiry approach rather than descriptive or performative storying" (p. 46). Further, Chang (2008) "expect[s] the stories of autoethnographers to be reflected upon, analyzed, and interpreted within their broader sociocultural context" (p. 46). Thus, for some, autoethnography focuses on a social scientific ethnographic process of analysis.

In contrast, Ellis (2004) asserts that the writing of an autoethnography itself is an analysis of the experience or data. Ellis (2004) declares that you should "show that there's something to be gained by saturating your observations with your own subjectivity" (p. 89). After all, we are writing about *our* real-world experience. We should own it. Further, Ellis (2004) realizes:

> In this space, we learn to live meaningfully in the stories of our lives. In this space, we learn to see and feel the world in a complicated manner and then reflexively turn that lens on ourselves. In this space, we access the material and talent to create and write evocative and engaging stories of our lived experiences. (pp. 98–99)

She refers to this as "story as analysis," a practice that should be encouraged within queer multicultural curriculum development. In this autoethnography, I combine social science prose and storying to reflect my voice.

Ultimately, in practice, an autoethnographer critically reflects on a lived experience while interjecting cultural analysis and implications. Indeed, narrative approaches, such as autoethnography, have "the possibility to transform everyday experience into insights with cultural, social, and educational significance" (Phillion et al., 2005, p. 1). To do this, the autoethnographer systematically collects data via, for example, field notes, journals, and photographs; "attempts to achieve understanding through analysis and interpretation" by "focusing on understanding of other (culture/society) through self"; and "uses their personal experiences as primary data" (Chang, 2008, pp. 48–49) to tell their story. By using narratives, we constructively "remember the past, turn life into language, and disclose to ourselves and others the truth of our experiences" (Ellis, 2004, p. 127; Bochner, 2001). *We write stories with a purpose.*

However, for narrative research to be effective, it must provide meaning and be *useful* to both the writer and the reader. Surely, "autoethnography requires a researcher to make personal experience meaningful for others, and, consequently, say something about cultural experience and/or motivate cultural change" (Adams, 2011, p. 158). Further, the process of conducting autoethnographic research "evokes self-reflection and self-analysis through which self-discovery becomes a possibility" (Chang, 2008, p. 41)—for both writers and readers. This is achieved when the work engages the reader and the reader engages with the work. One aspect of autoethnography that may help achieve this engagement is the freedom the researcher has from "the traditional conventions of [academic] writing." The author's "unique voicing—complete with colloquialisms, reverberations from multiple relationships, and emotional expressiveness—is honored." Thus, "the reader gains a sense of the writer as a full human being" (Gergen & Gergen, 2002, p. 14)—a colleague, peer, or even a mentor. "In autoethnography, we're usually writing about epiphanies in our lives and in doing so, we open ourselves up for criticism about how we've lived." By using authentic language and imagery of pure emotion, "you become your stories to your readers, and to yourself" (Ellis, 2004, pp. 33–34). Certainly, "readers, too, take a more active role as they are invited into the author's world, aroused [by] events being described, and stimulated to use what they learn there to reflect on, understand, and cope with their own lives" (Ellis, 2004, p. 46). These engaging aspects of autoethnography both comfort and absorb the writer and the reader as critical analysis occurs.

Indeed, "to write meaningfully and evocatively about topics that matter and may make a difference, to include sensory and emotional experience (Shelton, 1995), and to write from an ethic of care and concern (Denzin, 1997; Noddings, 1984; Richardson, 1997)" (Ellis, 2004, p. 46), opens ourselves up to such self-exploration and analysis. This practice may be especially pertinent when critically examining one's multicultural identities and may be particularly beneficial for educators—and their students. In this way, we advance our knowledge of self and others, as well as contribute to multicultural education development and scholarship. *We are not just telling stories about ourselves; we hope to create engagement and social change through our stories.*

In this way, autoethnography is a good fit for the present project. Teaching multicultural teacher education and developing multicultural curriculum requires identity awareness on behalf of the instructor (Banks, 2006b; Gollnick & Chinn, 2004; Grant & Sleeter, 2011a; Howard, 2006; Nieto & Bode, 2012). Grant and Sleeter (2011b) claim that "the sense you make of students and the work of teaching is filtered through your cultural lens: the beliefs, assumptions, and experiences you bring to the classroom" (p. 10). They add that it is impossible "to understand other people without first understanding yourself and how your perspective shapes how you interpret others" (p. 10). Further, education "researchers have a story to tell about themselves as well as their work" (Ladson-Billings, 1995, p. 470; Carter, 1993). As a queer scholar, I actively explore ways to understand my identities (e.g., race/ethnicity, socioeconomic status, exceptionality, religion, sexual orientation, and gender), why I hold certain perspectives, and how these outlooks impact my teaching and curriculum development. And as I develop curriculum, I do this to better understand and deliver course content, and to better relate to my students. Indeed, "[m]ost of the researchers within queer theory play with the author's self: It is rarely absent" (Plummer, 2011, p. 203).

Though it is a personal choice to critically explore one's identities, or to seek out methods with which to develop this awareness, I argue that it is the duty of educators (e.g., teacher educators, K–12 classroom teachers, coaches) to practice these methods and, furthermore, incorporate these techniques into their teaching practices (including multicultural education courses—thus providing K–12 teachers with tools for extending their identity awareness). By using critical autoethnography as a method to not only construct a curriculum, but also to explore self-identity and awareness as a means of knowing myself better, I hope to know my students better; build solid, strong relationships with my students; and increase student success. Additionally, I intend to model for future teachers how to use autoethnographic methods for similar outcomes. Autoethnographies outlining experiences of curriculum development are scarce or nonexistent. Therefore, by writing an autoethnography about my experience of developing queer multicultural teacher education curriculum as a means of learning more about my identities and the importance of identity awareness (of self and others), I am furthering narrative and social science research and contributing to the academy.

## QUEER(ING) CRITICAL AUTOETHNOGRAPHY

Personal experience narratives, such as autoethnography, share elements directly with critical theory. According to Boylorn and Orbe (2014), both seek to "understand the lived experience of real people in context, to examine social conditions and uncover oppressive power arrangement, and to fuse theory and action to challenge processes of domination" (p. 20). Moreover, autoethnography shares components directly with queer theory (a branch of critical theory). For example, like queer theory, autoethnographies may shape a critical awareness, disturb the status quo, and probe questions of identity (Spry, 2011). Given these correlations, the attributes of queer theory and autoethnography—as framework and methodology—complement each other with the goal of working toward social justice.

Mizzi and Stebbins (2010) assert that "when the term 'queer' is applied to 'autoethnography' to inquire into one's life experiences, it conjures meaningful possibilities for extending research into silenced and marginalized areas of qualitative research" (p. 25). Further, Bochner and Ellis (2016) recognize "that autoethnography has a wide appeal to people on the margins (e.g., working class, LGBTQ, and ethnic and racial minorities) because these populations often have been silenced, objectified, left out, or oppressed by value-free, disembodied social science" (p. 239). They claim that "if we relapse into traditional ways of assessing the value or validity of research, we risk delegitimizing the very essence of what makes the evocative autoethnography paradigm powerful"—its "capacity for self-reflective and self-critical accounts of experience that can heal, change, validate, and engage others" (p. 239).

Further, like queer theory, autoethnographic methods "showcase concrete *action*, dialogue, emotion, embodiment, spiritualty, and self-consciousness" (Ellis, 2004, p.38, italics added). "These features [...] are dialectically revealed through actions, feelings, thoughts, and language" (p. 38). In other words, autoethnography is a *performative* method. Chase (2011) affirms that "the goal of autoethnography [...] is to *show* rather than to *tell* (Denzin, 2003, p. 203; Saldaña, 2008, p. 201)" (p. 423, italics original). It is this queer, performative action that can "disrupt the politics of traditional research relationships, traditional forms of representation, and traditional social science orientation to audiences (Langellier & Peterson, 2006; Miller & Taylor, 2006)" (p. 423). These intended outcomes are parallel with Butler's (2005) theory of performativity. Indeed, as Madison and

Hamera (2006) maintain: "Performativity is the interconnected triad of identity, experience, and social relations" (p. xix). Thus, autoethnography is a performative—and queer—method because it encapsulates these characteristics.

Moreover, like queer theory, engaging in narrative research may change perspectives, ideologies, and actions. For example, Grace (2006) testifies that using autobiographical methods "is a quest to see whether [he has] reached a point where [his] own expanding knowledge, understanding and experience enable [him] to be a self-accepting, inclusive educator" (p. 827). These methods offer "an opportunity to grow as a teacher educator"—one "who has transgressed his history of internalized and overt homophobia"—and "is no longer bounded by the toxic politics of heteronormativity that assumes and privileges heterosexuality" (p. 827). These realizations are made possible through becoming aware of self and others.

Additionally, teacher educators Mulhern and Martinez (1999), who "educat[e] preservice elementary teachers about how they can help children understand the damaging effects of homophobia and the positive contributions of [LGBTQ people]," attest that "the decision to include sexual orientation in [their] multicultural education courses was easy;" but that "teaching queerly required more than a conviction" (p. 255). Admittedly, they were "[c]onfronted with a lack of knowledge and remnants of the homophobia [they] had grown up with," and they "had to peel back layers of fear and discomfort and educate [themselves]" (p. 255) to justly serve their students. Engaging in autoethnography is one way of "peeling back the layers" and educating oneself on these matters. Many educators have used autoethnographic methods to advance their self-awareness and, therefore, improve their teaching capabilities (Grace, 2006). *We share our stories as a means of personal growth and social justice advancement.*

Consistent with these observations, scholars within education, such as Adams (2011), Miller and Rodriguez (2016), and Pillay et al, (2016), *show* the connection between autoethnography and queer theory. Many educators and scholars also use autobiographical and other narrative approaches to write *about* their experiences of teaching multicultural education and of interacting with students (Bochner & Ellis, 2016; Chang, 2008; Ellis, 2004; Feuerverger, 2005). However, there appears to be relatively little *use* of queer autoethnography as a tool to *advance* education in the form of curriculum development. Through my review, I have not found any literature on using autoethnography as a curriculum development method. Thus, by using autoethnography to explore the experience of curriculum development, I am applying the method in a different, and possibly new, manner: further queering this already queer method by *using* it in a way for which it was not originally designed, and for which it has not been used—*queer curriculum development.*

More specifically, autoethnographic methods may be used to develop queer multicultural teacher education curriculum; thus, encouraging teacher educators (and classroom teachers) to critically examine their identities and document their experiences *while creating* multicultural curriculum. In contrast, *straight* curriculum development, in my experience, does not intend for curriculum workers to *perform* the lessons *as part of* the curriculum development process nor does it challenge the status quo. Indeed, there is no critical reflection occurring *before* the curriculum is implemented—this is how my proposed approach differs.

## STORIES AS CURRICULUM

*Curriculum* includes all our interactions with other beings (human and not) and our environment (natural and synthetic) that cause us to react and reflect. It includes what is learned within the confines of a school or institution (e.g., lessons, text, and hidden curricula) and related activities (e.g., going on field trips, attending mass, playing on sports teams); in addition, as Cary (2006) argues, *curriculum* is "more than a text book, more than a classroom, and more than teachers and students. It is all of the social influences, populist crises, military campaigns, and historical moments that shape our lives—when we are in school and in our lives beyond the classroom" (pp. xi-xii). Likewise, some scholars, including myself, "expand the definition [of curriculum] to encompass all formal and informal life experiences that contribute to [personal] growth, social consequence, and values" (Slattery, 2013, p. 298). In other words, all our collective interaction, experiences, and stories are *curricula*.

Certainly, all aspects of life are curricula; and therefore, we are all teachers and students in some capacity throughout our entire lives (Freire, 1970). *We call this living.* Dewey (1916) keenly writes that

> the dominant vocation of all human beings at all times is living—intellectual and moral growth. In childhood and youth, with their relative freedom from economic stress, this fact is naked and unconcealed. (p. 310)

To reiterate, as curriculum is defined as "living" experiences, we are all teachers in some capacity—maybe as a sibling, parent, friend, educator, boss, or mentor. *We are all teachers and learners simultaneously.*

*Queer explorations of identity awareness* is a curriculum that encourages explorers to engage in autoethnographic means to become aware of identities (of self and others). It is through our shared stories and experiences that we may advance our understanding of multicultural identities (e.g., socioeconomic statues, religion, sexual orientation, gender, race/ethnicity, and exceptionality) and their intersectionality with each other, as well as with other identities. Indeed, as Holman Jones (2016) asserts: "Stories also awaken us to the existence and experiences of others—especially those others who are different from us" (p. 230). Therefore, through these shared interactions and engagements, we may realize that identities, and the labels they are given, mean different things to different people, that language and identities are fluid, and that the assumptions we hold may be harmful (to self and others).

Moreover, it is important that we learn not to essentialize identities. As Letts (2002) so potently presents:

> Our intent in multiculturalism must be to better understand the complexities of these cultures and identity categories with an eye to recognizing but not essentializing difference, and without assuming that some "natural" order exists to them. We must advocate dialogue and exchange across differences, rather than trying to craft or impose some mythical set of shared values. This is not to wholly deny the utility of examining structural dynamics and power differentials in terms of categories (such as women, the rich, or lesbians), but only to signal quite strongly that an overreliance on these categories or an overattribution of what these categories "tell" us about people or what they "mean" to individuals would be a gross distortion of the limited use they have in these discussions. (p. 122)

These "complexities" and "differences" and their "overreliance" and "overattribution" may be realized through shared stories. This is congruent with what I argued in Part One: "Examining and developing identity awareness may be consistent with an ultimate desire to move past identity labels and identity politics" —but in the interim it is worth having discussions about and learning more about how we (and others) identify. Indeed, there are several benefits from sharing our stories as curriculum.

### Benefits of Sharing Our Stories

Because teachers walk into classrooms with lived experiences and prior knowledge, "a teacher's practice [and identity] is shaped in the intersection of the personal and the professional" (Grace, 2006, p. 827). Therefore, autoethnographic methods—which can bring attention to such intersections—may be "a particularly useful and powerful tool for researchers and practitioners [and educators] who deal with human relations in multicultural settings" (Chang, 2008, pp. 51–52). According to Chang (2008), the benefits of autoethnography lie in three areas:

> (1) it offers a research method friendly to researchers and readers; (2) it enhances cultural understanding of self and others; and (3) it has a potential to transform self and others to motivate them to work toward cross-cultural coalition building. (p. 52)

Certainly, autoethnographers benefit by "turn[ing] the analytic lens fully and specifically on themselves as they write, interpret, or perform narratives about their own culturally significant experiences" (Chase, 2011, p. 423). But these benefits may extend beyond the writer, and even the reader, of the research—they may impact our students.

Sharing our stories with our students—or at the very least, allowing our stories to influence our curriculum—may have a socially transformative effect. For example, Bickmore (1999) asserts:

If we hope that the new generation will recreate a social world that includes less sexism, homophobia, and bigotry, then we need to expose [students] to stories that suggest such a need, and such a possibility. (p. 22)

Further, by means of autoethnographic practices, multicultural educators "can get in touch with their own cultures and use the perspectives and insights they acquired as vehicles for helping them relate to and understand the culture of students" (Banks, 2013, p. 20). This can create a welcoming learning atmosphere and a culturally sustaining curriculum (Gay, 2010; Ladson-Billings, 1995, 2014; Paris, 2012; Paris & Alim, 2014).

Moreover, autoethnographic and reflective practices may encourage educators to confront their own biases—about themselves, their students and colleagues, and the world (Grace, 2006; Mulhern & Martinez, 1999). Bochner and Ellis (2016) explain:

The autoethnographies we write put us into dialogue with ourselves as we expose our vulnerabilities, conflicts, choices, and values. We take measure of our uncertainties, our mixed and amalgamated emotions, and the multiple layers of our consciousness of what happened to us. Our accounts seek to express the complexities and difficulties of coping and trying to feel resolved, showing how we changed over time as we struggled to make sense of our experience. Our accounts of ourselves are unflattering and imperfect, but human and believable. In this sense, we use autoethnographic text as an agent of self-understanding and ethical dialogue. (p. 71)

"This process is essential; if educators don't do this, think about how much damage we could do to the open, vulnerable minds of our students" (Pitt, 2016, p. 48). However, reporting this self-awareness may uncover information about ourselves that may put us at risk.

### Risks of Sharing Our Stories

Telling critical stories as a way of knowing oneself, and ultimately others, is a rigorous yet personal task. Indeed, engaging in autoethnographic practices is challenging, and possibly perilous, for a writer. Although critical autoethnography may be therapeutic for the writer (Bochner & Ellis, 2016; Ellis, 2004), sharing intimate details about experiences, critically analyzing oneself and one's actions, and resolving, at times, very personal tensions in one's life in a public forum may be risky, or even damaging. Bochner recognizes the "courage it takes to risk one's career to speak forbidden narratives." It "involves incredibly difficult choices; people need to be aware of the potential consequences in making the decision to publish or otherwise share [autoethnographic writings or experiences]" (Flemons & Green, 2002, p. 169).

Such risks occur when autoethnographers unveil tensions, feelings, and actions they were not expecting or intending to uncover and report. The topics of autoethnography are personal, real, and complex. Often, the author exposes delicate details about their life and the lives of those around them. Indeed, quality auto-ethnography is steeped in real-life happenings, emotions, and trauma. Yet, they may be important to share, as they may ignite tough, yet necessary, conversations. In the end, autoethnographers must determine whether the benefits outweigh the potential risks—and why we must be respectful of one's decision not to share.

*Our Stories, Our Prerogative*

While I performed the explorations developed for *Queer explorations of identity awareness*, I (like any performer would) had the freedom to choose how to perform and present each exploration, as well as from which perspective and lens to conduct the exploration. And though I share each of my performances in Part Two, you always have the option on how to share your performance (or you may choose not to share them—though I strongly urge you to do so). This autonomy may mitigate the risks involved with autoethnographic methods while increasing the potential benefits experienced through such methods of inquiry.

As you engage with the presentation of my explorations in Part Two, you will see that these tasks were not always easy for me to perform. For example, *Exploration 5: Religion and mortality* was a particularly sensitive exploration for me since I recently experienced the loss of my maternal grandmother, mother, and father. But as I explain in my reflection for Exploration 5, this exploration offered me an opportunity to subtly move through the grieving process. I wrote:

> This performance offered me a safe, yet focused project to begin advancing through my grieving process. I actively had to think about, remember, and write about my mom—things I try hard not to do. Because of these efforts, I have come up with further ideas on how to remember and learn about my mom.

Indeed, all the explorations granted me the autonomy to be reflective, creative, and self-supportive.

## CONCLUSION

As discussed, autoethnography engages and affects the reader. As Ellis et al. (2010) explain: "Personal narratives propose to understand a self or some aspect of a life as it intersects with a cultural context [...] and invite readers to enter the author's world and to use what they learn there to reflect on, understand, and cope with their own lives (Ellis, 2004, p. 46)" (paragraph 24). It is the engagement between the researcher and the audience, and the actions taken by both parties, that make autoethnography a powerful method. *By sharing my story, I hope to encourage self-awareness and queer curriculum development within multicultural learning spaces.* In Part Two, I present *Queer explorations of identity awareness*, and I share my performances and reflections in their entirety.

# PART 2

QUEER EXPLORATIONS OF IDENTITY AWARENESS:
QUEER CURRICULUM DEVELOPMENT THROUGH
PERFORMANCE

# QUEER EXPLORATIONS OF IDENTITY AWARENESS

## INTRODUCTION

*What is Queering?*

*Queering*, or *to queer*, is to take action against the normative and heteronorma- tive status quo. *Heteronormativity* dictates that being cisgender and heterosexual are the norm while it polices all other gender identities and sexual orientations. Thus, *queer curriculum* provokes critical questioning, critical reflection, and act- ing toward, the (de)construction of societal norms, identities, and ways of learn- ing.

As a curriculum worker, I queer multicultural social justice teacher education in a way that encourages learners to consider, question, and analyze how gender and sexual orientation—along with other multicultural identities (e.g., socioeconomic status, religion, race/ethnicity, and exceptionality)—interact with, influence, and maintain social power and control. In these explorations, I do so through autoeth- nographic methods—including storytelling—that encourage you to explore your own identities (as a way of knowing others), to question assumptions about self and others, and to examine how your identities impact your teaching practices.

*Queer Multicultural Social Justice Education: Curriculum (and Identity) Development Through Performance,* pages 51–55.

*What is Queer Multicultural Social Justice Teacher Education?*

Queer multicultural social justice teacher education is a critical approach that provides opportunities for and encourages educators to examine and (de)construct identity and its espoused privileges—thus allowing explorers, in part, to investigate ways to dismantle heteronormativity, rethink binary systems of identification, and deconstruct socially constructed identities. To be clear, the practice of analyzing and (de)constructing our identities is a queer approach to learning.

*How May Identity Awareness (of Self and Others) Promote Queer Multicultural Social Justice?*

Many multicultural education scholars agree that teachers must know who they are and who their students are—while understanding the changing nature and fluidity of identity—if they are going to be successful (Banks, 2006b; Grant & Sleeter, 2011a; Nieto & Bode, 2012).

*Queer explorations of identity awareness* is a set of explorations that provide opportunities to develop identity awareness (of self and others) as a means of promoting social justice. These performances encourage critical reflection, storytelling with a purpose (e.g., examining, deconstructing, and eradicating potential hostile presumptions present in our heteronormative society and within ourselves), and practices of identity awareness with a goal of promoting a more accepting, socially just, and multicultural society.

It is my hope that through writing and sharing your stories, you will make personal connections with each other, giving you a stake in what you are learning and how you are learning by (1) exploring identity and identity awareness through autoethnographical methods, (2) connecting personal experiences with the curriculum, and (3) making personal experiences *curricula*.

## INTENTIONS

*My Aim*

I want you to realize not only the importance of queer curricula, but the ease with which you may incorporate it into an already established curriculum and/or implement it on your own. I hope you find this curriculum unrestricted, flexible, and critical.

*The Explorers*

The explorations are aimed toward promoting social justice through identity awareness and exploration. The explorers, or performers of this curriculum, may include educators, life-long learners, parents, community members, or anyone interested in exploring identity and identity awareness as a means of promoting social justice.

*Intended Outcomes*

Explorers will:

- Understand the importance of queer(ing) curriculum by recognizing certain hostile presumptions present in our heteronormative society (and within ourselves) and the harm they cause;
- Realize that identity awareness (of self and others) through storytelling is key to contributing to and promoting a more accepting and socially just multicultural society; and
- Develop a multicultural teaching philosophy that recognizes the importance of identity awareness (of self and others) through storytelling as curriculum.

## ADAPTATIONS & SUGGESTIONS

*Learning Modalities*

I encourage you to use of a variety of discussion and presentation methods (which supports a broad range of learning methods). Further, elements of queer multicultural social justice education include being flexible and showing care for your needs.

*Adaptations*

This curriculum may be adapted to fit your needs and the resources available (e.g., technology, time).

*Word Wall*

A word wall is an interactive teaching and learning tool consisting of a collection of relevant words which may be displayed on a wall, bulletin board, in a virtual space, or in a personal journal. I invite you to create your own word wall, but some possible words include:

| | | |
|---|---|---|
| Assumptions | Ethnicity | Race |
| Autoethnography | Exceptionality | Reflection(s) |
| Awareness | Gender | Religion |
| Community | Ethnicity | Sexual orientation |
| Creativity | Identity/Identities | Social construct |
| Critical thinking | Identity awareness | Social justice |
| Curriculum | Multicultural education | Socioeconomic status |
| (De)Construct | Queer(ing) | Stories |

## ELEMENTS OF THE EXPLORATIONS

*Learning Outcomes*

Identity awareness can be achieved through methods like critical dialogue, critical reflection, critical thinking, and critical questioning (Nieto, 2003); therefore, you are encouraged to engage in these critical processes throughout this curriculum. Through these performative autoethnographic methods, you may realize how each exploration provokes identity awareness, and that identity is complicated, fluid, and ever changing. In the end, you should practice identity awareness and may ultimately appreciate that you may never fully know, understand, or define yourself (or others).

*Readings*

Each exploration consists of a reading list that may serve as a guide. These explorations may be paired with other multicultural texts, integrated with an already established curricula, or performed as a stand-alone set of inquiries.

*Prompt(s)*

Each exploration consists of one or more prompts for discussions and reflections, along with identity awareness explorations that provoke critical dialogue, reflection, thinking, and questioning.

*Discussion*

Discussions (e.g., large group, small group, partnered, online, internal) may consist of clarifying and defining the prompts and explorations.

*Presentation(s)*

Performances include but are not limited to traditional essays, comic strips, short stories, poems, photo essays, auto/photovoice, food essays, videos, drawings, paintings, or other methods through which you want to conduct and communicate your explorations. I encourage you to queer performances and presentations as these performative autoethnographic presentations are representations and reflections of you. Moreover, these presentations are not "finished" products. You need to understand that these explorations will always be works in progress.

*Sharing*

Performances and presentations must be shared with others. It is through these shared interactions that we get to know and learn from each other, where new knowledge is made, and when new perspectives are discovered. I encourage you to share your performances as presentations, written works, or artistic designs.

*Exploration Outline*

You may use the exploration outline as a guide in your explorations and to help narrow your focus. The format of the exploration outline may be queered as you see fit.

1. **Identity.** Describe your identity or identities. *How do I identify?*
2. **Initial questions.** Record any initial questions you plan to explore about your identity or identities. *What are my initial questions?*
3. **Preliminary resources/references.** Record any preliminary resources (e.g., family members, shared stories, recipes, photo collections) or references (e.g., articles, books, music) you intend to use or explore. *Where will I seek information?*
4. **Performance and presentation methods.** Record some method(s) for consideration. *How will I perform and present my exploration?*
5. **Additional questions.** Record any additional questions you asked as you performed the exploration. *What additional questions did I explore?*
6. **Further questions.** Record any questions you want explore in the future. *What are my further (future) questions?*
7. **All resources/references.** List all resources and references (e.g., formal, informal, academic) used during the exploration. *What resources did I use?*
8. **Sharing.** Share your performance with others. *How will I share this exploration?*

*Reaction/Reflection Responses*

You should critically respond to others' presentations (when applicable), reflect on the exploration and the readings, and address the reflection prompt(s) when offered. The goal here is to be aware of and reflect on your thoughts, vocabulary, feelings, and struggles.

# EXPLORATION 1

# WHY QUEER CURRICULUM?

*Exploration*

Share a time or times when you were affected by (e.g., a victim of, witnessed, and/or stood up to) hurtful, disrespectful, or violent normative or heteronormative behavior that occurred based on socioeconomic status, religion, gender, sexual orientation, race/ethnicity, and/or exceptionality in a school or learning atmosphere.

*Discussion*

Should include defining *heteronormativity*.

*Presentation*

Consider all options (e.g., a skit, essay, storytelling, graphic art, or comic strip).

*Reflection*

Critically respond to others' presentations (when applicable), reflect on the exploration and the readings, and address the following prompt: 1) How were you affected by telling your story? and, 2) How are you affected by others' stories?

*Queer Multicultural Social Justice Education: Curriculum (and Identity) Development Through Performance,* pages 57–62.
Copyright © 2021 by Information Age Publishing
57

*Readings*

*Introduction* section to curriculum.

Chan, M. (2015). My story of self-identity. In K. Jennings (Ed.), *One teacher in ten in the new millennium: LGBT educators speak out about what's gotten better . . . and what hasn't* (pp. 118–120). Beacon Press.

Gilbert, S. E. (2015). There is uncertainty, but there is also hope. In K. Jennings (Ed.), *One teacher in ten in the new millennium: LGBT educators speak out about what's gotten better . . . and what hasn't* (pp. 150–155). Beacon Press.

Knaier, M. L. (2016). A place where they can be themselves: Issues of LGBTQ students [Revisited]. In E. A. Mikulec and P. C. Miller (Eds.), *Queering classrooms: Personal narratives and educational practices to support LGBTQ youth in schools* (pp. 11–25). Information Age.

Letts, W. (2002). Revisioning multiculturalism in Teacher education: Isn't it queer? In R. M. Kissen (Ed.), *Getting ready for Benjamin: Preparing teachers for sexual diversity in the classroom* (pp. 119–131). Rowman & Littlefield.

Vàsquez, B. (2015). Questions to self: Being a queer Latino educator. In K. Jennings (Ed.), *One teacher in ten in the new millennium: LGBT educators speak out about what's gotten better . . . and what hasn't* (pp. 156–160). Beacon Press.

## TERRORIZED IN HIGH SCHOOL

High school. All four years. I graduated in 1990, but I still have reels of terror, violence, and abuse playing in my head. It plays like a movie-montage highlighting bullying, anti-LGBTQ, racist, misogynistic, and other hateful behaviors. All that was non-[hetero]normative was targeted by the "popular" students—the white, middle-class clique that ran the school. To be fair, we all had our cliques and our targets. My language used in this story (e.g., dirtbag, nerd, remedial student) illustrates this. We were known by these identity labels, whether we chose them or not.

I transferred to my public high school from a small parochial Catholic school. I know what you're thinking. I was a rich girl who attended a private school. No. I was a poor kid who attended a small Catholic school because it was convenient for my parents. The school was located three blocks away from my home, which meant I could walk to and from school. It also happened to be located at the corner of my grandmother's street. The location was beneficial because I could walk to my grandma's house after school and wait for my mother to get out of work. And when I became a bit older, I would walk home with my little sister. We were latchkey kids. I would watch over her, make dinner, and tend to housework until my mother arrived home from working her two jobs. I was an outsider in high school, in every way. A less than.

There are certain instances from my time in high school that haunt my mind—one being the daily bullying and taunting that occurred in Ms. H's science class. In this case, Ryan, a "dirtbag" or "head," was the tormentor. He was not a "popular" student. Ryan lashed out for other reasons—probably because he was bullied and abused. Anyway, he would pick on Sam, a "nerd," EVERY SINGLE DAY. He would make fun of Sam's last name, calling him "rye bread," and belittle Sam because he was overweight or because he wore glasses. In addition to bullying Sam, Ryan, for whatever reason, victimized Ms. H. (one of my female teachers who inspired me to become a science teacher). He would routinely taunt her and make her cry. He would constantly remind the class that she posed in Playboy or that she had small breasts. His misogynistic behavior usually got him kicked out of class. I always felt bad for Ms. H., but I was never strong enough to stick up for her, or for Sam. Honestly, I was glad I wasn't one of Ryan's victims.

I, too, endured a constant barrage of bullying from several classmates. One instance that is burned into my memory is a time when I was walking into a class-room and Lacey was walking out. We passed each other. She called me a "slut." And as I continued walking, I raised my left hand over my head, prominently giving her the middle finger and simply relied, "Fuck you." She bullied me every day, in and outside of school (e.g., at the local roller rink). I don't know why. Fortunately, during my sophomore year, I managed to befriend a girl from the "popular" group. We became best friends for the remainder of high school and a few years beyond. Mandy offered me quite a bit of protection, and somehow prevented Lacey from physically harming me on several occasions.

Another instance, and the final one that I will share in this exploration, plays out in the lunchroom. I sat with a group of my misfit friends, including one of the three black students in my entire school. At the table next to ours sat a group of re-medial-tracked students. My high school adhered to a tracking system: Advanced placement, Regents, regular, and Remedial. This caste system was another way to determine the "haves" from the "have-nots." I remember this group being made up of Mic and Jimmy amongst others. Mic, a neighbor of mine from the wrong part of town, had a reputation for being a troublemaker—and he was an asshole a lot of the time (for reasons unknown to me, but I suspect he didn't have an easy life). When Mic was bullied, he was explosive. The bullies at my school enjoyed a reactive subject. Jimmy suffered from a skin disease that emitted an unpleasant smell and caused his skin to flake, which he often ate in response to being bully-ing about his condition. He too was a volatile victim. They would get picked on daily, which caused them to act out and behave loudly and erratically. My friends and I were often annoyed by them and engaged in back-and-forth taunting and name-calling, which would usually end with one or more of them being removed from the lunchroom by a "rent-a-cop." It was a dog-eat-dog atmosphere—even among the have-nots.

These three recurring situations are burned into my memory. There are other moments, but these are the most vivid. My high school was a place where I, and others, were targeted because of our race or ethnicity (i.e., there was no short-age of Polish jokes); religion; gender, or sexual orientation (e.g., hearing "lezzy," "faggot," or "pussy" were daily occurrences); socioeconomic status (e. g., being picked on for not wearing the right clothes, for getting free or reduced lunch, or for being looked down upon because of the neighborhood in which we lived); or exceptionality (e. g., not being able to read aloud well or being enrolled in the remedial tract). And I can't recall any, or certain, instances when a teacher stepped in to stop or prevent harmful behavior, unless they were the target or there was a fistfight in the hallway.

I hated high school. It was not a safe space. And because of these and many other uncomfortable and terrifying experiences, I did not attend my high school graduation. Because, "fuck them!" I was not an accepted part of the class, so why pretend on that last day? I was even set to go up on stage and receive a small scholarship to put toward my college education that was awarded to those who wanted to pursue teaching. But I chose not to observe my graduation from a school that did not provide me with a safe, positive education equal to the one my fellow heteronormative, middle class peers received. It was my way of taking a stand after four years of abuse.

I will close by admitting that I did have some positive experiences throughout my tenure in high school. But the negative ones are what really affected me and impacted my teaching philosophy and focus of study. Because of my experiences, I vowed to be an educator that creates safe learning spaces and content for all students. I have spent my entire professional teaching career working toward just that. Students shouldn't have to wait until the last week of high school to hear a popular student say, "I wish I had gotten to know you sooner."

. . .

All names have been changed to protect the players' privacy and identity.

## REFLECTION

The readings I selected for Exploration 1 provide a foundation for the exploration by defining important terms and concepts and by offering relevant examples of teachers' stories. In "A place they can be themselves: Issues of LGBTQ students [Revisited]" (Knaier, 2017), I provide statistics supported by the literature show-ing why addressing the issues of LGBTQ students should be a vital aspect of teacher education. This chapter also defines *heteronormativity* and other relevant concepts (e.g., LGBTQ-inclusive curriculum), preventing me from having to [re] write a long introduction to my *Queer explorations of identity awareness* cur-riculum. However, because my chapter focuses on LGBTQ-inclusiveness with-out recognizing that LGBTQ-inclusiveness is embodied in queer multicultural curriculum, I chose "Revisioning Multiculturalism in Teacher Education: Isn't It Queer?" (Letts, 2002) to complement my work. In this chapter, Letts argues that LGBTQ-inclusiveness is not enough and that offering a queer multicultural teach-er education curriculum is key—and I agree. He provides three examples that teacher educators can incorporate into their queer multicultural education courses: autobiographical writing as a queer curriculum practice (which I adapted for this curriculum), a critical incidents paper, and the cultural plunge (both of which I will consider for future explorations). And finally, the three autobiographical stories from *One Teacher in Ten in the New Millennium* (Jennings, 2015) serve as examples of the type of writings I hope explorers produce for Exploration 1. These stories also show that LGBTQ educators and LGBTQ issues are prominent in schools, and that it is important to share our stories with other educators.

The story I wrote for this exploration shows how [hetero]normative bullying behavior affected me during my high school years. Because these memories are tragically engrained in my mind, and I "relive" them quite often, they were an obvious choice for me to share. However, I could have shared other experiences, like how I had to navigate being hit on by one of my community college professors; how I consistently heard preservice teachers (enrolled in the same teaching program as me) blurt out anti-LGBTQ taunts in the hallway; or how I was sexually harassed by a thirteen-year-old boy as a classroom teacher. My academic life is sprinkled with these terrible moments—something I will explore in another autoethnography. I chose to share the moments from high school because my time there greatly affected my choices for further education, career choice, and the way I choose to conduct my classroom, including my teaching style.

Full disclosure, this type of exercise is not new or original. I've been assigned this task, or exploration, in previous multicultural education classes. It is a good way to show that we all have stories to share—that we have something in common. We have all witnessed or experienced negative or violent behavior based on disrespectful or violent [hetero]normative behavior that occurred based on socioeconomic status, religion, gender, sexual orientation, race/ethnicity, and/or exceptionality in a school or learning atmosphere. It also provides us with a common goal: to stop this from happening in today's schools.

Connecting our personal experiences with the curriculum, and making our personal experiences *the* curriculum, helps us make connections with each other and allows us to have a stake in what we are learning and how we are learning (Dewey, 1938). These explorations will ultimately impact how we develop and deliver curriculum. These explorations of identity are not about me, the instructor, delivering lectures; they are about the students and me learning about, from, and with each other and our experiences. It is imperative that *our stories* are the focus of our learning in order to advance identity awareness (of self and others) as a means of promoting social justice.

## REFERENCES

Dewey, J. (1938). *Experience & education.* Simon & Schuster.

Jennings, K. (Ed.) (2015). *One teacher in ten in the new millennium: LGBT educators speak out about what's gotten better . . . and what hasn't.* Beacon Press.

Knaier, M. L. (2017). A place where they can be themselves: Issues of LGBTQ students [Revisited]. In E. A. Mikulec & P. C. Miller (Eds.), *Queering classrooms: Personal narratives and educational practices to support LGBTQ youth in schools* (pp. 11–25). Information Age.

Letts, W. (2002). Revisioning multiculturalism in Teacher education: Isn't it queer? In R. M. Kissen (Ed.), *Getting ready for Benjamin: Preparing teachers for sexual diversity in the classroom* (pp. 119–131). Rowman & Littlefield.

# EXPLORATION 2

# HOW DO YOU IDENTIFY?

*Exploration*

Reflect on your identity or identities for each of the multicultural identity categories (e.g., socioeconomic status, religion, gender, sexual orientation, race/ethnicity, and exceptionality). Then explore how each of these are represented in an aspect of your life (e.g., the books you read, the photographs you create, the movies you watch, the social media pages or groups you follow) and put together a presentation (e.g., a collection of quotes, portfolio, collage or word cloud) depicting these representations. (This exploration urges you to think about how you identify and provides a foundation for the following identity awareness explorations. But understand that through the course of these exercises your identities, and/or the language you use to describe yourself, may change.)

*Discussion*

Should include an overview of the multicultural identity categories.

*Presentation*

Consider all options (e.g., a collection of quotes, portfolio, collage, or word cloud).

*Queer Multicultural Social Justice Education: Curriculum (and Identity) Development Through Performance,* pages 63–71.
Copyright © 2021 by Information Age Publishing
**63**

*Reflection*

Critically respond to others' presentations (when applicable), reflect on the exploration and the readings, and address the following prompts: 1) Explain the purpose of multicultural education; 2) Discuss the multicultural identities listed as they pertain to you; 3) What did you learn about yourself?; and, 4) Discuss any difficulties or complexities of choosing a label or labels.

*Reading(s)*

Banks, J. A. (2016). Chapter 1: Multicultural education: Characteristics and goals. In J. A. Banks & C. A. McGee Banks (Eds.), *Multicultural education: Issues and perspectives* (9th ed.) (pp. 2–23). John Wiley & Sons.
Convertino, C., Levinson, B. A., & González, N. (2016). Chapter 2: Culture, Teaching, and learning. In J. A. Banks & C. A. McGee Banks (Eds.), *Multicultural education: Issues and perspectives* (9th ed.) (pp. 24–40). John Wiley & Sons.
Nieto, S. (2003). Chapter 2: Teaching as autobiography. In S. Nieto, *What keeps teachers going?* (pp. 22–36) Teachers College.

## IDENTITY REFLECTED IN MAGAZINES

Note: Image is of collage made from magazine clippings.

## REFLECTION

*Define and Discuss the Multicultural Identities Listed as They Pertain to You. What Did You Learn About Yourself?*

For this exploration, I chose to create a collage from magazines (e.g., *Women's Health*, *Skeptical Inquirer*, *Real Simple*, *Rolling Stone*, *Population Connection*,

*Vanguard: Los Angeles LGBT Center's Member Magazine, ZooNooz, Scientific American*) and journals (e.g., *The Science Teacher, Multicultural Education, Re-thinking Schools*) to which I presently subscribe and frequently read. As part of this reflection, I describe and discuss my collage in some detail since I do not have an audience to which to present. First, I identified my multicultural identities, along with subcategories or descriptions. They are listed here, however after some reflection, I moved the sub-categories of identities directly under the intended affiliated category.

### Socioeconomic Status

- Grew up poor
- Presently a person with means
- Fears becoming poor again

### Religion

- Atheist
- Science-minded & skeptical
- Raised Catholic, recovering

### Gender/Sexual Orientation

- Genderqueer-woman
  - Activist
  - Animal lover
  - Artist
  - Attracted to people of all genders
  - Avid reader
  - Business owner
  - Cat mama
  - Childless by choice
  - Buffalo, NY native
  - Corvette enthusiast
  - Fine art photographer
  - Gun enthusiast
  - Horror & true crime fan
  - Motorcyclist
  - Multicultural educator
  - Organized
  - Overweight
  - Partner
  - Prince fan
  - Science educator

- ○ Sister
- ○ Student
- ○ Unicorn lover
- ○ Woman
- ○ Writer
- Pansexual

### Race/Ethnicity

- White
- Polish-American
  - ○ Born in Buffalo, NY
  - ○ Raised in Depew, NY
  - ○ Identify as Polish-American
- German-America

### Exceptionality

- Suffers from depression & anxiety
- Undiagnosed dyslexia
- Undiagnosed Prosopagnosia (i.e., face-blindness)

Next, I examined my magazines and cut out images, titles, or headlines that represent one or more of my identities and created my collage. The discussion that follows highlights the images I included in my collage. Generally, I found images that represented some aspect of my identity descriptions. I also found images that illustrated different aspects within each multicultural identity category. I did not find or expect to find—or chose to cut out—images for every identity or sub-category of identities. Finally, I found that some of the images represent more than one of my identities—or an intersection of one or more of my identities.

### Socioeconomic Status

For my socioeconomic status category, I found images that represent various aspects of my identities. For example, I included images of the names and addresses of some of the organizations that I financially support through donations; images that support how I invest my money; and images of some of the consumer products on which I spend my money. These are examples of how multifaceted our identities may be within just one category.

For this category, I found it surprising just how many advertisements consisted of consumer products that I regularly buy and use. Though, maybe I shouldn't have been surprised by this given that the ads and featured reviews in *Real Simple* and *Women's Health*, for example, directly impact my buying practices. I trust these sources, and I am obviously a targeted demographic.

### Religion

I admit that I did not put much effort into finding images that represent my atheist, science-minded, and skeptical identities. I read *Scientific American* and *Skeptical Inquirer*, which consist of ideas and articles that support my ways of thought. Now that I reflect on it, I could have included images of Mars, highlighting the evidence of possible life on the planet and supporting the notion that "we are not alone." However, I did include images reflecting my support for science education, which broadly covers these ideas. But if I were to have dug deeper into the articles, I probably could have found arguments against religion being taught or practiced within the public-school system, something I strongly support.

### Gender/Sexual Orientation

This category overtook my collage. I identify so many parts of me, or my other identities, with my genderqueer-woman identity. I discuss this more under the *Intersectionality* heading below. Just by reading my list of identities and sub-identities, one can see that I pack a lot in to this multicultural identity category—for example, cat mama, photographer, motorcyclist, and science educator. Indeed, my identity as a genderqueer-woman is the most important, most performed, and most defended of all my identities. *I learned that my "genderqueer-woman" identity encompasses all my identities.*

### Race/Ethnicity

I included a couple of images of white women in my collage, though oddly not around the Race/Ethnicity section of the poster. Hmmm . . . it seems that "woman" trumped "white." As I was collecting images, I did notice the many white faces, but few seem to reflect me. In fact, the two that I pasted into my collage most closely represented my look and age, I guess that's why I included it in the "woman" section of my project. (There's much more to explore here regarding my whiteness.)

What I did not find *obviously* represented in my magazines were my Polish- and German- American identities. For example, none of my current magazines highlight Polish-American traditions or histories. (However, I do follow a couple of Polish-themed pages on Facebook.) Because of this acknowledgment, I was interested to learn if such magazines existed. I found the *Polish American Journal*, a monthly newspaper available for subscription through their website and through Amazon.com. I read the three reviews available on the Amazon website, and though warned by one critical Amazon subscriber that the "journal presents news and information regarding Poland and American Polonia from a very conservative, traditionalistic point of view," I bought a one-year subscription. I understand that the newspaper "present[s] news and opinion[s] from very conservative and far-right points of view," which are like the perspectives held by many of my Polish-American family members (e.g., aunts, uncles, cousins). Certainly, I am intrigued, and somewhat hopeful, because the reviewer also wrote that "there's also plenty of apolitical features on traditions and holidays." Nevertheless, I am heeding the reviewer's warning as a new subscriber. I realize that I will "be getting only a very conservative slant on Polish current events and history." I should receive my first *Polish American Journal* in March—maybe I will share my reaction to the newspaper when I perform the lesson on race/ethnicity.

And to be transparent, I've detached myself from my German-American identity since becoming estranged from my father over 20 years ago. Currently, I have little interest in learning about the paternal side of my family or my German heritage. But maybe this will change after recently connecting with aunts and uncles on my father's side of the family.

### Exceptionality

Many of the magazines and journals I read discuss (and advertise medications for) mental health issues, including depression and anxiety. They broach these topics from various perspectives which is helpful for someone who is interested in finding ways to cope, learning from others' stories and experiences, and understanding the biological and physiological systems at play.

### Intersectionality

Although I did not collect collage content that represented each of my identities (e.g., my Polish-American identity) or sub-identities (e.g., Corvette enthusiast), I did find that some of the images represent more than one of my identities. For example, "high school science education" reflects an intersection between my atheist and science-minded identities with my science educator identity. Another example is the image of the Giant Panda which represents my love of animals and my ability to financially contribute to conservation efforts—which I frequently do. Indeed, through critically reflecting on and analyzing my collage, I became aware of many intersections of my various identities—something I would hope those who perform this exploration will also realize as it shows the complexities of identity and identity awareness.

The greatest intersections connect my genderqueer-woman identity with all my other identities. Through this exercise, I realized that I am a genderqueer-woman above all else. My genderqueer-woman identity encompasses all other identities. For example, I am a genderqueer-woman who suffers from depression and anxiety; who invests her money but also supports wildlife conservation efforts; who likes to watch horror movies; who is a cat mama; who is a business owner; who is a science educator; who is a fine art photographer; and who rides a motorcycle. I recognize that all these identities, or sub-identities, are reflective of my genderqueer self.

## Discuss Any Difficulties or Complexities of Choosing a Label or Labels

As far as I know, there are no labels for a person who grew up poor, who now has means, and who is afraid of becoming poor again. Indeed, these explorations are not about finding, or even creating, labels. My (and your) identities are much more complex than a mere one- or two-word label or description. Further, the complexities of identity labels, or even recognition of certain identities, are tremendous. I found this exploration to be complicated, yet enjoyable. I liked that I got to choose the setting (e.g., my magazines and journals) for this exploration and I would perform this lesson again using a different set of criteria (e.g., my book library).

## Explain the Purpose of Multicultural Education

The purpose of multicultural education is to work toward creating curricula and school climates that encourage and support the teaching of all students. According to Banks (2016), "multicultural education is at least three things: an idea or concept, an educational reform movement, and a process" that "incorporates the idea that all students—regardless of their gender; sexual orientation; social class; and ethnic, racial, or cultural characteristics—should have an equal opportunity to learn in school" (p. 2). Further, because of these characteristics, some students "have a better chance to learn in schools as they are currently structured than do students who belong to other groups or who have different cultural characteristics" (p. 2). Indeed, "multicultural education is a broad concept with several different and important dimensions" (p. 16). These include content integration, the knowledge construction process, prejudice reduction, an equity pedagogy, and an empowering school culture and social structure (p. 16).

Along with these definitions of multicultural education, Banks (2016) provides a brief history of the development of multicultural education; an introduction of the nature of culture in the United States; a short discussion of the social construction of multicultural categories; and a glimpse of the implications these things have for education. I hoped that the section on the social construction of categories would offer a deeper understanding of each of the categories, but the content is very limited. I must admit that I was hoping for more guidance in the form of labels or sub-identities, especially for the socioeconomic status category. As alluded to earlier, I don't know where I fit in this category—but addressing these tensions is part of the multicultural education experience.

After reading "Chapter 2: Culture, Teaching, and Learning" (Convertino, Levinson, & González, 2016), I considered removing it from the reading list for Exploration 2, but then thought better of it. Although the content in Chapter 2 does not directly aid in the performance of Exploration 2, it does explain how culture and learning are intimately connected, and it provides examples that may "help educators make effective connections between their students' social lives and their learning in schools" (p. 24). And although I found the chapter to be a bit tedious, it presents meanings and uses of culture that are worth knowing and revisiting as an educator and curriculum worker. Indeed, the authors stress the importance of teachers having an "in-depth understanding of their students' participation in communities of practice outside of schools, derived from the teachers' own long-term observation of and participation in those communities" (p. 36). As classroom teachers know, these connections are imperative; and future teachers should be willing to engage with the communities in which they teach to achieve greater success in the classroom.

Another purpose of multicultural education, I would argue, is to offer teachers a chance to explore and develop an awareness of their multicultural identities and how these identities affect their teaching and learning philosophies. One of the outcomes of this curriculum is for educators to realize that identity awareness (of self and others) is key to contributing to a more accepting and socially just multicultural society. Tools, or methods, that may help with that are autoethnographical writings and practices. In one of the readings for this exploration, Nieto (2003) highlights the importance of teaching as autobiography. She writes, "I have come to believe that being aware of and valuing one's autobiography must be at the heart of teaching because . . . teaching is 'an encounter with self'" (p. 25). Her chapter repeatedly supports the idea that teachers bring their values, beliefs, and identities into the classroom with them; thus, these elements should be explored in order to be effective teachers. Further, the chapter consists of several autobiographical examples written by educators about what brought them to teaching. And though I use autoethnographical approaches (which connects self with culture), a term that until recently was not widely used in education research, these autobiographical writings serve as proper exemplars for explorers to refer to and learn from.

Additionally, queer multicultural social justice (teacher) education—a critical approach that breaks down, and may reach beyond, rigid identity labels by implementing methods such as autoethnography to provide learners with opportunities to investigate ways to dismantle heteronormativity, rethink binary systems of identification, and deconstruct socially constructed identities in personal and meaningful ways—helps to make connections between self and culture. By performing exercises that explore multicultural identities within their culture—including media outlets, social media, art, family traditions, school settings, and curricula—explorers may become of aware of social injustices and heteronormative policies and may take actions to diminish these inequalities in classrooms and in society at large.

## REFERENCES

Banks, J. A. (2016). Chapter 1: Multicultural education: Characteristics and goals. In J. A. Banks & C. A. McGee Banks (Eds.), *Multicultural education: Issues and perspectives* (9th ed., pp. 2–23). John Wiley & Sons.

Convertino, C., Levinson, B. A., & González, N. (2016). Chapter 2: Culture, Teaching, and learning. In J. A. Banks & C. A. McGee Banks (Eds.), *Multicultural education: Issues and perspectives* (9th ed.) (pp. 24–40). John Wiley & Sons.

Nieto, S. (2003). Chapter 2: Teaching as autobiography. In S. Nieto, *What keeps teachers going?* (pp. 22–36) Teachers College.

# INTERSECTIONALITY WITHIN ACTIVISM AND SUPPORT GROUPS

*Exploration*

Attend a protest, demonstration, march, sign making party, or support group (e.g., a protest related to "the wall," a march for LGBTQ rights, a March for Science, a trans* youth support group), as one who supports or protests—and/or identifies with—the cause or attend with a person who you want to support. Reflect on your experience.

*Discussion*

Should include defining *intersectionality*, determining appropriate events to attend, and understanding that this is not a "tourist" experience but an activist or supportive endeavor.

*Presentation*

Consider all options (e.g., a photo essay, video diary, blog post).

*Queer Multicultural Social Justice Education: Curriculum (and Identity) Development Through Performance,* pages 73–78.
Copyright © 2021 by Information Age Publishing
73

*Reflection*

Critically respond to others' presentations (when applicable), reflect on the exploration and the readings, and address the following prompts: 1) Describe your experience. What event did you attend? Why did you choose this event? Include details of the event and feelings you experienced before, during, or after the event; and, 2) Reflect on other experiences when you had difficulty separating one or more of your identities from your other identities (maybe this occurred while performing Exploration 2). If you did not already address it in your Exploration 2 reflection, discuss any critical awareness or conflict due to intersectionality you experienced when performing Exploration 2 or when attending your chosen event.

*Readings*

Lorde, A. (1988). I am your sister: Black Women organizing across sexualities. In A. Lorde (Ed.), *A burst of light: Essays by Audre Lorde* (pp. 19–26). Fireband.

Loutzenheiser, L. W. (2001). "If I teach about these issues they will burn down my house": The possibilities and tensions of queered, antiracist pedagogy. In K. K. Kumashiro (Ed.), *Troubling intersections by race and sexuality: Queer students of color and anti-oppressive education* (pp. 195–214). Rowman & Littlefield.

## WHY DO I RALLY FOR SCIENCE?

For Exploration 3 I chose to attend the San Diego Rally for Science on Saturday, May 4, 2019. The event took place in Waterfront Park in downtown San Diego. It's an event that I've wanted to attend in the past, and this exploration gave me more of a reason to participate. I chose this event because science plays an influential role in my life and I wanted to show my support for the discipline—especially during this politically hostile, anti-science climate.

From an early age, I was drawn to science—specifically to biology, zoology, and ecology—because of my love of and interest in animals and animal behavior. As a child, I would watch *Mutual of Omaha's Wild Kingdom* and collect mail-order animal fact cards. As an adult, I enjoy visiting zoos and safari parks and attending scientific lectures to learn more about animals, their behavior, and their habitats.

I have always preferred and enjoyed my science classes over others. Indeed, many women science teachers have had a profound impact on me throughout my schooling—including my undergraduate studies—as they acted as role models and mentors. In high school, I declared science as one of my major subjects of study. However, as a girl, being enrolled in these classes was not always easy. If I remember correctly, I was the only girl in my senior physics class. I recall feeling out of place—but I stuck with it. I eventually became a science teacher myself. Throughout my teaching career, I served in various middle and high school sciences classes.

Today, I partake in the life-long learning of science by attending, and occasionally speaking at, science- and evidence-based skeptic conferences (Knaier, 2014), supporting conservation efforts (e.g., donating to the Rhino Rescue Center), engaging in ecotourism and educational adventures (e.g., Great White Shark cage diving), and writing about queer and critical issues within science education (Knaier, 2019). To this day, science-centered spaces offer me a place to teach, learn, and explore. I frequently gather, study, and engage with others who share my interest in science—and that is why I rallied for science.

This was my first science rally. I was eager to be a part of a like-minded crowd, to participate in the march, and to proudly show my support for science! Unfortunately, I was disappointed by the low turnout, though I made the best of it. I stopped and spoke to the volunteers representing conservation groups and learned about their efforts. And I made small monetary contributions to each group.

I took notice of those who attended the rally. There were adults and children from various backgrounds and ethnicities, educators, scientists, and other members of the community. Before I arrived at the rally, I decided I would focus on and photograph the signs that participants carried. I wanted to visually show the diversity, and possible intersectionality, of the voices rallying for science—as science is a rather broad discipline. My goal was to capture and share images of the various approaches to, categories of, and politics of science supported by the crowd through their signs. Further, this project highlights the intersection between one's ideologies with one's support for science. I was also hoping to capture the signs of protestors, or anti-science, participants, but I did not see any. I thought photographing the signs would be a great way to share a part of the participants' stories. However, due to the scarce attendance, I photographed only nine different signs. With these images, I made a photo-collage for this exploration, titled *Signs for Science*. In part, the signs reflect support for women in science, science-based political reform (e.g., Green New Deal), and the everyday engagement with science. Although my sample is small, it does show various perspectives toward, and support, for science.

## SIGNS FOR SCIENCE

Note: Image collage of nine hand-made signs arranged in three columns and three rows. Top left: Image of sign that features hand drawn image of Rick and Morty giving the finger with text that reads "Hey Polititians! Peace among worlds! Top middle: Image of black sign that reads: "All you need is love & science." Top right: Image of sign that reads " Science needs dreamers." Second row left: Image of sign that features hand drawn planet earth with a red heart that reads "Make earth great again." Second row middle: Image of sign that reads "Green new deal now." Second row right: Image of bright green sign with hand drawn flask and graph that reads "More science less fiction." Bottom row left: Image of a woman wearing a black hat with a sign that reads "Stand up for science." Bottom row middle: Image of bright green sign that reads "Good politicians are not afraid of science." Bottom row right: Image of sign that reads "Science and everyday life cannot & should not be seperated ~Rosalind Franklin."

## REFLECTION

By performing this exploration, I experienced a potential problematic situation that other performers might experience—low attendance at an event. As an educator I would never penalize a student for something that is out of their control.

The assignment was to attend an event and reflect on it. And, although the event was not well-attended, I still met the exploration requirements as outlined in my performance.

The two readings I chose for this exploration highlight the tensions of *intersections* when teaching (a form of activism (Sleeter, 1996)) and discussing topics like race and sexuality. After reading these selections, I based the parameters of this exploration on them. Each reading shares personal accounts and offers suggestions and support for teaching important, yet difficult, topics.

The first reading is appropriate to include for three reasons. First, Loutzenheiser (2001) tells a story—her story, a personal story—about teaching secondary students and preservice teachers in ways that address and question intersections between race and sexuality. She shares successes of her students and mistakes made by her. She *shows* how she learns as she teaches. Loutzenheiser recognizes the importance of a teacher being a learner within her own classroom: "If I assume that I always have more to learn than I can ever know, especially about those less like me, those different from me, then I am never fooled into thinking that I am 'done'" (p. 199). Second, Loutzenheiser shares specific exercises she asked her students to perform (e.g., the index-card exercise and cultural autobiography), and though I do not prescribe these tasks in my curriculum, they give explorers additional ideas to perform themselves or try with their students. Finally, Loutzenheiser admits that there are no clean "Answers" to teaching about the intersections of race and sexuality. She argues that teachers need to be open and allow their lessons to flow and be guided by students—this is queer curriculum. Overall, Loutzenheiser highlights the difficulties and the importance of discussing the intersections between race and sexuality within classrooms and acknowledges that there is no one way to tackle the difficult lessons. She also points out that the lessons performed by her students in her classes are not enough. As Banks (1988, 1999, 2004, 2010, 2013, 2016) explains, these practices need to be nurtured across the curriculum and embedded within school culture.

In the second assigned reading, Lorde (1988) makes a powerful plea by asking Black women to come together despite sexual identity differences and acknowledges how heteronormative beliefs can hinder efforts to work together and may cause strife within minority groups (e.g., the Black community). Through sharing personal accounts, she proudly declares that she, a Black lesbian, has been working on the front lines of Black civil right movements—and that Black lesbians and gays have always been there fighting alongside their heterosexual brothers and sisters. Finally, she points out to her audience that heteronormative "stereotypes are yours to solve, not mine, and they are a terrible and wasteful barrier to our working together. I am not your enemy. We do not have to become each other's unique experience and insights in order to share what we have learned through our particular battles for survival as Black women" (Lorde, 1988, p. 26). Through this exploration (and others), I hope students will take heed of this powerful message as they engage with activists fighting for a common goal.

I do recognize that both assigned readings for this exploration address intersections between race—specifically those of color—and sexuality. As I progress through the development of this curriculum, I hope to find and include other readings for Exploration 3 to provide a more diverse reading list.

## REFERENCES

Banks, J. A. (1988). Approaches to multicultural curriculum reform. *Multicultural Leader* *1*(2), 1–3.

Banks, J. A. (1999). Chapter 5: Multicultural citizenship education. In Day, B. D. (Ed.), *Teaching & Learning in the New Millennium* (pp. 54–61). Kappa Delta Pi.

Banks, J. A. (2004). Multicultural Education: Historical Development, Dimensions, and Practice. In J. A. Banks & C. A. McGee Banks (Eds.), *Handbook of research on multicultural education* (pp. 3–29). Jossey-Bass.

Banks, J. A. (2010). Series forward. In G. Gay, *Culturally responsive teaching: Theory, research and practice* (2nd ed.), (pp. ix-xiii). Teachers College Press.

Banks, J. A. (2013). Chapter 1: Multicultural education: Characteristics and goals. In J. A. Banks & C. A. McGee Banks (Eds.), *Multicultural Education: Issues and Perspectives* (8th ed.), (pp. 3–22). Wiley.

Banks, J. A. (2016). Chapter 1: Multicultural education: Characteristics and goals. In J. A. Banks & C. A. McGee Banks (Eds.), *Multicultural Education: Issues and Perspectives* (9th ed.), (pp. 2–23). Wiley.

Knaier, M. L. (2014, July). *Teaching the nature of science: A social justice argument.* Paper presented at The Amazing Meeting 2014: Skepticism and the Brain, Las Vegas, NV.

Knaier, M. L. (2019). What makes *girls* and *boys* so desirable?: STEM education beyond gender binaries. In W. Letts & S. Fifield (Eds.), *STEM of Desire: Queer Theories in Science Education* (pp. 209–221). Koninklijke Brill.

Lorde, A. (1988). I am your sister: Black Women organizing across sexualities. In A. Lorde, *A burst of light: Essays by Audre Lorde* (pp. 19–26). Fireband.

Loutzenheiser, L. W. (2001). "If I teach about these issues they will burn down my house": The possibilities and tensions of queered, antiracist pedagogy. In K. K. Kumashiro (Ed.), *Troubling intersections by race and sexuality: Queer students of color and anti-oppressive education* (pp. 195–214). Rowman & Littlefield.

Sleeter, C. E. (1996). *Multicultural education as social activism.* State University of New York Press.

EXPLORATION 4

# SOCIOECONOMIC STATUS AND THE ARTS

*Exploration*

Explore your past and/or present socioeconomic status identity/identities in relation to the arts (e.g., writing stories or poetry, drawing or painting, photographing or digital designing, playing a musical instrument or singing, acting, or dancing). Explore and reflect on how your socioeconomic status, along with other (multi)cultural beliefs, customs, and/or practices (or other aspects of your life), may have influenced your artistic self. You may conduct this exploration in various ways (e.g., a story, photo essay, poem, video) and from many perspectives (e.g., as an artist, student, parent, art educator, your young self). When appropriate, include samples of artwork and/or performances.

You may use the exploration outline to guide your exploration. There is a lot to explore here, try to narrow your focus. Remember, you are choosing just one of many explorations that you may conduct.

*Discussion*

Clarify the prompt.

*Queer Multicultural Social Justice Education: Curriculum (and Identity) Development Through Performance,* pages 79–86.
Copyright © 2021 by Information Age Publishing
**79**

*Presentation*

Consider all options (e.g., a story, photo essay, poem, video, dance).

*Reflection*

Critically respond to others' presentations (when applicable), reflect on the exploration and the readings, and address the following prompt: Discuss ways in which you may be empathetic to socioeconomic differences of others.

*Readings*

Lorde, A. (1984). Age, race, class, and sex: Women redefining difference. In A. Lorde, *Sister/outsider: Essays and speeches* (pp. 114–123). Crossing.

Owens, J. (2013). Chapter 8: Not high school as you remember it. In J. Owens, *Confessions of a bad teacher: The shocking truth from the front lines of American public education* (pp. 127–135). Sourcebooks.

Ravitch, D. (2013). Chapter 10: How poverty affects academic achievement. In D. Ravitch, *Reign of error: The hoax of the privatization movement and the danger to America's public school* (pp. 91–98). Alfred A. Knopf.

Sapp, J. (2009). How school taught me I was poor. *Teaching Tolerance, 35,* 52–55.

## EXPLORATION 4 OUTLINE

1. **Identity.** *How do I identify?*
   - Grew up poor
   - Presently a person with means
   - Fears becoming poor again
2. **Initial questions.** *What are my initial questions?*
   - Did I have art-centered hobbies?
   - Was I encouraged to have them?
   - Why did I write poetry?
3. **Preliminary resources/references.** *Where will I seek information?*
   - My poetry notebook
   - Photo albums/boxes (digital and print)
   - My sister
4. **Performance and presentation methods.** *How will I perform and present my exploration?*
   - Poem supported by reflection and artifacts
5. **Additional questions.** *What additional questions did I explore?*
   - How did/does art help me?
   - Why don't I write poetry as often as I did?
   - How can I combine poem writing and photography?
6. **Further questions.** *What are my further (future) questions?*
   - What other artistic hobbies do I want to pursue?
   - As a photographer, how can I make a difference?

7. **All resources/references.** *What resources did I use?*
   - ○ The assigned readings
   - ○ My poetry notebook
8. **Sharing.** How *will I share this exploration?*
   - ○ Through writing and sharing this project.

## POVERTY AND POETRY

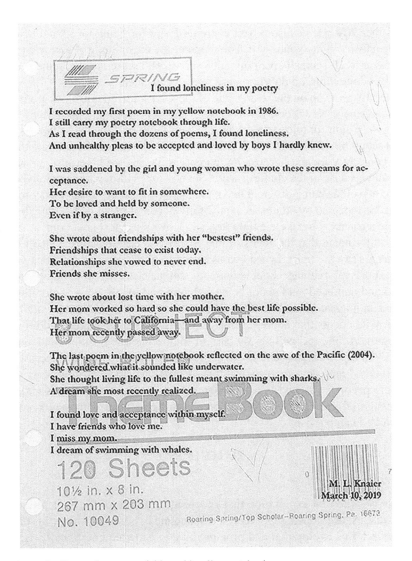

Note: Image is of a typed poem overlaid on old, yellow notebook cover.

For this exploration on socioeconomic status and the arts, I chose to write the poem, *I found loneliness in my poetry*. I wrote it after reading every poem I ever wrote between 1986 and 2004 in my yellow poem notebook. For the presentation, I overlaid my poem on an image of my yellow notebook.

The influence of poverty is certainly reflected in my writings. I grew up in a broken home—my parents divorced when I was nine. Throughout the notebook I wrote a lot about relationships and the desire to "expand" them; I wrote about feeling secure; and I wrote about my inability to express my love and gratitude toward others—sentiments brought on by having an absent father and a hard-working mother. My poems also reflect a strong desire for being loved and accepted and the naivety of my young self. These poems are the epitome of low self-esteem and insecurity. It seems I spent my adolescent years searching for some sense of security—something I didn't find until many years later.

I literally grew up on the wrong side of the tracks. I lived one block from Main Street in Depew, New York. It was a tough and poor neighborhood. Many of the houses were built for railroad workers and their families. I lived four houses away from a set of railroad tracks. (To this day, I refuse to live in earshot of train tracks.) I was constantly judged because my parents were divorced, because of where I lived, and because of the clothes I wore. Several times throughout my notebook, I refer to myself as being different and misunderstood. I feel the same way today. I want to be accepted by others. In some of my poems, I plead with certain boys to give me a chance—to take the time to get to know me. Most never did.

It's unfortunate that the focus of my poems was relationships. Since I didn't have access to a therapist, I wish I would have used this personal and creative outlet to express my feelings about being poor and unaccepted; about being sexually abused and confused; and about being different and lonely. This exploration has sparked an interest in me to further reflect on my childhood and early adulthood and to write poems that address some of the adversities I endured. Additionally, I have a hard time reconciling my current socioeconomic position, and a reflective look at my life's journey may help me come to terms with my successes and tribulations. I may develop a project that incorporates poem writing (e.g., verses from the poems I have written) and photography (e.g., images that capture the sentiments reflected in my words). Something I can share with others—maybe something I can publish.

## REFLECTION

### The Exploration Outline

This was the first exploration that encouraged the use of the exploration outline. And, just as I hoped, this exercise assisted me in brainstorming ideas on how to approach this exploration and prompted me to generate questions I wished to explore. I initially filled out the exploration outline before completing the readings (with a focus on my current artistic outlet, photography), but then I was inspired to conduct this exploration from another perspective (from when I was an adolescent girl who wrote poetry), so I went back and completed the exploration outline again. In fact, I updated it several times as I progressed through the performance—as I hope others will do during their explorations.

## The Readings

My exploration format, one which intersects a multicultural identity with a social or cultural practice or ideal (e.g., the arts) was envisioned while I read Lorde's (1984) essay, *Age, race, class, and sex: Women redefining difference*. Her words:

> Yet even the form our creativity takes is often a class issue. Of all the art forms, poetry is the most economical. It is the one which is the most secret, which requires the least physical labor, the least material, and the one which can be done between shifts, in the hospital pantry, on the subway, and on scraps of surplus paper. (p. 116)

This essay provoked me to reflect on my young self. As a poor, latchkey child, I often wrote poetry. All I needed was my notebook, a pen, and a bit of privacy. This essay also made me think about my current artistic self. I am a photographer. Lorde writes:

> The actual requirements to produce the visual arts also help determine, along class lines, whose art is whose. In this day of inflated prices for material, who are our sculptors, our painters, our photographers? (p. 116)

Lorde's work encouraged me to compare, and reflect on, my young, poor artistic self, with my current, privileged artistic self—including the modes, subjects, and purposes of my art.

Being a photographer can be expensive. I have spent thousands of dollars on my equipment over the past ten years. Though I am aware of how fortunate I am to be able to afford my photography equipment, Lorde's words affected me. Initially, I was going to explore my identity as a photographer for this lesson, but after completing the readings and through the process of filling out the exploration outline, I decided to pursue another path. I wanted to revisit the poetry I wrote as a young girl who was growing into adulthood. I wanted to rediscover my words and what was important to me then. I wanted to reflect on why I wrote poetry. I still have my yellow three-subject notebook that houses my poetry, and I decided to use it as a resource for this performance.

Lorde's essay also prompted me to clarify that through these explorations I am not asking the performers to separate out one identity from others, but maybe spotlight one within certain cultural aspects. As Lorde (1984) declares:

> As a Black lesbian feminist comfortable with the many different ingredients of my identity, and a woman committed to racial and sexual freedom from oppression, I find I am constantly being encouraged to pluck out some aspect of myself and present this as the meaningful whole, eclipsing or denying the other parts of self. But

this is a destructive and fragmenting way to live. My fullest concentration of energy is available to me only when I integrate all the parts of who I am, openly, allowing power from particular sources of my living to flow back and forth freely through all my different selves, without the restrictions of externally imposed definition. (pp. 120–121)

I want explorers to notice all their different selves and embrace the intersectionality of their selves while performing these explorations.

Further, since my original target audience was educators, including teacher educators and future classroom teachers, I wanted to expose explorers to real-world situations and challenges that occur in schools. In *Reign of Error*, Ravitch (2013) outlines how poverty affects children and their performances in school. She argues that "great" teachers cannot eliminate the achievement gap; and discusses how children of poverty may have more medical issues, less face time with working parents, and unfit learning and studying environments within the home. These are important issues that should be exposed to pre-service teachers. Future teachers need to understand how societal shortcomings, such as poverty, affect students. Further, they should be privy to the unrealistic expectations put on our teachers.

The importance of assigning and reading Owens' (2013) work is to illustrate drastic conditions between schools—even when the schools are housed in the same building. As I engaged with "Not High School as You Remember It" (Owens, 2013), I reflected on my time as a classroom teacher having served within two different charter schools. I witnessed first-hand how charter schools, within the same county, can be drastically different. Given our political climate and attitude toward the corporate interest in our school system, future teachers need to realize the potential flaws of charter schools and voucher systems.

For example, the first charter school I worked for consisted of seven trailers. Six of them served as classrooms and one trailer served as the main office. They were situated in a dirt lot not far from a non-charter, brick and mortar elementary school. Sadly, the school didn't have a library—aside from the classroom libraries maintained by teachers. Other resources were scare as well (e.g., physical education equipment, classroom funding). During my first year within the charter system, I chose to spend approximately $1000 of my personal money for furniture and other supplies that I needed and/or wanted for my classroom and my students—something not all teachers can afford to do. The school consisted of grades 6–12, and I served as a science teacher. I taught earth science (6th grade), life science (7th grade), physical science (8th grade), earth science (9th grade), forensic science (a high school elective that mainly served 11th and 12th grade students). This was not an easy teaching assignment. During my time there, I was expected to teach the sixth and seventh grade science classes in the same classroom during the same period. This situation did not serve my students well. Indeed, I could not serve my students well under these conditions. I chose to leave this school as soon as another opportunity presented itself.

In contrast, the second charter school I worked for had grown from similar temporary structures into a high-tech, beautiful college-like campus. I was first hired to serve as the tenth-grade computer applications and environmental chemistry teacher (a science class for non-science majors). After my first semester at that school, I was asked to be the school's eighth grade physical science teacher. In this role, I served approximately 135 students each year. Due to scheduling and the size of the school, I did not have my own classroom; nor did any other middle school science teacher on campus. Each of us had to "travel" at least one period a day, often into another building (for example, I taught one class a day in the high school building). As a science teacher who was expected to perform hands-on inquiries, traveling across campus with a cart packed with science equipment for my thirty-five or more students was cumbersome. I understand that there are teachers who are serving in deplorable conditions, but the situation I was in impacted my ability, and often my desire, to be the best teacher I could be. And this took a toll on me.

During my time serving in charter schools, I witnessed the dark side of the charter system. Schools were run like businesses with students serving as monetary pawns. Student enrollment and attendance allowances guided the way to getting creative with making up missed days. One solution was creating winter sessions and holding Saturday-school for those students who had a considerable amount of absences, in order to recoup funding. Students who were failing classes were also asked to attend these sessions to improve their grades and the school's statistics. Teachers had to supply individual lessons and assignments for each student that had incomplete work in the grade books. We were never asked to review or assess the work; however, we were instructed to change student grades. This did not sit well with me. There were other challenges, along with ethical and philosophical disagreements, that finally led to my departure.

Finally, Sapp's (2009) story provides a personal account and reminds us that not all students experience school the same way. His story highlights how students of poverty may navigate and experience learning. These students may have limited means and non-traditional family trees (e.g., single-parent families; foster parents). As teachers, we need to be aware of these potentials and offer experiences and activities that all students may equitably perform and enjoy. We may need to offer resources (e.g., art supplies, homework help, alternative methods) that support the engagement of all our students. Unfortunately, "school projects, holidays, extracurricular activities and field trips" often "send a surge of panic through" households "because they were yet another expense" (p. 55). This is unfair to our students who live in poverty. It is also unfair to the teachers who absorb extra costs so all their students can engage in an equal education.

In 2008, I left teaching. I was devastated. Lost. It was through photography that I found myself again. I took classes at my local community college. But I realized that this was not enough. I wanted to get back into teaching. It is my passion. So, I decided to move forward and pursue my Ph.D.—though I did earn my certificate in Fine Art Photography along the way. Having creative outlets, such as writing poems, photography, and even academic writing have played a large role in my life—maybe even a life-saving role. As educators we need to fight for the inclusion of such activities in our curriculum and as extracurricular activities that are available to all our students.

## REFERENCES

Lorde, A. (1984). Age, race, class, and sex: Women redefining difference. In A. Lorde, *Sister/outsider: Essays and speeches* (pp. 114–123). Crossing.

Owens, J. (2013). Chapter 8: Not high school as you remember it. In J. Owens, *Confessions of a bad teacher: The shocking truth from the front lines of American public education* (pp. 127–135). Sourcebooks.

Ravitch, D. (2013). Chapter 10: How poverty affects academic achievement. In D. Ravitch, *Reign of error: The hoax of the privatization movement and the danger to American's public school* (pp. 91–98). Alfred A. Knopf.

Sapp, J. (2009). How school taught me I was poor. *Teaching Tolerance, 35,* 52–55.

# EXPLORATION 5

# RELIGION AND MORTALITY

*Exploration*

Explore your religious affiliation(s) or religious identity/identities in relation to mortality (e.g., humanity, death). Explore and reflect on how your religion or absence of religion, along with other (multi)cultural beliefs, customs, and/or practices, or other aspects of your life, may have influenced your outlook on mortality. You may conduct this exploration in various ways (e.g., a children's story, scrapbook, memory box) and from many perspectives (e.g., as an educator, parent, daughter).

You may use the exploration outline to guide your exploration. There is a lot to explore here, try to narrow your focus. Remember, you are choosing just one of many explorations that you may conduct.

*Discussion*

Clarify the prompt.

*Presentation*

Consider all options (e.g., a children's story, scrapbook, memory box, photo essay).

*Reflection*

Critically respond to others' presentations (when applicable), reflect on the exploration and the readings, and address the following prompt: Explain any difficulties you had with the exploration.

*Queer Multicultural Social Justice Education: Curriculum (and Identity) Development Through Performance,* pages 87–101.
**87**

*Readings*

Brown, L. K. & Brown, M. (2009). *When dinosaurs die: A guide to understanding death.* Little, Brown, and Company.

González, X. (2017). *All around us.* Cinco Puntos Press.

Rowland, J. (2017). *The memory box: A book about grief.* Sparkhouse Family.

Wilcox, M. (2018). *After life: Ways we think about death.* Orca Book Publishers.

## EXPLORATION 5 OUTLINE

1. **Identity.** *How do I identify?*
   - Atheist
   - Science-minded, skeptical
   - Recovering Catholic
2. **Initial questions.** *What are my initial questions?*
   - How do those we lost live on after life?
   - How do/can I actively keep my mom's memory alive?
3. **Preliminary resources/references.** *Where will I seek information?*
   - Memories of my mom and grandmother
   - Photo albums/boxes (digital and print)
   - Artifacts of my mom
4. **Performance and presentation methods.** *How will I perform and present my exploration?*
   - Photo essay
5. **Additional questions.** *What additional questions did I explore?*
   - How will I concretely keep my mom's memory alive?
   - What other projects can I perform that involve my mom?
6. **Further questions.** *What are my further (future) questions?*
   - How will I be remembered?
   - How do I want to be remembered?
7. **All resources/references.** *What resources did I use?*
   - The assigned readings
   - Photographs
   - Talking with family
8. **Sharing.** How *will I share this exploration?*
   - Through writing and sharing this project.

## WE LIVE ON

I am an atheist. I believe that people live on through the art, photographs, and performances they leave behind. They also live on through the memories and actions of others. The living are vehicles for sustaining memories of the dead. My mom, Rose, lives on through the stories I hear, and the stories I tell, about her. She lives on through the sharing of scrapbooks and photobooks. She lives on through the love I feel, her love, when I wear a piece of jewelry that she gave me. And she lives on through the memories conjured when I hear one of her favorite songs. Sometimes

I cry—remembering how she used dance with my sister and me when we were young.

In Exploration 4, I revealed that I live in California, which was three thousand miles away from my mom. Throughout my adult life, I missed my mom often and very much. I always had an image of her around the house along with other mementos from when I was a child. But since my mom's death, I display more images of her around my home. I also incorporate some of her belongings into my décor to remind myself of her and to give her a presence in my life. My mom lives on through these actions—my actions.

For this performance, I created a series of images, titled *Remembering Mom*. These images include several of my mom's belongings, gifts from my mom, and other items that remind me of her that are purposefully placed throughout my home. Each image is accompanied by a title and short story about the objects featured.

When I first embarked on this project, I knew I would find several images (remember, I am a photographer) and a few items from my childhood spread throughout my house—but I found so much more. I found reminders of how much my mom loved me, how much she thought about me, and how much she still impacts my daily life. I miss her every day.

## REMEMBERING MOM:
## A COLLECTION OF IMAGES

*Mom's Room*
This is my guest room, but it was tailored mostly for my mom.
Her needs were considered when preparing this room; from the type of mattress
(firm) and showerhead (handheld) to other conveniences (shampoos) we provided,
we made sure my mom was comfortable when she visited.

***Three Generations of Mothers***
This vanity belonged to my great-grandmother. It resides in my guest room.
Draped over one side is a scarf that I bought for my grandmother when I was in
Paris. The scarf is adorned by one of my grandmother's rosaries. The jewelry box
belonged to my mother. On that same trip to Paris, I encountered the original
painting of the image on the box.

***Paper Princess***
Although I have had this toilet paper doll for years, which was hand-made by my
great-grandmother, Basi, I recently draped one of my grandmother's necklaces
around her. She is placed in my walk-in closet and I see her every day.
Another reminder of the generations of women who cared for me.

**Carousel Prints**

These framed images are monochrome prints I produced in the darkroom.
I gifted the set to my mom several years ago, and after she died,
I brought them home to display in my bedroom. Mom loved carousels
and she was the inspiration for these images.

**Mom's Three Little Pigs**

These piggy banks belonged to my mom. My father bought them for her
shortly after they got together. Throughout my childhood
(and beyond) these pigs sat on my mother's dresser.
She gifted them to me before she passed. They now sit on my dresser.

### *The Gift of Elvis*
The summer before my mom died, she gave this doll to me to
wrap up as a Christmas present for Bob, my husband. We didn't
know she wouldn't make it to Christmas at that time.

### *Los Angeles*
During mom's last visit we took a daytrip to Los Angeles where
she bought this hat. It now hangs on my coat rack by the front door.

***Joey and Rosie***
After my grandmother passed,
I brought home her photobook to archive the images.
This is a duplicate image of my Uncle Joey and my mom
that I kept from that process.

***My Workspace***
This is an alcove of my desk. This is where I write and work.
This image features an image of my sister, Sherry, my mom, and me from when we
visited the Carousel Museum in Western New York.
One of the last adventures the three of us took together.

***Fun Memories***
This bulletin board hangs in my home-office.
It is decorated with various memorabilia.
The center image (taken by Bob Knaier) is of my mom
and me on the beach during her last visit.

***Family Photos***
These images sit on a countertop in my upstairs hallway.
The child pictured on the left mug is me dressed up on an Easter Sunday,
and the child pictured on the right is my sister with her cat, Patches.
The image on the left is my grandma and my mom.

***Mom's Records***
Mom used to play her records so loud.
We would dance and laugh in our living room.
I now have custody of this vinyl
and can replay some of those happy memories.

***Coffee With Neighbors***
This is my coffee nook in my master bedroom.
I recently added the two coffee mugs.
They belonged to my mother. I remember her walking over to the
neighbor's house with her coffee in these mugs.

***A Small Gift***
This is a small resin box I bought for my mother, Rose.
It now sits on a table in my upstairs hallway.

***Remembering Mom***
This is a recently installed bulletin board in my exercise room.
The idea is to think about my mom as I exercise.
Something I often encouraged her to do.

***Alley Cat***
This is a poster from the '60s that belonged to my mom.
I had it framed and it hangs in my cats' bathroom.

***Celebrating Life***
This award-winning image was used on my mom's memory cards.
The cards were given out at the Celebration of Life event my
sister and I held to honor our mom.

*Life is Short*
This hourglass-pendent holds some of mom's ashes. It serves as a reminder that
life is short and to make the best use of my time. It is currently hanging in my
workspace.

## REFLECTION

I was raised Catholic. I remember attending a lot of funeral masses and wakes (i.e., visiting the body and paying respects with family members) for relatives who had passed (e.g., aunts, uncles, maternal grandfather) when I was young. These events seemed to be a large part of my childhood—I have a large extended family. But, until recently, nobody close to me has died in a long time. The last impactful death (prior to last year) was when my Auntie Irene died in 2010. I did not return to Buffalo for the services—but we toasted to her while drinking highballs, a drink she frequently enjoyed. Coincidently as I am writing this, my estranged father is laying brain-dead in a Buffalo hospital with only a few more days to live. I will not attend any services held for him either—but that's another story.

Presently, I am grieving the loss of two important women. I recently lost my maternal grandmother (February 2018) and my mother (November 2018), both who spent much of their lives caring for me and my sister, Sherry. When I first started to think about this project and curriculum, I planned on traveling to Buffalo to spend time with each of them to learn more about our family and about myself. I thought I'd be listening to stories, cooking traditional Polish foods, and reminiscing over old photographs with them. Unfortunately, those memories were never created. Instead, I must rely on secondhand stories, ancestry research projects, and my collected memories—while grieving my loss.

I did fly to Buffalo to be with my mom and sister shortly after my grandmother's death—though I chose not to attend my grandmother's funeral out of respect for her Catholic faith. My mother had a difficult time understanding my decision. As an atheist, I thought it was disrespectful to attend—and possibly psychologically harmful for me (as a former Catholic) to engage in such practices. But after a couple of tense conversations, and me relating that I did not want to disrespect my grandmother, I think my mom came to understand and accept my choice.

Then when my mother died (more rapidly than expected), my sister and I had to decide how to honor her. Because of my mom's untimely death, I needed time to arrange for travel, and we took some time to plan an event for four weeks after her passing. We chose to hold a secular Celebration of Life event—which was nontraditional (i.e., queer) considering we come from a Catholic family. We invited her family (mom was one of nine children) and her friends. We served coffee and desserts—mom's favorites. It was meant to be an uplifting event—a time to tell stories and remember my mom. I think she would have enjoyed it.

I spent the last year (February until November) helping my mom sort through my grandmother's stuff and aiding her in closing my gram's estate. I got to hear some stories about my grandparents, but it wasn't how I imagined it would be. Now I am helping my sister sort through my mom's estate (November-present). It all seems surreal. We have so many questions. We share memories, laughs, and tears. It's a small part of the healing process.

I recently spent some time in Buffalo helping Sherry. I asked my mom's two sisters to join Sherry and me for dinner because I wanted to learn more about my mom. Some of the stories they shared were fun, but others were heartbreaking. I learned more about some of the losses my mom endured throughout her life (e.g., losing the love of her life to the Vietnam War, losing two baby boys). One of my aunts described my mom as "broken." I knew she struggled after her first husband, Mickey, died, but until now, I didn't know to what extent. It was the first time I was told about my mom's "breakdowns." There is so much more I want to learn about my mom.

This performance offered me a safe, yet focused project to begin advancing through my grieving process. I actively had to think about, remember, and write about my mom—things I try hard not to do. Because of these efforts, I have come up with further ideas on how to remember and learn about my mom. One of the ideas came from the readings (Wilcox, 2018). I want to conduct a project that "introduces" my mom to others as a way of knowing her better. I haven't worked out the details yet, but it is something I am looking forward to exploring.

## The Readings

Dead bodies (human and nonhuman) make me uncomfortable. (Ok—they freak me out!) I have difficulty comprehending the once-living-to-being-dead phenomenon. But I accept that once a person's (or other animal's) brain stops working, they are dead. Further, I approach death (mine and others) secularly. I think a lot about death—mostly my own. I struggle with (at times, crippling) existential angst (another topic I want to research and write about). The four books

I chose to assign as reading for Exploration 5 offer varied multicultural perspectives about death. Each tells a story or stories about how to understand and cope with the loss of a loved one.

As a person who is fascinated by death, I found Wilcox's (2018) book, *After life: Ways we think about death*, informative, at times comforting, and rather interesting. She approaches death in a secular way, but also informs the reader how some religions, customs, and traditions celebrate, honor, or mourn the dead. She does this in a way that doesn't favor, condone, or condemn these actions. I found this book to be relatable and helpful during my time of grief.

In *When dinosaurs die: A guide to understanding death*, Brown and Brown (2009) offer age appropriate terminology (e.g., alive, death, funeral), illustrations, and methods for dealing with a loved one's death (e.g., drawing, punching a pillow, talking to friends). My concern about this book is that it favors Christian beliefs and traditions, such as heaven, funeral services, and prayers—though it does mention other traditions, mostly religious in nature (e.g., burning incense, sitting Shiva, singing at the grave). However, the parts of the book where different reasons for death (e.g., illness, violence, poverty, drug abuse) and feelings about death (e.g., sadness, fear, worry) are addressed have the potential for powerful discussions and teachable moments. Asking others about their encounters with death would prove helpful here.

González (2017) presents a beautifully written and illustrated book that tells a story of how one family reveres life, death, and our connection to earth. Based on some mestizo and Navajo beliefs and traditions (e.g., burying children's placentas), *All around us*, is an uplifting story presented through the interactions between a grandfather with his granddaughter. This book presents death as a part of life—a part of life that we can no longer see, but one that is relied on for growth. I found the story whimsical and the images mesmerizing—a must-have for any multicultural classroom library.

In *The memory box: A book about grief*, Rowland (2017) tells a story of a girl who tries to not forget a loved one who has passed, while creating and sharing new memories. She does this through creating a memory box—a box filled with things that represent past experiences with, and experiences that occurred after the passing of, a loved one. Though the book has a Christian tinge to it, the memory box idea aligns well with how I think about death. As mentioned above, I believe that we live on through the memories of others. My mom lives on through me, my thoughts of her, and my characteristics and behaviors that I inherited and learned from her. The idea of a memory box intrigues me. But as an adult without children (and nobody to hand the box down to), I display my memories of my mother throughout my house. And these are the artifacts I focused on for this performance.

*My Coping Methods*

It's telling that I chose children's literature for the readings for this exploration. One way I am coping with my recent loss is by reconciling these deaths with past deaths—those I am familiar with. I only know how to cope with human death as I did when I was a child. And, as a child, I really did not have to cope with it. I was exposed to death, but those who died really weren't a part of my everyday life, and they weren't close caregivers. Nonetheless, I find that I have regressed to my young self-identities (e.g., a granddaughter and a daughter) because this is how I know how to cope with death.

However, there is a tension between my young self and my adult self in this regard. As an adult I find myself not "dealing with" or "coping with" either of these deaths (e.g., I won't let myself cry or critically think about who or what I have lost). I am actively choosing not to fully process these losses. I keep telling myself I will grieve later—after my dissertation is complete. I have too much to do. I am coping, but maybe not in a sustainable manner. Overall, I found the reading of the children's books to be helpful, soothing, and reassuring. After all, my mom died—and I am forever her daughter.

. . .

It's obvious that these explorations are topics I want to personally explore. Some of the lessons include and address questions I have asked myself a time or two. But to be honest, if it weren't for this book and this curriculum, I probably would not have performed and reflected on these investigations—even as beginning investigations. Some of them are difficult and others are critically challenging. And although I am sharing these performances in a public platform, it is a safe, positive place to begin these explorations. I hope others will find that to be true as well.

### REFERENCES

Brown, L. K., & Brown, M. (2009). *When dinosaurs die: A guide to understanding death*. Little, Brown, and Company.

González, X. (2017). *All around us*. Cinco Puntos Press.

Rowland, J. (2017). *The memory box: A book about grief*. Sparkhouse Family.

Wilcox, M. (2018). *After life: Ways we think about death*. Orca Book Publishers.

## EXPLORATION 6

# GENDER AND/OR SEXUAL ORIENTATION AND VIOLENCE AWARENESS AND PREVENTION

*Exploration*

Explore your gender and/or sexual orientation identity/identities in relation to violence awareness and prevention. Explore and reflect on how your gender and/or sexual orientation identity/identities, along with other (multi)cultural beliefs, customs, and/or practices, or other aspects of your life, may have influenced your understanding of, or experience with, violence awareness and prevention. You may conduct this exploration in various ways (e.g., write a letter, create a poster, attend a Transgender Day of Remembrance (TDOR) event or a Safe Space Training) and from many perspectives (e.g., as a victim of violence, member of the #MeToo movement, trans-woman, member of the LGBTQ community, educator).

You may use the exploration outline to guide your exploration. There is a lot to explore here, try to narrow your focus. Remember, you are choosing just one of many explorations that you may conduct.

*Queer Multicultural Social Justice Education: Curriculum (and Identity) Development Through Performance,* pages 103–110.

*Discussion*

Clarify the prompt.

*Presentation*

Consider all options (e.g., write a letter, create a poster, attend a TDOR event).

*Reflection*

Critically respond to others' presentations (when applicable), reflect on the exploration and the readings, and address the following prompt: Explain any difficulties you had with the exploration.

*Readings*

Anonymous. (2018). "A thank you, with apologies." In L. Bean, *Written on the body: Letters from trans and non-binary survivors of sexual assault and domestic violence* (pp. 57–59). Jessica Kingsley Publishers.

Anonymous. (2018). To my humble front entrance. In L. Bean, *Written on the body: Letters from trans and non-binary survivors of sexual assault and domestic violence* (pp. 100–103). Jessica Kingsley Publishers.

Anonymous. (2018). Dear body. In L. Bean, *Written on the body: Letters from trans and non-binary survivors of sexual assault and domestic violence* (pp. 172–175). Jessica Kingsley Publishers.

Freitag, M. B. (2014). Chapter 17: Safety in Unity: One school's story of identity and community. In E. J. Meyer & D. Carlson (Eds.), *Gender and sexualities in education: A reader* (pp. 230–239). Peter Lang.

Knaier, M. L. (2019). What makes girls and boys so desirable?: STEM education beyond gender binaries. In W. Letts & S. Fifield (Eds.), *STEM of desire: Queer theories in science education* (pp. 209–221). Koninklijke Brill.

## EXPLORATION 6 OUTLINE

1. **Identity.** *How do I identify?*
   - ○ Genderqueer-woman
   - ○ Pansexual
2. **Initial questions.** *What are my initial questions?*
   - ○ How will this conference raise my awareness of LGBTQ violence?
   - ○ How will the information from this conference assist me in developing my curriculum?
3. **Preliminary resources/references.** *Where will I seek information?*
   - ○ #MeTooLGBTQ Conference
   - ○ Talking to presenters and other attendees
4. **Performance and presentation methods.** *How will I perform and present my exploration?*
   - ○ As a reflection/story

5. **Additional questions.** *What additional questions did I explore?*
   - ○ Should biological sex be included in multicultural education and/or multicultural identities?
   - ○ Do I identify as cisgender?
6. **Further questions.** *What are my further (future) questions?*
   - ○ In education, is there a need to know about one's body?
   - ○ Should bodied-identities be included in multicultural education?
7. **All resources/references.** *What resources did I use?*
   - ○ Conference sessions
   - ○ Talking to experts
8. **Sharing.** How *will I share this exploration?*
   - ○ Through writing and sharing this project.

## ME TOO

For this exploration, I attended the #MeTooLGBTQ Conference on April 27, 2019. The LGBTQ Survivor Task Force organized the conference, which was held at the San Diego LGBT Community Center. Although I had registered for the conference months before I developed the criteria for Exploration 6, I decided that attending the conference would be an appropriate way to perform it. However, I was uncertain of how or what to present. Initially, I considered creating a poster representing some of the information that was shared during the workshops. But this was the first time I attended this conference and I was not sure from whom or what I would be learning, so I kept an open mind. I knew the purpose for attending this conference was simply *awareness*; I just did not know what form that awareness would take. The following is my abridged account (and presentation) of what I experienced at the event.

After checking in, I surveyed the room and determined where would be the best place for me to sit. I wanted to make sure I could see the screen, sit at a corner of a table, and have my back to a wall. I scoped out a table near the center of the room. I introduced myself to the woman sitting next to me as I cleaned my section of the table with a wet wipe and unpacked my notebook and pen. Then I sat patiently, drank my Starbucks coffee, and waited for the *Welcoming remarks* to begin. During these comments, I learned that there were two presentations offered during each of the three workshop sessions. I noted which talks I planned to attend and where they were being held (e.g., library). I was eager to learn.

The first workshop, *Sexual violence in LGBQ+ communities: Why should your services address sexual assault trauma?*, started promptly at 9:45 am. The presenters shared statistics of LGBQ (lesbian, gay, bisexual, queer) violence compared to that toward cisgender heterosexuals; defined and offered examples of violence (e.g., stalking, rape, catcalls, victim blaming, child sexual abuse, and trafficking); and offered notable signs of when and how sexual violence occurs (e.g., a partner saying they are supposed to have sex, stealthing (having a partner remove a barrier during sex without warning), being sent porn or genital images they didn't want to see, getting unwillingly dosed at clubs). Additionally, they moderated a discussion to dispel myths and stereotypes about LGBQ+ communities. However, it was pointed out by an attendee that gay men were the abusers in each of their examples—another stereotype perpetuated. Overall, this workshop was a good introduction to the theme of the conference, especially for those who were never exposed to these statistics.

Next came the *Survivor Panel*. The panel consisted of four victims of sexual violence sharing their stories and answering questions about their experiences. The brave panelists—who are also social activists—shared their emotional accounts. It was an excellent example of *stories as curriculum*. Each story was unique. Each person was of a different gender and sexual orientation identity— though during lunch, one attendee loudly noted that Black LGBTQ victims were not represented. For me, each story was validating. It was during the last minutes of this panel that the emcee, Fernando, paused the conference to announce that there had been a shooting in a local synagogue and the shooter had fled the scene. My heart sank. When one marginalized group is attacked, we are all attacked. People started crying. Others checked their phones. I texted my partner. Some conference-goers left. The situation was shocking—and scary. It was decided that we would go on with our conference. News that the shooter was apprehended two miles from the scene was reported. And news about the victims trickled in throughout the afternoon. One woman was dead. Others were injured. The shooter was a nineteen-year old man. It was reported that he had allegedly tried to burn down a mosque the previous month in a neighboring community. When will the violence stop?

Time to break for lunch.

After a moment of silence for the victims of the shooting and the *Keynote address*, it was time for the *Second workshop session*. This is where *awareness* and my takeaway from this conference found me. I attended the *Sexual violence and the trans and nonbinary community* presentation. One of the presenters is the director for the Center for Gender Affirming Care at Rady's Children's Hospital. And the other is a psychotherapist. The first substantive slide read:

> Survivors of sexual violence navigate multiple webs of oppression in their daily lives. This is not to say that all survivors sharing similar social identities will be impacted by sexual assault in the same way; while it is important to historicize and contextualize survivor narratives, it is equally important not to make assumptions about a survivor's experience based on their perceived identities. Within these frameworks, every survivor experiences challenges in a unique way, and every narrative needs to be honored and respected.

I was hooked. It consisted of a quote from the FORGE website (https://forge-forward.org). FORGE is "a progressive organization whose mission is to support, educate and advocate for the rights and lives of transgender individuals" and their significant others, friends, family, and allies. The ideas of "webs of oppression" and respecting the "narrative" mirror my work on identity awareness, intersectionality, and autoethnography. They had my attention.

As the presentation progressed, the discussion included words and phrases that should be avoided—because these words may be construed as acts of erasure or even violence. It was when the term "biological sex" was included as an inappropriate term that I became puzzled. They suggest using "sex assigned at birth"—which added to my confusion. Through my research and experience I know that one's "assigned sex at birth" may be incorrectly determined and/or assigned. My brain rapidly tried to sort this out. I asked a question: "Why is *biological sex* inappropriate?" They gave a response. My rebuttal: "But don't we all have a biological sex?" It was obvious that they couldn't understand why I was asking these questions. Their response: "Well, yes, but it's complicated. Sex is not a binary. There are intersex people." "I know," I said, "So, how would you talk about one's body?" Their basic response was, "You shouldn't." This confused me even more. One of the attendees interjected, "When you talk about male and female sex you are buying into science as the norm for Truth." My thoughts swirled. I knew this wasn't the place to have a debate on whether science—evidence-based knowledge—was appropriate for determining biological categories—or Truth. Yes, science may be flawed. Science may be biased. But science is the best method we have for exploring and explaining our world. Another attendee spoke: "If you want to talk about bodies, you should be specific. For example, if you want to discuss menstruation, you should ask specially about that." I envisioned a laundry list of these "specific" questions—when one question would suffice. The presenters looked at me. It was clear that they wanted to move on, so I stifled my questioning—until after the presentation.

I couldn't concentrate on the rest of their presentation. My mind was racing. I struggled to understand—no *biological sex*? But isn't our bodied-identity part of our identities? The terms *cisgender* and *transgender* refer to alignment or lack thereof between one's gender and sex—biological sex or sex assigned at birth. I decided to approach the speakers after their talk. I wanted literature, resources—answers. They said that they didn't know of any literature on the topic. I clumsily tried to explain my research on identity awareness and wanted to know how or if *biological sex* fit in. They concluded that I should omit it from my research and focus on gender and sexual orientation. I raised the concern of conflating gender and sex. I did not want this to occur in my research like it does in such much educational research (see, Letts, 1999; Knaier, 2019)—which is why I specifically included *biological sex* in my curriculum.

The educator who mentioned the "specific questions" during the talk joined our discussion. We engaged in a somewhat lengthy conversation. They used themselves and their body as an example—telling me they had a double mastectomy. They, too, were frustrated about using language about biological sex and anatomy. They also explained that they didn't fully identify with the term "transgender." We both agreed that language is inadequate, but a necessary way to communicate (Meyer, 2007; Zacko-Smith & Smith, 2010). And that these topics are complicated. I continued to grapple with not including our bodied-selves as part of my curriculum on identity awareness. They made a good point: "Why do we [educators] need to know about each other's (or children's) bodies as their teachers?" I countered with my approach to identity awareness: "But we all have a biological sex or body." I explained that I accept that bodies do not necessarily fit into the female-male sex binary. But shouldn't this category be discussed and explored? I reflected quickly on what was being said. I pondered: Maybe a multicultural education class is not the appropriate time to discuss this topic.

Sexual orientation is based on the gender of the persons we are attracted to, not their bodied-selves (Killermann, 2017). And gender is (or can be) different from our biological or bodied-selves. So, their advice was to not include biological sex—as if it was not relevant. But then I was asked: "Do you also identify as a cisgender woman along with your genderqueer identity?" This baffled me because now they were asking me about my "irrelevant" bodied self. In the moment, I did not know how to answer this question. Am I *cisgender*? Upon further reflection, I would answer yes. I knew I did not identify as *transgender* even though I identify as *genderqueer*. I identify as a genderqueer-woman. And my genderqueer-woman identity aligns with my biological sex and my sex assigned at birth. So, I learned something new about my self-identity—I am cisgender. This identity now made me wonder: *Am I queer enough to be a part of the LGBTQ community?* Answer: *Fuck, yes!*

But should I include "biological sex" or "sex assigned at birth" in my curriculum as an identity category? I reflected. Because I do not identify as being transgender, I am privileged and comfortable talking about my biological sex. I lost sight of the fact that asking a transgender person about their body can be considered an act of violence. And asking children about their bodied-selves can be an act of violence. But, how do I omit *biological sex* from my curriculum without conflating it with gender? In two ways. One, I include a reading discussing the problem with conflating sex and gender; thus, I highlight the issue. And, two. I leave it to the explorers. Upon exploring gender identity, I let the participants decide whether they want to attach their gender to their body. For example, by using terms like *transgender* or *cisgender* they may provide the information about how *they* perceive themselves and how they negotiate their gender and sex. There are so many ways we can categorize gender. These identities include: agender, androgynous, bigender, cisgender, cisgender male, female to male, gender fluid, gender nonconforming, genderqueer, intergender, pangender, transgender, transmasculine, and Two-Spirit. It is not anyone's place to ask or make assumptions about others' bodies. And we must avoid conflating gender with sex. If necessary, we must change our ways of thinking about these concepts.

Through this performance, *my awareness* stemmed from engaging in conversations about harmful words or phrases. Words I directly used in the curriculum I am developing—this was difficult for me to remedy. Words I will now omit based on this performance. This (re)action is the reason why performing the curriculum while developing it is so urgent. Through exploring gender and violence awareness, I was able to stop myself from potentially acting in a violent manner—by directly asking about others' bodies. In addition, this performance helped me untangle ways I thought about the term *cisgender* and it made me realize my, although queer, cisgender identity. Just like in performing other lessons, reflecting on and sharing this experience is just the *beginning* of my investigation into this matter. This experience has prompted me to ask more questions, to search for literature, and to further research these concepts as they apply to multicultural education.

## REFLECTION

Unlike Explorations One-Five, I was not able to decide on the readings until I performed Explorations Six. Because there is so much to think about when exploring gender identity and sexual orientation, I wasn't sure which readings would be appropriate and helpful. But after I wrote my narrative, I knew I wanted to include a reading that addressed the conflation of sex and gender and how this may impact curriculum development. I chose to include my chapter, "What makes *girls* and *boys* so desirable? STEM education beyond gender binaries" (Knaier, 2019). In this chapter I explore and problematize the gendering of teaching techniques specifically prescribed in the *Next Generation Science Standards* (NGSS Lead States, 2013). And although I chose to omit "biological sex" from this exploration after performing it, I wanted to include problems of conflating sex and gender in the discussion. This reading helps to do that. It also addresses problems with gendering educational techniques, and furthermore, students. In it I explain that students may fall outside of the socially normative gender binary in complex ways and that we need to be aware of this as we develop curriculum so as to not exclude, or harm, any of our students.

Further, because Exploration 6 explores violence awareness and prevention, I included three narratives written by trans and non-binary survivors of sexual assault in the reading list. Each is a letter written to the bodies of the victims and describes violence the survivors experienced. One letter is addressed to one's body, and the other two letters are addressed to body parts (e.g., "my eyes" and "my humble front entrance"). Although these letters may be graphic and disturbing, they serve not only to inform about the violence trans and non-binary people experience, but also serve as models as ways of performing Exploration 6.

The final reading, "Safety in Unity: One school's story of identity and community," shares a study of what queering a school community may look like and why it is a good model to follow whether the students are part of the LGBTQ community or not. "The school was created as a response to the amount of bullying and harassment that went on in schools across the state" (Freitag, 2014, p. 232). And although the school does serve queer students, "any student that is looking for a safe, welcoming community" may enroll (p. 232). The study includes student and teacher narratives and highlights the need for and importance of safe spaces, emotional support, and allies within schools. Freitag (2014) writes: "Queering a school is about questioning and reframing the existing programs, policies, curricula, and support systems in or out of place" (p. 231). This chapter encourages readers to rethink, or queer, the purpose of schooling, how learning environments should be constructed, and our roll as educators.

By prompting explorers to think about their identities in relation to other social aspects, in this case gender identity and sexual orientation and violence awareness and prevention, it is my hope that awareness will commence. For me, by attending the conference I became aware of potentially violent, or at the very least inappropriate, language. Language I had intended to use in my curriculum and its development. My point being that it was one line on one slide that began my questioning. It is my hope that through performing and sharing these explorations that we become aware of our misconceptions and question our assumptions.

## REFERENCES

Anonymous. (2018). "A thank you, with apologies." In L. Bean, *Written on the body: Letters from trans and non-binary survivors of sexual assault and domestic violence* (pp. 57–59). Jessica Kingsley Publishers.

Anonymous. (2018). To my humble front entrance. In L. Bean, *Written on the body: Letters from trans and non-binary survivors of sexual assault and domestic violence* (pp. 100–103). Jessica Kingsley Publishers.

Anonymous. (2018). Dear body. In L. Bean, *Written on the body: Letters from trans and non-binary survivors of sexual assault and domestic violence* (pp. 172–175). Jessica Kingsley Publishers.

Freitag, M. B. (2014). Chapter 17: Safety in Unity: One school's story of identity and community. In E. J. Meyer & D. Carlson (Eds.), *Gender and sexualities in education: A reader* (pp. 230–239). Peter Lang.

Killermann, S. (2017). *A guide to gender: The social justice advocate's handbook.* Impetus Books.

Knaier, M. L. (2019). What makes girls and boys so desirable?: STEM education beyond gender binaries. In W. Letts & S. Fifield (Eds.), *STEM of desire: Queer theories in science education* (pp. 209–221). Koninklijke Brill.

Letts, W. J. (1999). How to make "boys" and "girls" in the classroom: The heteronormative nature of elementary-school science. In W. Letts & J. Sears (Eds.), *Queering elementary education: Advancing the dialogue about sexualities and schooling* (pp. 97–110). Rowman & Littlefield.

NGSS Lead States. (2013). *Next generation science standards: For states, by states.* www.nextgenscience.org

# RACE AND/OR ETHNICITY AND (HI)STORY AND HERITAGE

*Exploration*

Explore your race and/or ethnic identity/identities in relation to (hi)story and/or heritage. Explore and reflect on how your race and/or ethnicity/ethnicities, along with other (multi)cultural beliefs, customs, and/or practices, or other aspects of your life, may have influenced your understanding of (hi)story and/or heritage. You may conduct this exploration in various ways (e.g., a detailed family tree or photo album, story or poem, lesson plan) and from many perspectives (e.g., as part of your chosen family, as a parent, as an educator).

You may use the exploration outline to guide your exploration. There is a lot to explore here, try to narrow your focus. Remember, you are choosing just one of many explorations that you may conduct.

*Discussion*

Clarify the prompt.

*Queer Multicultural Social Justice Education: Curriculum (and Identity) Development Through Performance,* pages 111–118.
Copyright © 2021 by Information Age Publishing
**111**

*Presentation*

Consider all options (e.g., a detailed family tree or photo album, a story or poem, a lesson plan).

*Reflection*

Critically respond to others' presentations (when applicable), reflect on the exploration and the readings, and address the following prompt: Explain any difficulties you had with the exploration.

*Readings*

Hazzard, D. (2018). Queering Black history and getting free. In D. Watson, J. Hagopian, & W. Au (Eds.)., *Teaching for Black lives* (pp. 325–329). Rethinking Schools.

Nicola, M. (2018). Rethinking identity: Afro-Mexican history. In D. Watson, J. Hagopian, & W. Au (Eds.)., *Teaching for Black lives* (pp. 340- 347). Rethinking Schools.

Nodding, N., & Brooks, L. (2017). Chapter five: Race. In N. Noddings & L. Brooks, *Teaching controversial issues: The case for critical thinking and moral commitment in the classroom* (pp. 47–62). Teachers College Press.

## EXPLORATION 7 OUTLINE

1. **Identity.** *How do I identify?*
   - White
   - Polish-American
   - German-American
2. **Initial questions.** *What are my initial questions?*
   - How do/can I learn about lost (hi)stories now that my grandmother and mother have passed?
   - What do I remember about customs/traditions?
   - What local resources are available?
3. **Preliminary resources/references.** *Where will I seek information?*
   - Talking to family members (e.g., my sister, my aunts)
   - The *Polish-American Journal*
   - Books on Polish traditions
4. **Performance and presentation methods.** *How will I perform and present my exploration?*
   - As a reflective essay
5. **Additional questions.** *What additional questions did I explore?*
   - How/where will I start my own traditions?
   - What other resources are available to me?
6. **Further questions.** *What are my further (future) questions?*
   - Where did my family originate?
   - Is it possible to visit the villages of my ancestors?

7.  **All resources/references.** *What resources did I use?*
    ○   Assigned readings
    ○   The *Polish American Journal*
8.  **Sharing.** How *will I share this exploration?*
    ○   Through writing and sharing this project.

*I Want to Learn More About Being a Polish-American*

Determining how to perform this exploration was difficult for me. When I first proposed this project, I imagined that I would be making trips to Buffalo, New York to ask my grandma and mom about who I am—and about who they are. I wanted to learn more about my great-grandparents coming over from Poland. I wanted to spend time making pierogi and learning family secrets. I wanted to know who was featured in old photographs. And although I have asked these questions many times before, I thought this project would be a reason for them to share parts of their lives with me—the parts they have been hesitant about sharing. Over the years, I hadn't had much luck getting them to talk openly about their childhoods, marriages, or even their present day lives—at least not in much detail. But surely, they would be willing to talk if I approached them under the guise of this project. My grandma and mom were always willing to help. This is how I imagined I would learn about my family and its (hi)stories.

But if you read my prior explorations, you know that I lost both my grandma and mom last year (2018). I am still processing my loss. And through the process, I am realizing that I have many questions about my Polish heritage (e.g., about the Polish town where my family is from, food, traditions), our past socioeconomic status (e.g., How poor were we? What sort of public assistance did we receive? Did my father ever pay child support?), and my grandma's and mom's happiness (e.g., Were they happy? Did they want to be parents?). My gram and mom did not share their worries and woes with us (e.g., children and grandchildren)—not even when asked. They didn't share much about the good times either. And now that they have passed, I am at a loss on how to obtain answers. I'm not even certain what the questions are.

So, in order to perform this lesson, I had to rework, or queer, the way I intended to perform it. This reflection is my way of doing just that. I relied on learning about my ethnic heritage from my grandma and mom, but now I must explore my identities and (hi)stories in other ways—in queered ways. My mind is reeling. The possibilities are pulling me in many directions. To begin, I reflected on my memories. I recall a handful of Polish traditions that we partook in at Easter (e.g., "duck blood soup" and a plate of blessed food) and Christmas (e.g., attending mass, and Polish Christmas wafers (Oplatki)). I vaguely remember attending Catholic funerals and Polish weddings when I was a child where some Polish traditions were recognized and celebrated (e.g., something about a funny wedding hat comes to mind). And, of course, I know one Polish swear word that I heard my grandma and mom use many times—often lovingly: *Dupa* (ass). My cats probably think it's their name because I use it so often—lovingly. But my memories mostly lead me to dysfunction and abuse—places I do not want to go. So, I chose an alternative route.

I decided to look up some demographic information about the Buffalo, New York area, and specifically the Village of Depew, where I grew up. According to Wikipedia (a site I generally despise), I learned that Buffalo is the sister city to Rzeszow, Poland, and it ranks seventh in the country for the highest number of Pole residents (34,254 or 11.7%). Depew, however, has a Pole population of 31.2%. This explains why most of the names in my yearbooks end in *ski*. But it doesn't tell me much about my family history.

So, me being me, I bought some books. I read excerpts from Bukowczyk's (2009) *A History of the Polish Americans*. Because the book is scholarly and very dense, I couldn't read it in its entirely for this lesson—but I will revisit it in the future. According to the author, the book "allows readers to glimpse the intersection of a set of political strands, with a group of historiographical developments, with a moment in the history of an American ethnic group" (p. xvi). Further, "the book recounts a commonplace aspect of the immigrant/ethnic story—the struggle by decent people to achieve a decent life" (p. xvi). Buffalo, New York is referenced several times throughout the book. Indeed, there is even an image of the famed Broadway market where even today "thousands of Polish-Americans buy meat, produce, and ethnic baked goods" (p. 64). I remember going there during Eastertime with my mom when I was a child. I have only been there a couple of times as an adult—Polish traditions faded in my family.

Bukowczyk (2009) may have provided some insight as to why this was. According to an unpublished study conducted in 1936, Buffalo Poles "considered themselves full-fledged Americans (53.6%) [rather] than either 'Polish-Americans' (11.8%), 'American Poles' (26.8%), or just plain 'Poles' (7.8%)" (p. 71). American assimilation was taking hold "in large measure because Polonia's parents had grown too casual about adhering to and passing on Polish customs" (p. 74). This is probably what my grandmother, my mother, and I experienced—a gradual loss of Polish traditions and customs through four generations.

Because this exploration is about race and ethnic (hi)stories, it's worth revealing that along with such "acculturization" came racism (p. 99). I remember my father, a German-American, frequently saying that he loved Black people. He declared, "Everyone should own one!" My family (extended and nuclear) was (is) racist. I am racist, though I work hard not to be. Bukowczyk (2009) reports that a study conducted between 1926 and 1928 found that "native-born Poles . . . [had] begun to acquire a prejudice [toward the Negro] which their parents evidently did not possess" (p. 99). This "competitive animosity" between Blacks and Poles was driven by the struggles faced in industrial cities (p. 99). This history is important to learn and reflect on but given the scope of this exercise I cannot genuinely cover practices of "Negro removal" and "white flight" to an acceptable standard. This ugly past that has bled into the present will have to be revisited and studied through other explorations. But before I move on, I would like to mention that "in 1972 in Buffalo, twenty prominent Blacks and Polish-Americans joined together to seek 'some common ground' and 'ways and means of working together for the common good of Buffalo'" (p. 129). Presumably, some "Blacks and Polish-Americans realized that both groups shared common ground around issues of identity and powerlessness and that neither had caused the other's problems" (p. 140). This sort of coming together is prevalent within civil rights movements and histories (Pollard, 2013). Further, in "1984, the Black/Polish Coalition of Buffalo was formed in order to try to build bridges between the two previously warring groups" (Bukowczyk, 2009, p. 140).

As I mentioned in my performance of Exploration 2, I subscribed to the *Polish American Journal*. For this exploration, I finally took the time to read the four issues I have since received. Although there is an obvious right-leaning slant with Catholic overtones, I found the journal enjoyable. By ignoring the religious origins of many of the traditions and customs, and by focusing on secular aspects of the activities, I found them quite endearing. The journal not only offers old-world explanations for holiday traditions, it also provides authentic recipes—some with a modern twist. There's also a calendar section that highlights important dates for the month and a listing of nationwide celebrations and festivals, many of which take place in Buffalo, New York. I also learned that a branch of the Polish-American Association is in San Diego. I particularly like the column dedicated to genealogy. The author outlines tips from how to talk to relatives and record their stories to how to navigate ancestry websites and searches. This journal will be an invaluable tool as I move forward with future explorations.

A Polish Bishop once remarked, "If we forget our Polish heritage we become nothing but ships in the wind without anchors" (Bukowczyk, 2009, p. 69). I have often felt like I was drifting through life without an anchor. My life was virtually void of Polish culture and tradition, let alone family dinners and quality time. But I am a proud Pole who is looking forward to wearing babushkas in my old age. Working through this exploration made me realize that maybe my grandmother and mother did not hold the answers I am searching for. It's possible that stories stopped being shared generations ago. Now, I need to seek answers in nontraditional, or queer, spaces.

Recently, my partner and I have proverbially set anchor. We moved to a rural community where we plan to participate in community events and be involved with wildfire safety standards and action. Further, we both want to actively learn more about our heritage and incorporate both Polish and German traditions and art into our household. And since both of us are from Depew, New York, we plan to visit local resources, such as the Broadway market and Polish Community Center, and to attend events like the Polish Heritage Festival to learn more. Additionally, we will seek out Polish resources and restaurants in San Diego County, like the Polish-American Association and the Romeo and Juliet Wine Café. All of which I learned about through this investigation. I will also reach out to elder family members and ask them to share their stories before it's too late. Although I have not found answers to my many questions, through this exploration, I found resources where I can begin to search for those answers.

### Reflection

In "Queering Black history and getting free," Hazzard (2018) writes about queering the Black history that we teach. She urges us to "complicat[e] the stories of the historical figures" (p. 326). This includes "having conversations about the role of the Black freedom movement in bringing about trans liberation today" (p. 325). She reminds us that "queering" means "reworking" (p. 326); and that "we must rework and complicate the stories we tell about the Black figures we are familiar with" (e.g., Rosa Parks, Billie Holiday) (p. 326). Further she declares:

> We also have to study and celebrate the Black people who have been erased, hidden from our collective memories . . . We have to look beyond the cracks and find our incarcerated heroes, our undocumented leaders, our luminary sex workers, the people who systems of oppression most desperately want us to forget. And we have to teach those stories to others. (p. 326)

She also urges us to remember "everyday people" and to tell the stories of their struggles and "the work they did" (p. 328). It is my hope that this work will inspire readers to explore queer(ing) Black history and incorporate it into their lesson plans. Taken further, we should queer all the racial and ethnic histories presented in our classrooms—including our own.

Pairing Hazzard's work with Nicola's (2018), "Rethinking identity: Afro-Mexican history," seems ideal. In her chapter, Nicola writes about her experiences developing lessons for her students who are "heritage language speakers" (p. 340). She explains that "heritage students have both a cultural and linguistic connection to a language other than English" (p. 340). One of the tasks she includes in the lessons she shared is having the students "collect stories" and make connections between Africa and what they consider to be "Mexican" culture (p. 342). Nicola's account includes examples of how her students make personal connections and share personal stories and experiences.

Moreover, her curriculum takes up the notion of racial categories, including their invention, elimination, and reinstatement in Mexico. Goals of the unit include "rethinking identity, identifying ways that Afro-Mexicans helped shape the nation, and reflecting on the present-day implications of Afro-Mexican invisibility" (p. 347). Indeed, this reading serves as a model on how to incorporate race and ethnicity and (hi)stories and identities into student-centered curriculum and planning. It is also an exemplar of how students may make personal connections to what they are learning. Further, Nicola highlights teaching techniques (e.g., note-taking strategies and group work) which may serve as a review and reminder for future teachers as they engage with multiculturalism. And she notes the importance of giving her students time to journal and self-reflect, thus allowing them an opportunity "to question assumptions they had about themselves, and the groups they identify with" (p. 347). This reinforces the foundational philosophies and goals of the curriculum developed for this project.

Finally, in their chapter "Race," Noddings and Brooks (2017) recommend that we teach race and race relations—including race in relation to the history of our country and within the history of Black education—within social studies classes, as well as integrated across the curriculum (e.g., in language arts, science, and art classes). And they remind us that

> History reflects culture and philosophy of the era in which it is written or displayed as well as personal beliefs and preconceptions of the writer and presenter and thus may contain commentary on moral lessons learned or to be learned from past acts. (p. 49)

These caveats remind educators and students to critically think about and interpret history and question the motives of who is telling it. Further they remind us that

> Teachers should explore local resources such as museums, parks, and monuments for examples of underreported minority achievement, the suppression of actions the majority is not proud of, and local myths and legends. (pp. 49–50)

These explorations will allow educators and students to see how thinking, culture, and stories have evolved within their own communities, and possibly within their own families. It will also encourage learners to rethink the way they remember and experience history.

These readings inspired and energized me. It was from their collective messages that I constructed my reflective exploration for Exploration 7. First, Hazzard reminds us to remember "everyday people" and their struggles and (hi)stories. These ideas brought me back to my mom, grandmother, and great-grandmother—though they are no longer with us it is important for me to remember, learn, and share their stories. But even more broadly, I'm eager to learn about the (hi)stories of Polish-Americans, particularly in Western New York. In Nicola's work, I found an exemplar of how to incorporate students' (and those of the community) identities—something I do not recall being a part of my school experiences (at least not in a positive way—I heard plenty of Polish jokes growing up). And finally, Noddings and Brooks reinforce the practice of integrated curriculum, public resources, and the importance of local histories. This made me wonder if there are public resources reflecting Polish-American (hi)stories. So, for this performance, I chose to reflect on where to search for answers, to read about Polish-American (hi)stories specific to Western New York, and to search for local (e.g., Depew, Buffalo, and San Diego) resources that will support my investigations. Maybe I'll learn something that will help me understand my family's heritage, language, and customs; learn more about the struggles and accomplishments of Polish-Americans; and navigate all those Polish jokes (which are still prevalent in Western New York).

## REFERENCES

Bukowczyk, J. J. (2009). *A history of the Polish Americans*. Transaction Publishers.

Hazzard, D. (2018). Queering Black history and getting free. In D. Watson, J. Hagopian, & W. Au (Eds.)., *Teaching for Black lives* (pp. 325–329). Rethinking Schools.

Nicola, M. (2018). Rethinking identity: Afro-Mexican history. In D. Watson, J. Hagopian, & W. Au (Eds.)., *Teaching for Black lives* (pp. 340- 347). Rethinking Schools.

Nodding, N., & Brooks, L. (2017). Chapter five: Race. In N. Noddings & L. Brooks, *Teaching controversial issues: The case for critical thinking and moral commitment in the classroom* (pp. 47–62). Teachers College Press.

# EXPLORATION 8

# EXCEPTIONALITY AND DIGITAL TECHNOLOGY

*Exploration*

Explore your exceptionality identity/identities in relation to your use of digital technologies (e.g., video gaming, social media, learning devices). Explore and reflect on how your exceptionality identity/identities, along with other (multi)cultural beliefs, customs, and/or practices, or other aspects of your life, may have influenced your use of digital technologies (e.g., teaching and learning styles, personal and professional communications, mental well-being). You may conduct this exploration in various ways (e.g., a fictional story, photo essay, demonstration of a task using digital technology) and from many perspectives (e.g., educator, learner, worker).

You may use the exploration outline to guide your exploration. There is a lot to explore here, try to narrow your focus. Remember, you are choosing just one of many explorations that you may conduct.

*Discussion*

Clarify the prompt.

*Presentation*

Consider all options (e.g., a fictional story, a photo essay, demonstration of a task using digital technology).

*Queer Multicultural Social Justice Education: Curriculum (and Identity) Development Through Performance,* pages 119–128.
Copyright © 2021 by Information Age Publishing

*Reflection*

Critically respond to others' presentations (when applicable), reflect on the exploration and the readings, and address the following prompt: Explain any difficulties you had with the exploration.

*Readings*

Ander, C. J. (2015). Rat catcher's yellows. In D. H. Wilson & J. J. Adams (Eds.), *Press start to play* (pp. 73–88). Vintage Books.

Bacigalupa, C. (2016). Partnering with families through photo collages. *Early Childhood Education, 44,* 317–323.

Doody, K. R. (2015). GrAPPling with how to teach social skills? Try tapping into digital technology. *Journal of Special Education Technology, 30*(2), 122–127.

## EXPLORATION 8 OUTLINE

1.  **Identity.** *How do I identify?*
    - Abled-bodied
    - Depression & Anxiety (e.g., self-doubt)
    - Undiagnosed Dyslexia
    - Undiagnosed Prosopagnosia (i.e., face-blindness)
2.  **Initial questions.** *What are my initial questions?*
    - How does the term *exceptional* apply to me?
    - How do I use digital technology in relation to exceptionality?
3.  **Preliminary resources/references.** *Where will I seek information?*
    - Explore my social media platforms
    - Reflect on my digital technology use and needs
4.  **Performance and presentation methods.** *How will I perform and present my exploration?*
    - Through screenshots of my Facebook posts and reflective essay
5.  **Additional questions.** *What additional questions did I explore?*
    - Are there other technologies, including social media platforms, that may help me?
    - What other, non-digital, support tools available to me?
6.  **Further questions.** *What are my further (future) questions?*
    - How has my depression and anxiety impacted my work?
7.  **All resources/references.** *What resources did I use?*
    - Assigned readings
    - My social media account
    - My digital technologies and tools
8.  **Sharing.** How *will I share this exploration?*
    - Through writing and sharing this project.

## DEPRESSED AND ANXIOUS SEEKS DIGITAL SUPPORT

I don't consider myself to be *exceptional*. As far as I know, as a student I was never labeled as gifted or talented or diagnosed as having learning disabilities; I was never placed in remedial classes, nor was I ever offered special assistance. However, as an eighth grader, I was chosen to be a member of a small group of students who attended ninth-grade second-language classes (French, in my case) at St. Mary's High School, the school was located across the street from my K–8 Catholic School. Reflecting on this it strikes me as odd because I often earned "C's" for reading throughout my elementary and early secondary years. But I excelled in French—a skill I still practice today.

As an adult I was diagnosed with depression and anxiety. I have been on and off medications for both ailments for the good part of twenty years. I am currently off daily medications. In addition, as part of my treatment I intermittently sought help and support from therapists. I am currently not seeing a therapist. In the beginning, I sought help to work through some childhood issues that continued to affect me as an adult (e.g., the sexual abuse I experienced, the situations I was put in due to my parents' divorce, the guilt ingrained in me from attending Catholic school). During these sessions, I learned coping methods (e. g., positive self-talk) that I still practice daily. I also manage my anxiety by spending time with my cats instead of with people and by pursuing hobbies (e.g., photography, scrapbooking) that allow me to lose myself in creativity.

There were times during my undergraduate and graduate schooling when I shared with my professors my feelings of being overwhelmed. I was often offered verbal support or a deadline extension. In one instance, I was allowed a second chance to write an in-class essay outside of class so I could rely on a word processor to organize my thoughts. Because of this allowance, my grade went from a D to an A on that assignment. I was very grateful for that opportunity.

As I read the readings for this exploration, my use of Facebook as a means of digital support came to mind. And as I developed and performed this exploration, I felt it was worth looking at my use of Facebook, as I do use it to practice self-support, validation, and mental health awareness. In addition, I use Facebook to support others who share their feelings about, and experiences with, mental health or other conditions (e.g., autism). Further, I often use Facebook as a communication station for issues on depression, anxiety, and introversion (an aspect of my personality). My admission of my struggles with these ailments and/or characteristics is a way for me to openly help dismiss the stigmas that go along with mental illnesses and personality attributes.

As an introvert, I do not always seek interpersonal connection or communication. I do, however, find comfort in memes on Facebook. They make me feel less alone. For this exploration, I captured screens shots of every meme I shared on Facebook since the beginning of the year (2019) that I felt comforted by, found support in, or realized a connection with related to my depression and anxiety. The following seventeen images are those captures in reverse chronological order. The prominent theme of these memes is positive self-talk (e.g., Captures 1, 3, 5, 6, 8, 9, 10, 12, 13, 14, 15, 16, and 17), something I practice daily—specifically to aid in my getting out of bed and being somewhat productive.

These memes also speak to my many different anxieties. For example, Capture 2 shows how I was able to send a message to my loved ones on how they can support me and others who experience anxiety—something I have a hard time articulating. And Capture 4 highlights why I find comfort in watching re-runs of my favorite shows (e.g., The Big Bang Theory, The Office). Again, this is something I have tried to explain to my partner many times. He has often expressed that watching re-runs is a waste of his time. I hope he now has a better understanding of why I enjoy it so much. And Capture 7 portrays something I would do if I thought my cat would possibly be stepped on. I worry about the well-being of my cats a lot.

Further, Capture 8 depicts how my friends can support my and others' queer lifestyles. Stereotypes, particularly gender stereotypes, are something I am forever pushing back on as a woman who identities as genderqueer. Other themes found in these memes are positive self-talk regarding the self-doubt or shame I often feel (e.g., Captures, 3, 6, 14, 15, 17); my introvert personality (e.g., Captures 5, 9); healthy self-validation (e.g., Captures 10, 12 ); and the importance of self-care (e.g., Captures 11, 13, 16). Overall, I found this exploration engaging. It was a fun, yet meaningful, way to explore and share my use of digital technologies in relation to my exceptionality identities.

## DIGITAL SUPPORT

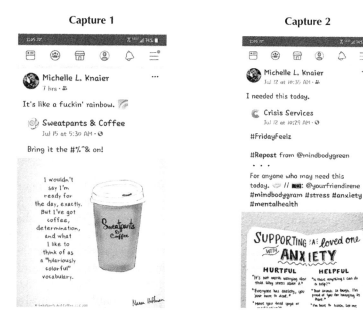

**Capture 1**

**Capture 2**

## Capture 3

**Michelle L. Knaier**
Jul 6 at 1:15 PM · 👥

Note to self: Stop battering yourself and bloom...

**Sweatpants & Coffee**
Jul 6 at 12:00 PM · 🌐

See what blooms when you stop shaming yourself.

No one is motivated to become better or more productive while being battered with shame and guilt. Especially if that person is you. Stop. Be kind. Be brave. See what blooms.

## Capture 4

**Michelle L. Knaier**
Jul 6 at 1:13 PM · 👥

The Big Bang Theory, The Office, and Modern Family are my hugs.

TODAY.COM     *i* About this website

**How watching 'comfort' TV can help ease an anxiety flare up**

## Capture 5

**Michelle L. Knaier**
Jun 24 at 6:06 AM · 👥

A child sneezed on my leg this morning...

**Sweatpants & Coffee**
Jun 24 at 5:30 AM · 🌐

Truth time.

TRUTH TIME:

1. Yes, it really is Monday.

2. You're probably going to have to interact with people.

3. No, you can't kick them in the shins.

4. You're so going to need this coffee.

## Capture 6

**Michelle L. Knaier**
Jun 14 at 2:36 PM · 👥

Floating...

**Sweatpants & Coffee**
Jun 14 at 1:35 PM · 🌐

#FlashbackFriday reminder for anyone who needs it. 💜

If you're feeling discouraged, remember you don't have to paddle every second. Sometimes you float, and that's good enough.

## Capture 7

Michelle L. Knaier
May 29 at 6:31 PM · 👥

Love this

KitNipBox
May 29 at 9:00 AM · 🌐

That's one good cat momma! 😻

[via Introvert Crazy Cat Lady with a sarcastic twist]

## Capture 8

Michelle L. Knaier
May 25 at 3:55 AM · 👥

Girl Inside
May 20 at 7:10 AM · 🌐

by Serah Eley

**Things Queer Culture Teaches
That Straight Culture Doesn't:**

- You don't have to get married if you don't want to.
- You don't have to have kids if you don't want to.
- It's nobody's job to flirt with you or be flirted with. If you're into someone, do the work and tell them.
- People will judge you and myself you without knowing you. That isn't your fault. You're not their responsibility.
- Your clothing and hair and other style choices are to make YOU feel good first and foremost.
- Signaling to your people is the secondary job of hair and clothes. But don't dress for them. Be you, they'll see it.
- Anyone who judges you badly for your hair and clothes is not your people and can fuck off.
- Physical affection in public is an act of deliberate courage.
- Family is a matter of choice. Loyalty is a two-way street.
- Mental health is important and it's hard. Anxiety and depression are natural reactions to the world.
- Sensitivity isn't weakness. It just means you pay attention.
- It's alright to think "just" also means a path in a vagina or penis silly. They aren't the only option you have.
- Everyone who's interesting reinvented themselves after their world fell apart. Just like you did.
- Community is a safety net from an unfair world. Let it catch you when you need it. Catch others when you can.
- Don't live your life for anyone else's happiness. Live for your own, and share it.

## Capture 9

Michelle L. Knaier
May 20 at 7:59 AM · 👥

I'm enjoying all three . . .

Sweatpants & Coffee
May 20 at 5:30 AM · 🌐

Favorite things.

## Capture 10

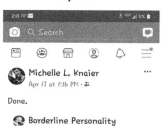

Michelle L. Knaier
Apr 17 at 1:16 PM · 👥

Done.

Borderline Personality
Disorder Memeposting
Apr 16 at 10:20 PM · 🌐

## Capture 11

## Capture 12

## Capture 13

## Capture 14

## Capture 15

## Capture 16

## Capture 17

## REFLECTION

According to Bicard and Heward (2016), "when the term *exceptional* is used to describe students, it includes children who have difficulty learning and children whose performance is advanced" (p. 214). Based on this statement, I would argue that all children—or all learners—are exceptional under different circumstances. But Bicard and Heward (2016) continue, explaining:

> The performance of *exceptional children* differs from the norm (either above or below) to such an extent that individualized programs of special education are necessary to meet their diverse needs. (p. 214, italics original)

I agree with this notion; however, the philosophy of some schools, including a charter school in which I taught, provides and orchestrates learning experiences based on individual education plans (IEP) for each student—again allowing the term *exceptional* to be applied to all students. In my experience with this, although IEPs were not physically created for each student, teachers were expected to consider the strengths and weaknesses of every student in the classroom when creating and implementing lesson plans. Further, if a student required special assistance or extra support *beyond* what a classroom teacher could provide in order to be successful, then an IEP was officially created by a taskforce of stakeholders in that child's educational progress.

Sometimes digital technology and other tools were included in IEPs. During my teaching tenure, I had students who relied on additional technologies, such as laptop computers to aid in notetaking, for example. Another resource that I personally offered to exceptional students was frequent communication with caretakers, including daily emails or phone calls. Therefore, based on my experiences, I wanted to pair *exceptionality* with technology for this exploration. After discussing my general idea for the exploration with my partner, he told me about a science fiction short story he recently read, "Rat catcher's yellows," by Anders (2015). It was at the close of this brainstorming session that I formulated my exploration plan and decided to pair *exceptionality* with *digital technologies*.

Digital technologies may be described as electronic tools, systems, devices, and resources that generate, store, or process data (e.g., social media, online games, mobile phones). I chose two articles that articulate the use of various methods of digital technologies to support exceptional students. One example of how digital tools may help children with autism spectrum disorder (ASD) improve empathy and communication skills is addressed by Doody (2015). She describes the use of social narratives "to help students with [ASD] acknowledge the feelings of another, thereby increasing and improving appropriate social interactions with peers" (p. 123). More specifically, a social narrative "is a written story, describing and illustrating a target behavior that is socially appropriate" (p. 123). Further, a "social narrative is able to utilize the visual strengths children with ASD possess through use of photographs, written narrative, and other graphics" (p. 124). Though originally designed to be read to students, "digital presentations delivered through hand-held devices, particularly when voiceover narration is included, allow the children to independently access the social narrative without the assistance or physical proximity of an adult, thereby making the intervention more suitable and naturalistic for a child with ASD" (p. 124).

Another digital mode of communication presented by Bacigalupa (2016) highlights the usefulness of digital photo collages as tools to communicate with parents of children attending a university-based child-care center. Although the photo collage tool was not used in a special education setting, in this case the staff team "believed that photos of the children would be an effective way to show what children were doing every day and to demonstrate the benefits of play-based curriculum" (p. 318). I was intrigued with using this method, as it could have strong implications if used to inform parents of special needs students, in lieu of a phone call, for example. As a former science teacher, I could envision using this strategy as an effective way of communicating with families. Photo collages would allow caregivers a chance to see what students are learning and performing in the classroom, thus opening the lines of communication between students, caretakers, and educators (Bacigalupa, 2016)—an element imperative to student success.

Finally, I assigned Anders' (2015) story as a reading for Exploration 8 because it was the inspiration for this exploration. Indeed, the use of a fictional story is also applicable to autoethnographic performances and serves as a model for explorers. In "Rat catcher's yellows," Anders (2015) highlights possibilities and applications of both present and future digital technologies and platforms. In sum, the story centers around the use and implications of a game, *Divine right of cats*, for those affected by dementia. In the story, the game can be customized to include names of loved ones, details of meaningful events, and other specifics that would allow a connection from the real-world with the virtual world. Although the story is heartbreaking, it is also a beautiful representation of how two women share a connection despite the deteriorating effects of a disease. It also speaks to the importance of support needed by caregivers during trying times. Finally, it serves as a reminder that support, both personal and digital, is available. Based on these readings and my experiences, I chose to reflect on my Facebook posts alluding to my depression and anxiety—two mental impairments that often cripple my productivity and learning experiences.

## REFERENCES

Anders, C. J. (2015). Rat catcher's yellows. In D. H. Wilson & J. J. Adams (Eds.), *Press start to play* (pp. 73–88). Vintage Books.

Bacigalupa, C. (2016). Partnering with families through photo collages. *Early Childhood Education, 44*, 317–323.

Bicard, S. C., & Heward, W. L. (2016). Chapter 12: Educational equality for students with disabilities. In J. A. Banks & C. A. McGee Banks (Eds.), Multicultural education: Issues and perspectives (9th ed., pp. 213–234). John Wiley & Sons.

Doody, K. R. (2015). GrAPPling with how to teach social skills? Try tapping into digital technology. *Journal of Special Education Technology, 30*(2), 122–127.

# CREATING A QUEER MULTICULTURAL SOCIAL JUSTICE TEACHING PHILOSOPHY

*Exploration*

Create a teaching philosophy reflective of your experiences of performing these explorations.

*Discussion*

Clarify the prompt.

*Presentation*

Consider all options (e.g., a(n) poem, photo essay, autoethnography, philosophical statements).

*Reflection*

Critically reflect on how performing the *Queer explorations of identity awareness* curriculum influenced your teaching philosophy.

*Queer Multicultural Social Justice Education: Curriculum (and Identity) Development Through Performance*, pages 129–132.
Copyright © 2021 by Information Age Publishing
**129**

*Readings*

Mayo, C. (2016). Chapter 8: Queer lessons: Sexual and gender minorities in multicultural education. In J. A. Banks & C. A. McGee Banks (Eds.), *Multicultural education: Issues and perspectives* (9th ed., pp. 132–148). John Wiley & Sons.
Nieto, S., & Bode, P. (2016). Chapter 14: School reform and student learning: A multicultural perspective. In J. A. Banks & C. A. McGee Banks (Eds.), *Multicultural education: Issues and perspectives* (9th ed., pp. 258–274). John Wiley & Sons.

## QUEER MULTICULTURAL SOCIAL JUSTICE EDUCATION PHILOSOPHY STATEMENT

When I think about multiculturalism, I think about differences—differences between people, cultures, and ideologies. Encouraging K–12 classroom teachers, support staff, and caregivers to explore and accept these differences is complicated and necessary. For me to be an effective queer multicultural social justice teacher educator, I consistently explore my identities and my position within the classroom. By exploring and (de)constructing my identities through autoethnographic performances, I establish an elementary understanding of myself as a way of better understanding others. As I continue to become aware of myself—including my privilege, power, and purpose—I become more cognizant of others.

Upon further practice of autoethnographic methods, I continue to negotiate and clarify my ideas and beliefs about myself and others. And as I reflect on who I am, I often wonder how I will express my identities as a queer multicultural educator—identities that reflect my understanding of myself, others, and my multicultural ideologies. I continue to ask: *How will I explore multicultural education issues with my students? How will I create spaces that safely allow my students to explore and share their identities?*

One role as a queer multicultural social justice teacher education professor is to consistently determine where to begin with my students. In other words, I need to be aware of my students' prior knowledge, expertise, and values. Further, I must encourage them to explore how they identify and to listen to the voices of others. It is by knowing my students that I know myself better—thus becoming a more effective multicultural educator. I nurture this knowledge through critical reflection.

Another role is to provide and encourage the critical dialogue of diverse perspectives. The goal is to encourage students to think critically, to be skeptical, and to integrate their experiences to construct new information. By asking and learning about student identities (e.g., socioeconomic status, religion, gender, sexual orientation, race/ethnicity, and exceptionality) and by practicing awareness of our own biases, privilege, and limitations, educators, myself included, may learn how these attributes affect us, our teaching practices, and our students.

As a queer multicultural social justice teacher education instructor, I draw on and share my experiences of being a classroom teacher. Throughout my K–12 teaching career, I witnessed diverse learning environments—some more equitable than others. To be certain, our schools are not yet where they need to be as far as delivering a multicultural education, but it is my quest as a queer multicultural social justice teacher educator to guide preservice teachers toward practices that promote social justice. By drawing on my experiences, I can convey practical anecdotes along with theoretical ideals in a meaningful manner.

In sum, my queer multicultural social justice education philosophy is *activating awareness:* by actively and critically exploring, understanding, and articulating how I identify; by being aware of the language and teaching practices I use; by creating lessons that are queer and inclusive; by queering safe learning spaces and school policies; by engaging and promoting queer critical dialogue and reflection; by queering teaching by continuously learning; by checking my privilege and my assumptions of others; and by including students, caretakers, and other stakeholders in queer curriculum development processes.

## REFLECTION

For the readings for Exploration 9, the final exploration, I chose two chapters from *Multicultural education: Issues and perspectives* (Banks & McGee Banks, 2016). In "Queer lessons: Sexual and gender minorities in multicultural education," Mayo affirms that: "Queer is a concept and identity that works against problematic forms of normalization, troubling the exclusions that any category of identity may enact" (p. 134). I chose this chapter because Mayo (2016) reiterates why queer multicultural education is needed—a message that should not be lost through the course of this curriculum. Further, she reminds us that "some categories of identity such as those related to gender identity and minority sexuality are often not part of the official school curriculum or multicultural education" (p. 132). And she confirms that the "intersections of categories of identity [...] must become central to how educators think and learn before they can begin to teach their students" (p. 140). These ideas are pertinent to the philosophy of generating queer multicultural social justice curricula.

The second reading, "School reform and student learning: A multicultural perspective" by Nieto and Bode (2016), addresses the idea that "education is part and parcel of larger societal and political forces, such as inequality based on stratification due to race, social-class, gender, and other differences" in a *sociopolitical context* (Nieto & Bode, 2012) (p. 260). "Given this perspective, decisions concerning such practices as ability tracking, high-stakes testing, native language instruction, retention, curriculum reform, and pedagogy are all influenced by broader social policies" (p. 260). Indeed, like Mayo who reminds us that heterosexism is rampant within our education system, Nieto and Bode remind us that "institutionalized racism is alive and well" (p. 262). To combat such practices, they stress that "teachers need to become aware of how their own biases can act as barriers to student learning" (p. 266). Further, "teachers also need to consider how their students best learn and how their own pedagogical practices need to change as a result" (p. 266). One of the practices Nieto and Bode (2016) support is "using students as collaborators in developing the curriculum," as it may help promote learning (p. 266). These ideas are also pertinent to developing queer multicultural social justice curricula.

To conclude, both chapters encourage the reader to adopt different, or queer, perspectives when thinking about multicultural education, including one's own place within the field and within teaching/learning spaces. "*To queer something* means to challenge its core meaning" (Mayo, 2016, p. 144, italics original). The explorations of *Queer explorations of identity awareness* encouraged me, and may encourage others, to queer how curriculum is performed and developed. It is my hope that through these methods, explorers will develop a sustainable, queer teaching philosophy.

## REFERENCES

Banks, J. A., & McGee Banks, C. A. (Eds.). (2016). *Multicultural Education: Issues and Perspectives* (9th ed.). Wiley.

Mayo, C. (2016). Chapter 8: Queer lessons: Sexual and gender minorities in multicultural education. In J. A. Banks & C. A. McGee Banks (Eds.), *Multicultural education: Issues and perspectives* (9th ed.) (pp. 132–148). John Wiley & Sons.

Nieto, S., & Bode, P. (2016). Chapter 14: School reform and student learning: A multicultural perspective. In J. A. Banks & C. A. McGee Banks (Eds.), *Multicultural education: Issues and perspectives* (9th ed.) (pp. 258–274). John Wiley & Sons.

# PART 3

## REFLECTIVE ANALYSIS AND DISCUSSION

# CHAPTER 4

# QUEER CURRICULUM DEVELOPMENT

**(Em)Bodied**

Throughout this process, I lost sight of my purpose.

This story is about queer curriculum development.
This story is not about the future act of teaching the curriculum.
Stories will be told.
Lessons will be learned.

This story is about queer curriculum development.
This story is not about creating a queer curriculum.
Impossible task.
I cannot create a queer curriculum.
I can queer a curriculum.
*To take action against the normative.*

This story is about queer curriculum development.
The process.
Step One.
Create a curriculum.

*Queer Multicultural Social Justice Education: Curriculum (and Identity) Development Through Performance*, pages 135–154.

Much like Dr. Frankenstein (Shelley & Hindle, 2003), I "bodied" my curriculum.
*To give form to something abstract.*
Constructed from various theories.
Social justice harvested from multicultural education.
Sewn together with queer theory.
And dressed in autoethnographic storytelling.
Only to find that I created a *straight* monster.

It's alive!

Step Two.
Queer the fucker.

It is my creature.
I am its parent.
Its blood is my past, present, and future.[1]

My explorations "embodied" queer curriculum development.
*Gave a tangible form to [queer] theory.*
It is null until it is performed (Butler, 1990).

Perform it.
(stories, photographs, poems)
Nurture it.
(remove violent language, allow freedoms)
Develop it.

## PERFORMANCES AS ANALYSIS

This story is about queer curriculum development. As presented in Chapter Three, there are various approaches to analysis in autoethnographic writing (Chang, 2008; Ellis, 2004), and they may be performed in numerous ways. Since the format of this project is a queered social science prose, my analytical approach is blended. First, performance and analysis concurrently occurred throughout the duration of this project (e.g., performing the explorations and writing this autoethnographic story). And second, a reflective and reflexive analysis is presently occurring—processes that "aid in making visible the practice and construction of knowledge within research in order to produce more accurate analyses of our research" (Pillow, 2003, p. 178). These modes of analyses encapsulate both Ellis' (2004) "story as analysis"—for me, an alluring feature of autoethnographic work—and Chang's (2008) subsequent forms of autoethnographic analysis.

Further, "theory and story exist in a mutually influential relationship" within critical autoethnography (Holman Jones, 2016, p. 229). As Holman Jones (2016) points out, "theory is *not* an add-on to story" (p. 229, emphasis original). She goes to explain:

---

[1] Maybe there is a bit of Pinar (2004) running through its veins.

We cannot write our stories and then begin the search for a theory to "fit" them, outside of the cultures and politics and contexts. Instead, theory is a language for thinking with and through, asking questions about, and acting on—the experiences and happenings in our stories. (p. 229)

Indeed, queer theory is infused in my knowledge-building and my storytelling. It is with these approaches that I write my story and address the question guiding this study:

How may queering critical autoethnography and using it as a queer curriculum development method provide an opportunity for becoming more aware of, and for working toward, an understanding of identities (e.g., socioeconomic status, religion, sexual orientation, gender, race/ethnicity, and exceptionality), as well as impact curriculum development?

My analytical narrative encompasses ideas presented in multicultural social justice education, as introduced in Chapter One (see, Grant, 2012; Grant & Sleeter, 2013; Nieto, 2012), three principles of queer theory as highlighted in Chapter Two (i.e., interrupting heteronormativity, fracturing binary systems, and deconstructing socially constructed aspects of identity (Snyder & Broadway, 2004)), and autoethnographic storytelling as presented in Chapter Three (see, Chang, 2008; Ellis, 2004; Phillion, 2002; Phillion, He, & Connelly, 2005).

I present this analysis in four sections. First in *Queer multicultural social justice teacher education*, I reflect on the intended outcomes written for the *Queer explorations of identity awareness* curriculum and the need for such curriculum, with a short recap of how that need grew from becoming cognizant of our intersecting identities (see, Gay, 2010, Grant & Sleeter, 1985; Lorde, 1984; Sleeter, 1996) and our common goals as civil rights activists (see, Banks, 2006b; Gay, 1983; Pollard, 2013; Sleeter, 1996). Indeed, as educators, we are activists (Freire, 1970; Sleeter, 1996). Second, in *Breaking the norm*, I reflect on some of the tensions I wrestled with during the development of the (un)structured nature of the curriculum as I took steps to interrupt the (hetero)normative practices to which I was accustomed (Sullivan, 2003; Sumara & Davis, 1999). Third, in *Breaking a binary*, I identify myself as a teacher and a student simultaneously (Freire, 1970) and reflect on this extraordinary experience. And finally, in *Breaking down (de)constructions*, I reflect on my use of language and my curriculum development practices. I conclude this chapter with a section titled *(Non)conclusion*, where I reflect on the fluid, never-ending endeavors of practicing identity awareness and curriculum development (Banks, 2006b; Britzman, 1995; Grant & Sleeter, 2011a; Loutzenheiser, 2001; Nieto, 2010; Nieto & Bode, 2012; Oliva & Gordon, 2013; Whitlock, 2010).

### No, I Do Not March

I do not march for LGBTQ rights.
I do not march because Black Lives Matter.
I do not march in support of women's right to choose.

But I am an activist.

I teach.
I teach to defend civil rights.
I teach to promote social justice.
I teach to interrupt heteronormativity.

## QUEER MULTICULTURAL SOCIAL JUSTICE TEACHER EDUCATION

In Part One, I laid the foundation for this project based on theories contending that educators must explore and understand themselves, and the impact of their perspectives on their teaching practices, before they can effectively learn about and teach others (Gay, 2010, Grant & Sleeter, 1985; Lorde, 1984; Sleeter, 1996). After sharing (hi)stories of multicultural education, queer theory, and autoethnography, I synthesized these movements, ideologies, and methods in what I termed *queer multicultural social justice teacher education*. I define it as "a critical approach that provides opportunities for, and encourages, educators to examine and (de)construct identity and its espoused privileges—thus allowing explorers, in part, to investigate ways to dismantle heteronormativity, rethink binary systems of identification, and deconstruct socially constructed identities." We can do this "by implementing methods, such as autoethnography which may provide learners with opportunities to investigate ... identities in personal and meaningful ways" (Knaier, 2020, p. 147).

As an experienced classroom teacher and teacher educator, I am aware of the white, middle-class, and heteronormative resistance I will face from explorers (e.g., students) who are asked to perform such exercises (hooks, 1994). Indeed, as I confess below in *Breaking the Norm*, I was one of those students. But now, I am up to the challenge of welcoming such resistance as a queer educator. As Britzman (1995) explains:

> Pedagogical thought must begin to acknowledge that receiving knowledge is a problem for the learner and the teacher, particularly when the knowledge one already possesses or is possessed by works as an entitlement to one's ignorance or when the knowledge encountered cannot be incorporated because it disrupts how the self might imagine itself and others. These dynamics, quite familiar in contexts where multiculturalism is constituted as a special interest, are not resistance to knowledge. Rather, it is knowledge that is a form of resistance. (p. 159)

By encountering others and engaging with their stories, specifically those developed and performed based on the *Queer explorations of identity awareness* curriculum, knowledge is being shared, (re)shaped, and disruptive.

Indeed, these explorations reflect my desire to promote and fight for social justice and interrupt heteronormativity. By recognizing how the intersectionality of our identities influences the way we seek justice, we can actively pursue our common goals as civil rights activists (Banks, 2006b; Gay, 1983; Sleeter, 1996;

Pollard, 2013). We, educators, are activists (Freire, 1970; Sleeter, 1996). These ideas are implicated throughout the explorations and the processes used to create them. Moreover, by performing the *Queer explorations of identity awareness* curriculum and through sharing our stories, we can get closer to creating curricula and school climates that encourage and support the teaching all of students—as a form of social justice.

As part of the curriculum development process, I wrote three "intended outcomes" that move us closer to achieving these goals as we begin to better understand ourselves and others. They read that explorers will:

1. Understand the importance of queer(ing) curriculum by recognizing certain hostile presumptions present in our heteronormative society (and within ourselves) and the harm they cause.
2. Realize that identity awareness (of self and others) through storytelling is key to contributing to and promoting a more accepting and socially just multicultural society.
3. Develop a multicultural teaching philosophy that recognizes the importance of identity awareness (of self and others) through storytelling as curriculum.

In the following sections, based on my experience, I share three examples of how my performances address each of these objectives and the queer implications filtered through each.

*Intended Outcome 1*

Regarding hostile presumptions present in *society*, in Part 1 I argue the need for queered curriculum based in part on research conducted and presented by the Gay, Lesbian & Straight Education Network (GLSEN) (Kosciw et al., 2018). For almost two decades I have relied on their work on studying the learning atmospheres of LGBTQ youth as the basis of pursing my passions of creating queer, safe learning spaces, conducting and publishing queer research, and nurturing my identity as a queer educator. As a victim of bullying and jarred by the research presented by GLSEN (Kosciw et al., 2018), Iannotti (2006), and others, I have presented my own research on the matter with the intention of bringing about *awareness* (see, Knaier, 2003, 2013, 2017).

These experiences and studies have certainly impacted my teaching practices and philosophies as evidenced by the stories told throughout this book and by the first exploration prompt featured in *Queer explorations of identity awareness*. It reads:

> Share a time or times when you were affected by (e.g., a victim of, witnessed, and/or stood up to) hurtful, disrespectful, or violent normative or heteronormative behavior that occurred based on socioeconomic status, religion, gender, sexual orientation, race/ethnicity, and/or exceptionality in a school or learning atmosphere.

As I point out in my reflection for Exploration 1, I am not the first educator to use such a prompt; indeed, many scholars use prompts like this in their teaching and research (e.g., Letts, 2002); and, as a student, I have performed this autobiographical exercise several times throughout my teacher education. However, it is worth reiterating that, unfortunately, there is still a need for such prompts, as presented in the readings for Exploration 1 (Chan, 2015; Gilbert, 2015; Vàsquez, 2015).

My reason for using this as the first prompt is for us to make connections to one another—although we are different, we all experience hurtful situations based on (hetero)normative policing or bullying (Martino & Pallotta-Chiarolli, 2003). And by recognizing these commonalities, we may realize that we are indeed working toward common goals (Lorde, 1984; Mayo, 2014). Since these explorations involve critical, emotional, and personal affects, a sense of understanding and similarity will make learning spaces more comfortable. Indeed, we need to learn how to create safe learning spaces and opportunities for each other. *This is an integral part of our fight toward queer social justice and LGBTQ equality.*

But the first intended outcome is not only about recognizing hostile presumptions in society; it is also about us taking a reflexive look within ourselves and identifying our harmful beliefs and practices. Unquestionably, through my performance of Exploration 6, I recognized hostile assumptions, and ignorance, within myself—and the harm they could have caused if I had not addressed them. Through this performance, I acknowledged that some of the language I had chosen was potentially harmful and could "certainly lead to oppression, injustice, and violence" (Zacko-Smith & Smith, 2010, p. 7). Based on this realization, I omitted it from the exploration (and curriculum). Indeed, it was through this queered, performative approach to curriculum development that I became aware of my potentially violent actions and heteronormative language. "Through exploring gender and violence awareness, I was able to stop myself from potentially acting in a violent manner—by directly asking about others' bodies." If I had not performed this exploration, I may have caused harm to you and other explorers.

## Intended Outcome 2

As part of my curriculum development process, I interreacted with others (e.g., my partner and editor, colleagues, and peers), shared my ideas and stories, and considered all constructive feedback. Through these (inter)actions, I understood that identity awareness through storytelling contributed to the development of this curriculum—which is a tool for promoting a more accepting and socially just multicultural society.

During the time I was developing the *Queer exploration of identity awareness* curriculum, I was given the opportunity to share my early processes and progress of the work with some colleagues at the annual American Educational Research Association (AERA) conference (Knaier, 2019a). As I read the passage below to my peers, I could literally feel connections being made. People were shaking their heads acknowledging my hardships as I shared:

As a poor, latchkey child, I often wrote poetry. All I needed was my notebook, a pen, and a bit of privacy. Thus, in developing [Exploration 4], I performed it, reflecting on how poverty influenced my writings. In part I wrote:

> I grew up in a broken home—my parents divorced when I was nine. Throughout [my poetry] notebook I wrote a lot about relationships and the desire to "expand" them; I wrote about feeling secure; and I wrote about my inability to express my love and gratitude toward others—sentiments brought on by having an absent father and a hard-working mother. My poems also reflect a strong desire for being loved and accepted and the naivety of my young self. These poems are the epitome of low self-esteem and insecurity. It seems I spent my adolescent years searching for some sense of security—something I didn't find until many years later.

Through sharing such self-realizations, I connect with my readers, and ultimately with my students. (Knaier, 2020, p. 150)

Afterward, some of those with whom I shared these reflections revealed that they too found solace in poetry. Others validated my work by telling me how important my stories are and that they would like to use my curriculum in their courses. *I was grateful for the welcoming reception of my work.*

Further, by taking this project on the road, I learned how to succinctly describe my processes and the elements of the embodied curriculum. Again these (inter) actions were pertinent to my curriculum development process, as I usually work solely with my in-house editor (and partner). I graciously appreciated the interactive and constructive feedback I received from my colleagues. Based on this feedback, my work was validated and further developed.

I must confess that these early exposures of my work helped me realize, or at the very least refocus on, its purpose: To tell a story about queer curriculum development. Prior to these presentations, I had difficulty separating the work of curriculum development with the future act of the teaching the curriculum (which is not a part of this project and may be the focus of future research projects). To be clear, this narrative is not about student response or engagement; it is about the way *I* developed, performed, and engaged with the *Queer explorations of identity awareness* curriculum. It is about the foundational research that lead me along a path, and my experiences, including struggles and realizations, along the way.

I mention these interactions because they are important, even imperative, to this project. Moving forward, as I implement and perform these explorations as part of my queer curriculum development process, I am hopeful that opportunities like these between colleagues, students, and myself will generate new ideas about clarifying language, identity awareness, and cultural pairings (Jagose, 1996). Moreover, once this story is told, my engagement with you—the reader of this work—will also serve to advance it (Ellis, 2004). Indeed, I hope you find this project helpful and affirming—*a story you can relate and react to*—as you travel along your path through queer curriculum development. *I have much to learn from you.*

*Intended Outcome 3*

As I learn (e.g., through research, teaching, listening to your stories, or other experiences) my perspectives change. I change—consequently, my teaching philosophy changes. Therefore, I revisit, reflection on, and update my teaching philosophy periodically. After completing the first eight explorations of the *Queer explorations of identity awareness* curriculum, I felt it was sensible to revisit and (re)create my teaching philosophy as the performance for Exploration 9 and meet the third intended outcome:

> My queer multicultural social justice education philosophy is *activating awareness*: by actively and critically exploring, understanding, and articulating how I identify; by being aware of the language and teaching practices I use; by creating lessons that are queer and inclusive; by queering safe learning spaces and school policies; by engaging and promoting queer critical dialogue and reflection; by queering teaching by continuously learning; by checking my privilege and my assumptions of others; and by including students, caretakers, and other stakeholders in queer curriculum development processes.

These practices will guide me through my journey of knowing myself as a way of knowing others "both for the purpose of building relationships that work, and also for the purpose of designing curriculum and pedagogical strategies that are responsive to, and honoring of, our students' actual lived experiences" (Howard, 2006, p. 132).

My current teaching philosophy was influenced by this project, with both its queer curriculum development processes and the performances of the developed curriculum—a queer multicultural social justice education curriculum which bloomed out of multicultural social justice education (see, Gay, 2004; Grant & Sleeter, 2013; Nieto & Bode, 2012). The goals of multicultural social justice education "are to reduce prejudice and discrimination against oppressed groups, to work toward equal opportunity and social justice for all groups, and to affect an equitable distribution of power among members of different cultural groups" (Grant & Sleeter, 2013, p. 49). *Queer* multicultural social justice education attempts to meet these goals by disrupting heteronormative practices, language, and assumptions otherwise experienced as the societal status quo.

**One Times One is One**
Rote
Memorize
Repeat

Two times two is four
Conditioning
Obedient
Enslaved citizenship

Three times three is nine
Fuckery
Anger
Rebel

One plus two multiplied by three equals
Queer
Imaginaries
Freedom

## BREAKING THE NORM

For the last eighteen years, I have practiced queering my learning, teaching, and research practices (see, Knaier, 2003, 2013, 2014, 2015, 2017, 2020)—and I am still realizing that aspects of my learning, teaching, and research behaviors are severely (hetero)normative. Though I am adamant about exploring and implementing queer approaches, it is evident by my performance throughout this project that I am still unlearning years of (hetero)normative ways of conducting myself.

As a student, even into adulthood, I wanted everything spelled out for me. *Tell me what you want, and I will deliver!* I excelled in structure and order—not in flexibility and freedom. I wanted to learn in ways with which I was familiar—through memorization and regurgitation—through transmission (King, 1993). I was resistant to change (hooks, 1994). I liked the ease, comfort, and lack of critical thinking found in the traditional teaching methods I had experienced. Freire (1970) refers to this oppressive form of teaching as the "banking" system where knowledge is essentially transferred from teacher to student. Indeed, the tensions between my experiences as a student and my experiences of becoming a classroom science teacher were (and, at times, still are) difficult to resolve. But given the new approaches to learning and teaching (e.g., reflective, critical thinking exercises) implemented by my teacher educators, I had to learn how to navigate, succeed, and excel in a new learning space. And, after some push back and struggling, I did.

Throughout my teacher education, which was steeped in social justice and reflective practices, I was expected to write, and excel at writing, very precise lesson plans. Plans that often included exactly what the teacher was to say and how students were expected to respond, so that anyone (e.g., a substitute teacher, administrator) should be able to pick them up implement them. And I excelled at this practice. *But as I reflect on these practices, they seem contrary to the constructivist theories to which I was also being exposed* (Dewey, 1938).

Once I became a science teacher, I tried to practice and implement constructivist methods. However, I found that my lessons were constructed of cement scaffolding. As I explained in the Introduction, I did the best I could at that time—but it was not enough. Indeed, my teaching practices were impacted by the hardships experienced by teachers (e.g., unrealistic expectations, personal costs [time and money], and lack of respect). Though these experiences were touched upon in some of the explorations, a deeper discussion of such issues is beyond the scope of this project. *Funny thing about this type of inquiry, I did not expect these realizations to come out. But this is now part of my process of developing this curriculum—and getting to know myself* (Chang, 2008; Conle, 1996).

This is the (hi)story I bring to this project. Relying on my education and past experiences (Ladson-Billings, 1995), I assigned myself the task of creating a queer multicultural social justice teacher education curriculum. I was excited about being, and expected to be, queer and creative. However, I had a difficult time reconciling queerness with pragmatism. I could not envision a queer curriculum that would realistically be used in a teacher education program. Rodriguez (2007) termed this the "pedagogical search for theory" (p. 293). Which begs the question, once again: "Is there a queer pedagogy?" (Britzman, 1995). But, after suffering some major existential angst and pondering my success as a queer educator, I put my anxieties aside (or tempered them with Xanax) and I started typing. *Or, should I say, pouring cement.*

The first draft of my queer curriculum included required readings, oppressive language, and **bold due dates**. It was steeped in heteronormativity and was unwaveringly rigid. My second attempt was not much better. Though more relaxed, it included harmful language and strict directives surrounding the heart of queer, creative prompts that I wanted you to perform freely. It was confusingly tyrannical. I realized, like Dr. Frankenstein (Shelley & Hindle, 2003), that what I created—through incorporating the best parts of multicultural social justice education, sewing them together with queer theory, and dressing it in autoethnography—wasn't quite right. The complexities of developing a structured, yet unstructured, queer curriculum fucked with my rationalities. *I had failed.*

But Halberstam (2011) whispered I my ear: "Under certain circumstances failing, losing, forgetting, unmaking, undoing, unbecoming, not knowing may in fact offer more creative, more cooperative, more surprising ways of being in the world" (pp. 2–3). And it dawned on me that I had given myself an impossible task. I cannot *create* queer curriculum . . .

Indeed, queer theory does not allow the tangible (or pragmatic); queer theory as described by Golding (1993) is a technique: "a 'route,' a mapping, an impossible geography—impossible not because it does not exist, but because *it exists and does not exist exactly at the same time*" (as cited in Britzman, 1995, p. 155, emphasis original). *For a moment, I took pride in my failure.*

. . . but I can *queer* a curriculum even in unstable, fluid formats (Britzman, 1995). So, to make this newly drafted curriculum *(Dare I refer to it as a misunderstood monster?)* into a viable body of work, I had to queer it. This was only possible once my theories were embodied in a living curriculum, because now I could perform it, analyze it, and develop it (Butler, 1990). I could take actions to queer it (Mayo, 2014). *Some queer theorists may argue that my approach to exploring identities maintains the status quo of the construction, and policing, of identities, identifications, and self-identifying practices. But the tensions between pragmatic teaching practices and queer theorizing is where I currently find myself.*

## Queer Explorations . . .

"Queer theory offers [...] a lens through which educators can transform their praxis so as to explore and celebrate the tensions and new understandings created by teaching new ways of seeing the world" (Meyer, 2007, p. 15). Indeed, as I progress through this project, the tensions between the educator I was and the one I am becoming are evident. But my initial assumption and determination that this curriculum needed to be delivered in an institutional setting only to preservice teachers might have been the most detrimental setback. Indeed, these explorations are intended for all educators in all learning spaces. This notion of equal access was evident even in my early (failed) conceptions of this curriculum as I urged performers to utilize various perspectives (e.g., educator, child, artist, victim) throughout the explorations. Further, although I clearly approached this project from the perspective of a teacher educator, this curriculum is not designed only for teacher educators and future K–12 classroom teachers. *I want you to utilize it in any, and all, learning spaces without limitation.*

Since this realization, I chose different, more inclusive, language to refer to the performers of this curriculum—I replaced "students" with the broader term "explorers." "Student" gives the connotation of a young person sitting behind a desk within a formal classroom setting. *Not queer.* But an "explorer" is a person on an adventure.

Given that you were no longer "students," I also abandoned the term "lesson(s)" and replaced it with "exploration(s)." The term "lesson" was always a misnomer in this context. *I do not intend on teaching you a lesson.* I want you to freely perform these explorations, to seek answers to questions only you can ask, and to share your stories with others. *That's the adventure!* It will be through these actions that insights—queer and unique to everyone—will be gained and the intended outcomes of this curriculum achieved. Because you, as an explorer, are simply offered exploration and reflection prompts, you are free to create your own investigations, inquiries, and stories. It is not my want to tell you what to learn. I can only offer guidance (King, 1993). *I will finally be that "guide on the side." Maybe I've found my constructivist self after all.*

Now that I was using different language to describe you and your actions, I had to rework some of my actions, including the construction of the elements of the explorations. Based on my experiences as a curriculum planner, I included several traditional elements in my curriculum (e.g., learning outcomes, readings, prompts, discussions, assessments) but retained flexibility through ambiguity. One of the first features developed for a curriculum are the learning outcomes. These are often referred to as "objectives" which may serve as a map for curriculum workers. Tyler (1949) explains that "educational objectives become the criteria by which materials are selected, content is outlined, instructional procedures are developed and tests and examinations are prepared" (p. 3). Though I already address the formally stated intended outcomes above (see, Queer Multicultural Social Justice Teacher Education), I summarize them here:

> Through these performative autoethnographic methods, you may realize how each exploration provokes identity awareness, and that identity is complicated, fluid, and ever changing. In the end, you should practice identity awareness and may ultimately appreciate that you may never fully know, understand, or define yourself (or others).

These purposefully ambiguous learning objectives allow you to pursue various perspectives, methods, and inquiries. Indeed, as Cranton (2001) supports: "both providing choices for ways of participating in an activity and modeling the engagement of multiple ways of knowing in keeping with our own personality and cultural backgrounds in our own efforts to be authentic tend to dissipate resistance" (as cited by Tisdell & Tolliver, 2009, p. 99). Moreover, these options, along with modeled engagement, allow you to create your own map for this journey.

Further, due to this ambiguity, I initially suggested that the explorations be assessed as (in)complete and/or (un)satisfactory instead of on a traditional grading scale; however, upon further queering, I decided that there should be no assessment at all. *I cannot measure your realization of identity awareness or your appreciation for such matters.* Moreover, another queer aspect of these explorations is that your performances will never be "finished" and therefore cannot be assessed. These performed explorations are the beginnings of critical self-awareness and will always be a work in progress—much like queer curriculum and its development.

In addition to omitting the assessment factor, I also removed time restrictions (e.g., class time, discussion time, performance time, and presentation time), minimum word and page requirements, and the required submission of the exploration outline for Explorations Four through Eight (*For fuck's sake, I actually had you putting your identities into little boxes!* (Butler, 1993; Fausto-Sterling, 2000)) Traditionally these elements may often serve as a guide and are prominent in education programs and teacher education curricula (Oliva & Gordon, 2013). However, these factors are oppressive—to teachers, students, and explorers—though my initial cemented intent was good. My hope is that you will perform the explorations to the best of your ability—with the understanding that "the best of your ability" may change from day to day. Overall, I want you to examine and reflect on your own disposition and confront queer issues (Murray, 2015) as you engage with queer curriculum.

### . . . and readings

Again, as a normative practice, my first intent to was adhere a single text (aided by secondary texts) to my curriculum that would serve as a guide for your journey. I initially chose *Multicultural education: Issues and perspectives* (Banks & Mc-

Gee Banks, 2016), because I relied heavily on Banks' (1988, 1993, 1994, 1996, 1999, 2004, 2006a, 2006b, 2010, 2013, 2016) work for setting the foundation for this project. Throughout the curriculum development process, I continued to read the corresponding chapters from *Multicultural education: Issues and perspectives* (Banks & McGee Banks, 2016); however, I found that this body of work is not queer enough for my means—indeed, it may not be queer at all. (The non-inclusive definition of "multicultural education," as mentioned in Chapter One [see, The Evolution of Multicultural Education], should have tipped me off.) *It was clear that most of the authors featured in the text were not familiar with the queer terrain that lay ahead.*

However, I did use three chapters from the Banks and McGee Banks (2016) textbook. For Exploration 2, I chose Banks' "Chapter 1: Multicultural education: Characteristics and goals," because, as explained in my reflection in part, he "provides a brief history of the development of multicultural education" and "a short discussion of the social construction of multicultural categories." I also thought this chapter would be relevant, even helpful, because I chose to focus on these six socially constructed multicultural categories: socioeconomic status, religion, gender, sexual orientation, race/ethnicity, and exceptionality, as Banks (2016) describes, for my curriculum project on identity awareness.

It was not until my final exploration, *Exploration 9: Creating a queer multicultural social justice teaching philosophy*, that I included two more chapters from the *Multicultural education* text. "Both chapters encourage the reader to adopt different, or queer, perspectives when thinking about multicultural education, including one's own place within the field and within classrooms." These perspectives may prove helpful as you develop your queer multicultural social justice teaching philosophy (the objective of Exploration 9). In the first, "Chapter 8: Queer lessons: Sexual and gender minorities in multicultural education," Mayo (2016) "reiterates why queer multicultural education is needed—a message that should not be lost through the course of this curriculum." And in the second, "Chapter 14: School reform and student learning: A multicultural perspective," Nieto and Bode (2016) stress that "teachers need to become aware of how their own biases can act as barriers to student learning" (p. 266). In short, I chose these chapters because they complement the goals of my queer multicultural social justice education agenda and may be pertinent to developing your teaching philosophy.

Next, I set out in search of queer texts that would guide you through the explorations. For example, I reached out to two Facebook groups, *Queer Ph.D. Network* and *Queer Studies SIG: American Educational Research Association*, and asked: Can you recommend any articles or books on what heteronormativity looks like within schools and/or curriculum? At the time, I was specifically looking for readings that I could use for *Exploration 1: Why queer curriculum?* I received several responses. One person suggested *Queering classrooms: Personal narratives and educational practice to support LGBTQ youth in schools* (Mikulec & Miller, 2017). *I thought to myself, I know that book.* I saw it perched in the hutch of my desk, and that is when I decided to use my chapter, "A place they can be themselves: Issues of LGBTQ students [Revisited]" (Knaier, 2017), as a reading for Exploration 1.

I continued my quest for finding queer texts throughout the curriculum development process—a task I did not take lightly. I reached out to colleagues a couple of times for book or article suggestions but to no avail. So, I relied heavily on my personal queer library and my university's online library. I selected a diverse set of readings, genres, and authors, with the purpose of being inclusive and offering a queer multicultural space in which to engage with voices that are not usually heard. If you are interested in learning more about why I chose each of the readings, please revisit Part Two of this book, as I included short descriptions of each of the readings and reasons why they were included.

**Looking in the mirror**
Do I exist outside of your constructed language?
Do I exist outside of your defined performances?
Do I exist outside of your unfounded assumptions?
Do I exist outside of your described feelings?
"I am something that you'll never understand" (Nelson, 1984).

## BREAKING A . . .

During my teacher education I was often told to review all the materials (e.g., readings, movies, documents) before sharing them with my students. And even though we get busy and overwhelmed, please heed this advice! *Learn from my mistakes—and from the others that came before me. The last thing you want to experience is a naked lady (picture the opening scene from Jaws) and products from a sex shop (imagine life-like rubber fists for punching sharks) on the screen in your classroom in front of 37 eighth graders. It happened! I was mortified. Thanks, MythBusters!* Since such experiences can be prevented, I now review all materials before sharing them with my students.

However, this project delves deeper than merely reviewing materials; it required performing the curriculum as others would. Indeed, as Cranton (2001) discusses, "it is important that teachers and facilitators develop activities that they themselves also participate in to model some sense of engaging completely and authentically in such learning" (as cited by Tisdell & Tolliver, 2009, p. 99). My hope is that by performing these vulnerable tasks (e.g., performing the explorations and sharing my stories) alongside others, critical learning about ourselves and our assumptions (of self and others) may occur (Bochner & Ellis, 2016; Dewey, 1938; Ngunjiri, Hernandez, & Chang, 2010; Rosenberg, 2016).

Further, we can encourage and model engagement, by exploring ourselves and our world together (both as teachers and learners), by sharing our stories, and by being the teacher and the student simultaneously. As realized by Freire (1970), "the teacher is no longer merely the-one-who-teaches, but one who is himself taught in dialogue with the students, who in turn being taught also teach" (p. 80). Through performing the *Queer explorations of identity awareness* curriculum, I had opportunities to create, share, and model my performances; to engage with the curriculum as others would; and to use various perspectives and modes for learning and teaching—all of which contributed to its development. Through these actions, I became mindful of the intersectionality of teaching and learning. *I was not doing one or the other. I was doing both.*

## A BREAK TO PONDER

According to Luhmann (1998), "both queer theory and pedagogy argue that the process of main (sense) of selves relies on binaries such as homo-hetero, ignorance-knowledge, learner-teacher, reader-writer, and so on" (p. 150). Further, "queer theory and pedagogy place at stake the desire to deconstruct binaries central to Western modes of meaning making, learning, teaching and doing politics" (pp. 150–151). Indeed, "both desire to subvert the processes of normalization" (p. 151). But how does queer theory present, *show*, or even perform these deconstructions? And does *deconstruction* mean *destruction*? Could it mean a *construction* of something new?

Queer theorists find the decentering and deconstruction of binaries essential to the denormalization of those identities (Derrida & Spivak, 2016), or identifications (Luhmann, 1998), that are presently in power. But how does queer theory *signify* a false dichotomy like teacher-learner? If we are both teachers and learners simultaneously (Freire, 1970), there would not be a hard shift from one position (teacher) to another (learner). Based on my experiences, I view it as a fluidity between the two (teacher ~ ~ learner).[2] Is this what Luhmann (1998) tries to convey? She states: "Queer tries to interrupt these modes of making selves and making sense by refusing stable identities and by producing new identifications that lie outside binary modes of gender and sexuality" (p. 151). Could then my *teacher ~ ~ learner* be a new way of presenting this identity? *I'm sure these ideas are not new. I do not recall reading about them. Maybe I have not read about them. It was just something I was pondering as part of this process.*

## . . . BINARY

Indeed, through this queer curriculum development process, I was acutely aware that I was actively playing the role of teacher and learner simultaneously (Freire, 1970). When I crossed obstacles as a learner, I had to be understanding as a teacher. And through this practice, I gained an appreciation for what I am asking you to do. *This self as teacher ~ ~ learner dynamic was fascinating. I have never been so self-forgiving and self-understanding before.*

---

[2] I am using the symbol, ~ ~ ,to show the fluidity between two or more identities, in this case between teacher and learner.

I illustrate this empathetic approach in my reflection for Exploration 3. To re-cap, I was disappointed after attending the San Diego March for Science because of the low attendance rate. Indeed, "by performing this exploration, I experienced a potential problematic situation that other performers might experience." And, "as an educator I would never penalize a student for something that is out of their control." After all, "I still met the exploration requirements as outlined above." Initially, I blamed myself for choosing the event, but then I realized, I would never blame a student for such a choice. I would be understanding and tell the student to make the best out of the experience—just as I did. *We must be understanding when explorers (including ourselves) experience unfortunate circumstances. By the way, talking about myself in both roles was trippy.*

## BREAKING DOWN (DE)CONSTRUCTIONS

Throughout my queer curriculum development process and analyses, I reflected on, and attempted to deconstruct and understand my use of language and my cur-riculum development practices.

### Use of Language

The greatest impact on rethinking my use of language within this project was through performing *Exploration 6: Gender and/or sexual orientation and violence awareness and prevention.* Indeed, what I learned through that performance about the harmful language I intended to use, my assumptions, and myself, prevented me from potentially committing acts of violence toward gender nonconforming, non-binary, and transgender people. *This would have shown a much worse lack of judgment than the MythBusters fiasco.*

Another insightful incident that occurred regarding my language use was an in-teraction with a colleague. It was kindly pointed out to me that the way I original-ly wrote the explorations would not yield the results I imagined. In other words, I used very *straight* language in my very *straight* directives but expected queer results for the performances. After this enlightenment, I queered my curriculum further (see, Appendix). The changes I made included identifying and changing qualifying, restrictive, and harmful language in my directives. For example, the reflection directive initially read, "Positively respond to others' presentations . . .." I later changed them to read, "Critically respond to others' presentations . . .." Indeed, not all responses have to be "positive," but they all should be "critical."

As I reflect on the language changes I made throughout the curriculum, I feel as though *I* would not have performed them any differently, but the reformed directives more accurately articulate my intentions—those being that explorers conduct their explorations freely, openly, and with little, to no, restrictions. In-deed, by having the courage to ask questions, to engage in constructive conversa-tions, and to address my heteronormative actions, I was able to better understand, change, and learn from the choices I had made regarding language use within my curriculum. *We must practice questioning and changing our heteronormative beliefs and actions.*

## The Heart of My Curriculum Development[3]

As illustrated, it was challenging to construct a viable curriculum around a heart consisting of queer, creative prompts. The prompts explored in *Queer exploration of identity awareness* were conceived while reading Lorde's (1984) essay, "Age, race, class, and sex: Women redefining difference." Indeed, her words inspired me to explore the intersectionality between multicultural identities (e.g., socioeconomic status, religion, gender, sexual orientation, race/ethnicity, and exceptionality) and social or cultural practices or ideals (e.g., socioeconomic status and the arts, religion and mortality). She asserts that "even the form our creativity takes is often a class issue" (p. 116). She goes on to clarify: "Of all the art forms, poetry is the most economical. It is the one which is the most secret, which requires the least physical labor, the least material, and the one which can be done between shifts [...], on the subway, and on scraps of surplus paper" (p. 116). I was immediately transported to a time when, "as a poor, latchkey child, I often wrote poetry. All I needed was my notebook, a pen, and a bit of privacy" (Knaier, 2020, p. 150). Even before I "created" the prompts, I was performing them. I used Lorde's work as an exemplar in my search for other queer readings—readings that would spark my—and your—imagination. I wanted the prompts to be meaningful. I wanted them to provoke heartfelt responses. I wanted them to be challenging and enlightening—just as Lorde's work was for me. *I responded to Lorde's story by enveloping it with my own—this is the impact of autoethnographic writing and story sharing.*

Lorde's essay also prompted some conflict within me. She challenged me "to compare, and reflect on, my young, poor artistic self, with my current, privileged artistic self—including the modes, subjects, and purposes of my art" (Knaier, 2020, p. 151). Almost accusingly, she wrote:

> The actual requirements to produce the visual arts also help determine, along class lines, whose art is whose. In this day of inflated prices for material, who are our sculptors, our painters, our photographers? (Lorde, 1984, p. 116)

Indeed, I have struggled to reconcile my current socioeconomic position with the one in which I was raised (a topic I plan to explore further). Through these reflections, I am prompted into *action*; these explorations are the *beginnings* of self-awareness and include prompts for life-long journeys of realizing who I am—and who we are.

Finally, Lorde (1984) also impacted my perspective of how to explore my identities and their intersectionality. Indeed, through her direct explanation . . .

---

[3] Parts of this section were published in "Our stories *as* curriculum" (Knaier, 2020).

As a Black lesbian feminist comfortable with the many different ingredients of my identity, and a woman committed to racial and sexual freedom from oppression, I find I am constantly being encouraged to pluck out some aspect of myself and present this as the meaningful whole, eclipsing or denying the other parts of self. But this is a destructive and fragmenting way to live. My fullest concentration of energy is available to me only when I integrate all the parts of who I am, openly, allowing power from particular sources of my living to flow back and forth freely through all my different selves, without the restrictions of externally imposed definition. (pp. 120–121)

. . . she "prompted me to clarify that … I am not asking [you] to separate out one identity from others." (Knaier, 2020, p. 151). I clearly realize how "plucking out" one aspect of oneself may be "destructive." Indeed, I want explorers to notice all their different selves and embrace the intersectionality of their selves while performing these explorations. *Lorde is at the heart of this curriculum.*

## MY SELVES ARE EMBODIED, YET FLUID

## (NON)CONCLUSION

As I stated in the Introduction, I hope to advance the kind of multicultural education that provides opportunities for and encourages educators (e.g., K–12 classroom teachers, caregivers, artists) to examine and explore their identities and the way they teach (e.g., develop curriculum, nurture relationships with students, and learn from others) in conjunction with their identities. Further, I want explorers to move beyond conversation, texts, and videos that simply tell us that we are different from one another. I want us to interact, engage, and discuss our differences, rethink our assumptions, and promote *our stories as curriculum* together. These are the notions reflected in *Queer exploration of identity awareness*. Indeed, as Murray (2015) acknowledges, these types of queer methods (e.g., autoethnography, autobiography) are "logically housed in [multicultural curricula] because in addition to examining a range of sexualities, teacher candidates can analyze intersections of class, race, ethnicity, gender, language, and ability" (p. 196). Further, "this explicit, though undervalued, stance can allow students to engage in more generative modes of thinking about the ways that difference matters" (Letts, 2002, p. 128, as cited in Murray 2015, p. 196). *Through sharing our stories, we will make personal connections with each other, giving each of us a stake in what and how we are learning.*

Within queer pedagogy, Pitt (1995) maintains that "learning about content is not the same thing as learning from it. In other words . . . learning is something more than a series of encounters with knowledge; learning entails, rather, the messier and less predictable process of becoming implicated in knowledge (p. 298)" (as cited by Luhmann, 1998, p. 150). Further, Luhmann (1998) cautions:

> what is at stake in a queer pedagogy is not the application of queer theory (as a new knowledge) onto pedagogy, nor the application of pedagogy (as a new method) for the dissemination of queer theory and knowledge. Instead, at stake are the implications of queer theory and pedagogy for the messy processes of learning and teaching, reading and writing. Instead of posing (the right) knowledge as answer or solution, queer theory and the pedagogy I have outlined here pose knowledge as an interminable question. (p. 151)

This is the type of teaching ~ ~ learning I prescribe here. Messy. Unpredictable. Queer.

Throughout this project, I have tried to identify and disrupt potentially harmful (hetero)normative behaviors in the way I create curriculum (e.g., language use, personal assumptions), including the (un)structuredness of curriculum. And through reflective and reflexive practices (e.g., engaging with others and listening to and sharing stories) and narrative inquiry (e.g., autoethnography, storytelling), I have explored my identities, questioned my assumptions, and changed my use of harmful language within my practices of curriculum development and beyond. If we all practiced curriculum development and explored ourselves in these ways, maybe we could gain an understanding of, and stop the bullying, judging, and policing of, each other's (and our own) performances (Butler, 1990).

In sum, this project reveals the first step in developing the *Queer explorations of identity awareness* curriculum (Oliva & Gordon, 2013). Going forward, we must share *our stories as curriculum* (Knaier, 2020). I need to share my stories, and I need to hear the stories of others—that is when connections, engagement, and awareness occur. This book represents just one performance. Next, this queer multicultural social justice education curriculum needs to be implemented, (re) performed, and (re)developed (Oliva & Gordon, 2013). It is a living curriculum that will change as we change—as society changes. Tyler (1949) determined:

> Because contemporary life is so complex and because life is continually changing, it is very necessary to focus educational efforts upon the critical aspects of this complex life and upon those aspects that are of importance today so that we do not waste the time of students in learning things that were important fifty years ago but no longer have significance at the same time that we are neglecting areas of life that are now important and for which the schools provide no preparation. (p. 17)

Moreover, Banks (2016) reminds us: "Multicultural education must be viewed as an ongoing process, not as something that we 'do' and thereby solve the problems that are the targets of multicultural education reform" (p. 3). We change. Our perspectives shift. And our stories evolve. We are always becoming (Freire, 1970, p. 84).

# CHAPTER 5

# OUR STORIES CONTINUE

Although this is the last chapter in this book, I hope our journey together will continue. As I mentioned throughout, this work is not complete until it is responded to, used by, and reflected upon by you—the reader. Indeed, your interaction and engagement are imperative to the success of this project. *Think of it as paying it forward.* It will be through the sharing of *your* stories that I will get another step closer to addressing my guiding question for this project.

Since engagement with the reader, and my fellow explorer, is essential, I have kept you in mind throughout the entire process. I truly hope you find this work helpful and affirming—*a story you can relate and react to*—as you teach ~ ~ learn and develop curricula. Indeed, I, as "the autoethnographic storyteller," want "you to interact *with* the story, to plunge in, using all the senses available to you, feeling the story's tensions, experiencing its dilemmas or contradictions, and living in its reality." Magically, "when you engage *with* a story in this way, you allow yourself to consider the ways in which this story relates to your life and to find in that connection some truth about yourself—especially the good that you are seeking" (Bochner & Ellis, 2016, p. 219, emphasis original). Further, this engagement may also ignite memories and spark stories of your own as you make connections with, or resonate with, my story and the stories of others (Conle, 1996). *As I have reported, I have felt such connections, including transports in time and transformative shifts in my perspectives, with others' stories.*

*Queer Multicultural Social Justice Education: Curriculum (and Identity) Development Through Performance,* pages 155–160.
Copyright © 2021 by Information Age Publishing

Moreover, this project has implications beyond my queer curriculum development practices. It has changed me, my perspectives, and my identity. Through the process of performance, I learned about myself and my family, and I discovered resources that will lead to answers and future questions. And, because I am sharing this story with you, I hope you will incorporate it in *your* story.

## (UN)FINISHED

As I review my performances, I am unsettled, yet excited, that there is so much more to reflect on, analyze, and share. *There are many more stories to tell.* But first, I would like to take a moment to step away from this project. *A moment for me. A moment to grieve. A moment to smile.* Then, I plan to write more autoethnography. Further stories, reflections, and studies will be developed as I implement this curriculum and these queer curriculum development practices; new (hi) stories will be told as I—we—(re)perform it and (re)develop it; new topics will be added; new perspectives will be utilized; and new identities will be explored. Indeed, as I continue to become a queer educator, I will continue to work on ways to represent this curriculum—to queerly convey and extend the critical imagination as evidenced through my performances to the very foundations of what constitutes curriculum and education (Dewey, 1934).

Moreover, my performances for this project deserve to be nurtured. I plan to revisit each of them and offer more of my time and engagement. Surely, I will (re)perform some of the explorations through different perspectives and modes. And some of my performances will be revised as future projects, presentations, and publications—as they serve as methods of inquiry (Richardson, 2011). For example, I am drawn to revisit *Exploration 5: Religion and mortality,* as I am still grieving my loss. I would like to engage in a project that allows me to stay in touch with my mom; and I foresee this future performance as being therapeutic (Bochner & Ellis, 2016; Ellis, 2004; Richardson, 2011).

## LEARNING THROUGH LIFE

I am a life-longer learner on a quest for self-understanding: "The kind of self-understanding [...] that comes from understanding our personal lives, identities, and feelings as deeply connected to and in large part constituted by—and in turn helping to constitute—the sociocultural contexts in which we live" (Anderson, 2006, p. 390). Indeed, learning and living are not two separate actions (Dewey, 1916, 1938). They are intertwined. *All life experiences are curricula.*

The lucid awareness of being a teacher ~ ~ learner that I experienced during this project was surreal. Along with this realization, I am also beginning to understand and navigate a learning ~ ~ living approach to being. This notion is not new to me, but I consciously experienced the learning ~ ~ living fluidity throughout this project. The autoethnographic methods I chose emboldened reflexivity and allowed a natural (e)mergence between my research and my life. Indeed, by recognizing that I cannot separate my professional self (academic) from my other selves (partner, daughter, photographer, genderqueer-woman), I allowed myself to be (re)present(ed) throughout the curriculum development process and within the curriculum (Whitlock, 2010). Again, these ideas about my intersectional selves are not new to me; however, the notion of self (re)present(ation) within curriculum is a new practice for me—one, I have found, that is essential in queer multicultural social justice education and queer curriculum development. And, one that I hope you will explore and nurture as you develop curriculum. *Allow yourself to be present and represented.*

In a postscript to my Exploration 5 reflection, I openly confessed that "these explorations are topics I want to personally explore." Indeed, "some of the explorations include and address questions I have asked myself [before]." I go on to admit that "if it wasn't for this project . . ., I probably would not have performed and reflected on these investigations. [...] Some of them are difficult and others are critically challenging." This admission exudes vulnerability—an attribute we tend not to reveal, model, or discuss in our work (Bochner & Ellis, 2016; Ngunjiri, Hernandez, & Chang, 2010; Rosenberg, 2016). But these confessions and vulnerabilities are imperative to share. As Tisdell and Tolliver (2009) contend:

> going beyond what is expected and generally accepted as the norm for content and presentation in the conventional classroom can often open the learning space for the voices and participation of those who have been underrepresented in the academy. (p. 98)

So, by telling my story and by being open, and at times showing vulnerabilities, I am using my voice as a queer educator. Further, Grace (2006) recognizes that such writing "helps [him], and hopefully those who read [his] work, to come face-to-face with the intricacies of attempting to make meaning and sense of a queer life in educational and other structured sociocultural spaces" (p. 828). "Stories are our *way in* to understanding—to theorizing, and thus to knowing and working to change—our cultures and ourselves" (Holman Jones, 2016, p. 230, emphasis original). *My final confession: Throughout the process, I questioned my intentions as a queer educator, my practices as a queer curriculum worker, and my overall queerness. What kind of queer educator was I becoming?*

Finally, these queer curriculum development methods and explorations encourage explorers—*you*—to reflect on everyday experiences, inquiries, and practices (i.e., life) through autoethnographic means, thus providing a "possibility to transform everyday experience into insights with cultural, social, and educational significance" (Phillion, He, & Connelly, 2005, p. 1). As a queer educator, I am passionate, and excited, to move "beyond accepted boundaries" (hooks, 1994, p. 7), to step outside classrooms, and to extend learning to include "everyday experiences." Indeed, hooks (1994) proclaims that "there must be an ongoing recognition that everyone influences the classroom [or learning] dynamic, that everyone contributed. *These contributions are resources.* Used constructively they enhance the capacity of any class [or learning space] to create an open learning community." And "before this process can begin there has to be some deconstruction of the traditional notion that only the professor is responsible for classroom [or learning] dynamics" (p. 8, emphasis added). Indeed, I encourage you to "step outside classrooms" and realize that learning takes place everywhere. *We have much to learn from one another.*

## MORE MICHELLENESS

As I stated in my introduction, my Michelleness is not limited to, or confined by, the multicultural identities (e.g., socioeconomic status, religion, gender, sexual orientation, race/ethnicity, and exceptionality) explored in this project. We are more complex than these six rudimentary identity categories. And though the central focus was on these six categories, the explorations beg for explorers to intersect their other selves. Indeed, as Sedgwick (1990) points out, these categories,

> with the associated demonstrations of the mechanisms by which they are constructed and reproduced, are indispensable, and they may indeed override all or some other forms of difference and similarity. But the sister or brother, the best friend, the classmate, the parent, the child, the lover, the ex-: our families, loves, and enmities alike, not to mention the strange relations of our work, play, and activism, prove that even people who share all or most of our own positionings along these crude axes may still be different enough from us, and from each other, to seem like all but different species. (p. 22)

The intersectionality of our identities cannot be overlooked when performing these explorations. From the reason you chose to engage with these explorations (e.g., as a student, adult educator) to the perspective you chose when performing them (e.g., parent, artist), and the methods of performance and presentation (e.g., photography, story)—many of your "selves" are working together to achieve these goals.

Indeed, due to the normative restraints I knowingly placed upon myself, I struggled to realize, and necessarily had to omit or closet, many of my identities throughout this project. For example, exploring the intersectionality between being an educator and a heavily tattooed genderqueer-woman would make for a colorful story. And as much as I would have liked to stray from the (hetero)norm, this project was not the place for me to reflect on these queer(er) stories—they did not completely fit into the narrative I wanted to tell. However, I am certain that many queer projects will branch from this work. *Stories that will be told through other queer autoethnographic projects.*

For example, an essay, inspired by my Exploration 6 performance, tentatively titled "Am I really a cis-genderqueer-woman?" will explore my revelations into identifying as a cis-gender person, along with the taboo of including biological sex as an identity. Another autoethnographic book project that has spun off from this one, tentatively titled *Student/teacher, Lost/found, Story/curriculum*, explores my journey through my formal education experiences, beginning with my years attending Catholic school and ending with earning my doctorate degree. Truth be told, I am in awe of the queer possibilities that await. *I am also eager to hear your stories.*

Indeed, the explorations performed for this project, along with the project itself, are unfinished products. They are merely beginnings. They generate questions to be pondered. They are adventures in knowing oneself (and others). These performances are drafts of future curriculum, projects, and publications. They empower me to seek and discover, to question, and to embark on new adventures. They may also encourage others to do the same. To humbly borrow the insightful words of Shafak (2007): "Every book is a journey, a map into the complexities of the human mind and soul. This one is no different. Every reader therefore is a traveler of a sort" (p. xii). May this book serve as a scratched treasure map to knowing oneself. *I have more stories to tell—and so do you.*

## (UN)SATISFIED

Ladson-Billings (2014) warns: Sometimes our work has "no definitive or prescriptive solutions, and, for some, that will be deeply unsatisfying. However, those who do this work understand that not knowing is one of the most powerful tools and motivators for doing more and doing it better" (p. 82). There are, indeed, so many more aspects of this research I want to discuss, analyze, and change. And after spending such an extended amount of time on it, it is difficult, yet satisfying, to bring it to a close. However, as I stated throughout—this is just the beginning. Throughout the book, I have left breadcrumbs on topics and additional explorations in which I would like to engage. And I have highlighted your responsibility as the reader of this work. Indeed, it is not crucial, or even beneficial to you or to me, that I reiterate or discuss my future research plans or ideas—though I introduced some ideas here. That is not how I want to leave you. I want to leave you with the gift of not knowing. *Go out and explore!*

. . .

## WHO THE FUCK CARES?

Recently, I shared this book with some colleagues in a space where we were able to engage in a critical, open conversation. It was a safe space where we could be vulnerable and supportive of one another—and candid when needed. Indeed, near the close of our conversation, one of them frankly posed the question: *Who the fuck cares?* Academics (e.g., writers, presenters, and performers) are often asked, or we self-reflect upon, this brutal question. It is one we must consider when formulating our work and putting it out into the world. *Why should educators (and others) care about this project?*

Initially and momentarily, I was taken aback by the question (though I had posed it to myself countless times throughout the writing process). I had just written hundreds of heartfelt pages, including what I thought was a solid foundation and reasoning for why this work matters. Indeed, not only does the scholarship support it, it calls for it. I managed to clumsily reiterate the importance of my work, and we closed the conversation. Now, as I am preparing to publish this book, I am reflecting upon my colleague's question once more. I knew I had to address at least a derivative of this blunt question within these pages. In short, my answer is: *Everyone should fucking care.*

You see, I want you (and others) to engage with the (hi)stories, and, hopefully, start sharing your own stories. As you progressed through this book, I hope you began to understand my (and began to form your own) queer multicultural social justice education philosophy. In sum, mine is *activating awareness*. As I reflect on in Chapter Four, we do this by actively and critically exploring, understanding, and articulating how we identify; by being aware of the language and teaching practices we use; by creating lessons that are queer and inclusive; by queering safe learning spaces and school policies; by engaging and promoting queer critical dialogue and reflection; by queering teaching by continuously learning; by checking our privilege and our assumptions of others; and by including students, caretakers, and other stakeholders in queer curriculum development processes. This work *shows* you how I performed these tasks. It also serves as a guide for you to perform and explore them.

But like a pesky six-year old we continue to ask: *Why?* Why is this important? It is important for the same reasons that multicultural education was first developed (see, Chapter One). We continue to observe xenophobic, homophobic, transphobic, and racist actions, behaviors, and ideologies within our society. Indeed, our cultural and political climates are explosive. It is important because queering our teaching practices, including our curriculum development, may bring about the awareness necessary for change. Maybe by engaging with the theories and frameworks presented here (see, Chapter Two), and by practicing queer multicultural social justice curriculum development strategies, we can nurture our understanding, empathy, and support for others. And finally, it is important because telling our stories and listening to each other's stories are ways of knowing ourselves and others (see, Chapter Three). By engaging with each other, learning from each other, and respecting each other, we may become aware of and confront our personal shortcomings (see, Chapter Four). *We should all want to become more (multi)culturally aware of ourselves and others in order to advance our understanding of social justice and to make our world a safer, happier place to live. We should all fucking care.*

# REFERENCES

Adams, T. E. (2011). *Narrating the closet: An autoethnography of same-sex attraction.* Routledge.

Adams, T. E., & Holman Jones, S. (2008). Autoethnography is queer. In N. K. Denzin, Y. S. Lincoln, & L. T. Smith (Eds.), *Handbook of critical and indigenous methodologies* (pp. 373–390). Sage.

Anderson, L. (2006). Analytic autoethnography. *Journal of Contemporary Ethnography, 35*(4), 373–395.

Apple, M. W., & Weis, L. (Eds.). (1983). *Ideology & Practice in schooling.* Temple University Press.

Aronson, J., & Steele, C. M. (2005). Stereotypes and the fragility of academic competence, motivation, and self-concept. In A. J. Elliot & C. S. Dweck (Eds.), *Handbook of competence and motivation* (pp. 436–456). Guilford Press.

Ayers, W. C. (2006). Trudge toward freedom: Educational research in the public interest. In G. Ladson-Billings. & W. F. Tate (Eds.), *Education research in the public interest: Social justice, action, and policy* (pp. 81–97). Teachers College Press.

Baker, G. C. (1973, December). Multicultural Training for Student Teachers. *Journal of Teacher Education, 24,* 306–307.

Baker, G. C. (1994). *Planning and organizing for multicultural instruction.* (2nd ed.). Addison-Wesley.

Banks, J. A. (1988). Approaches to multicultural curriculum reform. *Multicultural Leader 1*(2), 1–3.

*Queer Multicultural Social Justice Education: Curriculum (and Identity) Development Through Performance,* pages 161–170.

Banks, J. A. (1993). The canon debate, knowledge construction, and multicultural education. *Educational Researcher, 22*(5), 4–14.

Banks, J. A. (1994). *Multiethnic education: Theory and practice* (3rd ed.). Allyn & Bacon.

Banks, J. A. (Ed.). (1996). *Multicultural education, transformative knowledge, and action: Historical and contemporary perspectives* (Multicultural education series). Teachers College Press.

Banks, J. A. (1999). Chapter 5: Multicultural citizenship education. In B. D. Day (Ed.), *Teaching & Learning in the New Millennium* (pp. 54–61). Kappa Delta Pi.

Banks, J. A. (2004). Multicultural education: Historical development, dimensions, and practice. In J. A. Banks & C. A. McGee Banks (Eds.), *Handbook of research on multicultural education* (pp. 3–29). Jossey-Bass.

Banks, J. A. (2006a). *Cultural diversity and education: Foundation, curriculum, and teaching* (5th ed.). Allyn and Bacon.

Banks, J. A. (2006b). *Race, culture, and education: The selected works of James A. Banks*. Routledge.

Banks, J. A. (2010). Series forward. In G. Gay, *Culturally responsive teaching: Theory, research and practice* (2nd ed., pp. ix–xiii). Teachers College Press.

Banks, J. A. (2013). Chapter 1: Multicultural education: Characteristics and goals. In J. A. Banks & C. A. McGee Banks (Eds.), *Multicultural education: Issues and perspectives* (8th ed., pp. 3–22). Wiley.

Banks, J. A. (2016). Chapter 1: Multicultural education: Characteristics and goals. In J. A. Banks & C. A. McGee Banks (Eds.), *Multicultural education: Issues and perspectives* (9th ed., pp. 2–23). Wiley.

Banks, J. A., & McGee Banks, C. A. (Eds.). (2013). *Multicultural Education: Issues and Perspectives* (8th ed.). Wiley.

Banks, J. A., & McGee Banks, C. A. (Eds.). (2016). *Multicultural Education: Issues and Perspectives* (9th ed.). Wiley.

Berlak, A., & Moyenda, S. (2001). *Taking it personally: Racism in the classroom from kindergarten to college*. Temple University Press.

Bickmore, K. (1999). Why discuss sexuality in elementary school? In W. J. Letts & J. T. Sears (Eds.), *Queering elementary education: Advancing the dialogue about sexualities and schooling* (pp. 15–25). Rowman & Littlefield.

Bochner, A. (2001). Narrative's virtues. *Qualitative Inquiry, 7*, 131–157.

Bochner, A. P., & Ellis, C. (2016). *Evocative autoethnography: Writing lives and telling stories*. Routledge.

Bornstein, K. (1994). *Gender outlaw: On men, women, and the rest of us*. Vintage.

Boylorn, R. M., & Orbe, M. P. (2014). Introduction: Critical autoethnography as method of choice. In R. M. Boylorn & M. P. Orbe (Eds.), *Critical autoethnography: Intersecting cultural identities in everyday life* (pp. 13–32). Left Coast Press.

Britzman, D. (1995). Is there a queer pedagogy? Or, stop reading straight. *Educational Theory, 45*(2), 151–165.

Bronner, S. E. (2011). *Critical theory: A very short introduction*. Oxford University Press.

Burke Johnson, R., & Christensen, L. B. (2014). *Educational research: Quantitative, qualitative, and mixed approaches* (5th ed.). Sage.

Butler, J. (1990/2006). *Gender trouble: Feminism and the subversion of identity*. Routledge.

Butler, J. (1993). *Bodies that matter: On the discursive limits of "sex."* Routledge.

Butler, J. (2004). *Undoing gender*. Routledge.

Butler, J. (2005). *Giving an account of oneself*. Fordham University Press.

Carrera, M., DePalma, R., & Lameiras, M. (2012). Sex/gender identity: Moving beyond fixed and 'natural' categories. *Sexualities, 15*(8), 995–1016.

Carter, K. (1993). The place of story in the study of teaching and teacher education. *Educational Researcher, 22*(1), 5–12, 18.

Cary, L. J. (2006). *Curriculum spaces: Discourses, postmodern theory and educational research*. Peter Lang.

Chan, M. (2015). My story of self-identity. In K. Jennings (Ed.), *One teacher in ten in the new millennium: LGBT educators speak out about what's gotten better . . . and what hasn't* (pp. 118–120). Beacon Press.

Chang, H. (2008). *Autoethnography as method*. Left Coast Press.

Chase, S. (2011). Narrative inquiry: Still a filed in the making. In N. K. Denzin & Y. S. Lincoln (Eds.), *The SAGE handbook of qualitative research* (pp. 421–434). Sage.

Combahee River Collective. (1982). A Black feminist statement. In B. Smith, P. B. Scott, & G. T. Hul (Eds.), *All the women are White, all the men are Black, but some of us are brave: Black women's studies* (pp. 13–22). Feminist Press.

Comber, B. (2001). Critical literacies and local action: Teacher knowledge and a "new" research agenda. In B. Comber & A. Simpson (Eds.), *Negotiating critical literacies in classrooms* (pp. 301–314). Lawrence Erlbaum.

Conerly, G. (2000). "Are you black first or are you queer?" In D. Simms (Ed.), *The greatest taboo: Homosexuality in black communities* (pp. 7–23). Alyson Books.

Conle, C. (1996). Resonance in preservice teacher inquiry. *American Educational Research Journal, 33*(2), 297–325.

DePalma, R., & Atkinson, E. (2006). The sound of silence: Talking about sexual orientation and schooling. *Sex Education, 6*(4), 333–349.

de Lauretis, T. (1991). Queer theory: Lesbian and gay sexualities: An introduction. *differences, 3*(2), iii–xviii.

Derman-Sparks, L. (2004). Culturally relevant anti-bias education with young children. In W. G. Stephan & W. P. Vogt (Eds.), *Education programs for improving intergroup relations: Theory, research, and practice* (pp. 19–36). Teacher College Press.

Derrida, J., & Spivak, G. C. (2016). *Of grammatology*. John Hopkins University.

Dewey, J. (1916). *Democracy and education: An introduction to the philosophy of education*. The Free Press.

Dewey, J. (1934). *Art as experience*. Penguin Group.

Dewey, J. (1938). *Experience & education*. Simon & Schuster.

Ellis, C. (2004). *The ethnographic I: A methodological novel about autoethnography*. AltaMira Press.

Ellis, C, Adams. T. E., & Bochner, A. P. (2010). Autoethnography: An overview [40 paragraphs]. *Forum Qualitative Sozialforschung/Forum: Qualitative Social Research, 12*(10), Art. 10. http://nbn-resolving.de/urn:nbn:de:0114-fqs1101108.

Fausto-Sterling, A. (2000). *Sexing the body: Gender politics and the construction of sexuality*. Basic Books.

Ferfolja, T., & Robinson, K. H. (2004). Why anti-homophobia education in teacher education? Perspectives from Australian teacher educators. *Teacher Education, 15*(1), 9–27.

Feuerverger, G. (2005). Multicultural perspectives in teacher development. In J. Phillion, M. F. He, & F. M. Connelly (Eds.), *Narrative & experience in multicultural education* (pp. 175–199). Sage.

Fifield, S., & Letts, W. (2014). [Re]considering queer theories in science education. *Cultural Studies of Science Education, 9*, 393–407.

Flemons, D., & Green, S. (2002) Stories that conform/stories that transform: A conversation in four parts. In A. P. Bochner & C. Ellis (Eds.), *Ethnographically speaking: Autoethnography, literature, and aesthetics* (pp. 165–169). AltaMira Press.

Freire, P. (1970). *Pedagogy of the oppressed.* Seabury Press.

Fuss, D. (Ed.). (1991). *Inside/out: Lesbian theories, gay theories.* Routledge.

Gay, G. (1983). Multiethnic education: historical developments and future prospects. *Phi Delta Kappa International, 64*, 560–563.

Gay, G. (2002). Preparing for culturally responsive teaching. *Journal of Teacher Education, 53*(2), 106–116.

Gay, G. (2004). Curriculum, theory and multicultural education. In J. A. Banks & C. A. McGee Banks (Eds.), *Handbook of research on multicultural education* (pp. 30–49). Jossey-Bass.

Gay, G. (2010). *Culturally responsive teaching: Theory, research and practice* (2nd ed.). Teachers College Press.

Gergen, M. M., & Gergen, J. G. (2002). Ethnographic representation as relationship. In Bochner, A. P. & Ellis, C. (Eds.), *Ethnographically speaking: Autoethnography, literature, and aesthetics* (pp. 11–33). AltaMira Press.

Giffney, N. (2009) Introduction: The 'q' word. In N. Giffney & M. O'Rourke (Eds.), *The Ashgate research companion to queer theory* (pp. 1–12). Ashgate Publishing.

Gilbert, S. E. (2015). There is uncertainty, but there is also hope. In K. Jennings (Ed.), *One teacher in ten in the new millennium: LGBT educators speak out about what's gotten better . . . and what hasn't* (pp. 150–155). Beacon Press.

Gillborn, D. (2008). Developing antiracist school policy. In M. Pollock (Ed.), *Everyday antiracism: Getting real about race in school* (pp. 246–251). Basic Books.

Gollnick, D. M., & Chinn, P. C. (2004). *Multicultural education in a pluralistic society* (6th ed.). Pearson.

Grace, A. P. (2006). Writing the queer self: Using autobiography to mediate inclusive teacher education in Canada. *Teaching and Teaching Education, 22*, 826–834.

Grant, C. A. (2012). Cultivating flourishing lives: A robust social justice vision of education. *American Educational Research Journal, 49*(5), 910–934.

Grant, C. A., Elsbree, A. R., & Fondrie, S. (2004). A decade of research on the changing terrain of multicultural education research. In J. A. Banks & C. A. McGee Banks (Eds.), *Handbook of research on multicultural education* (pp. 184–207). Jossey-Bass.

Grant, C. A., & Sleeter, C. E. (1985). The literature on multicultural education: Review and analysis. *Educational Review, 37*(2), 97–118. https://doi.org/10.1080/0013191850370202

Grant, C. A., & Sleeter, C. E. (2011a). *Doing multicultural education for achievement and equity* (2nd ed.). Taylor & Francis.

Grant, C. A., & Sleeter, C. E. (2011b). Your world: The identity and culture you bring. In C. A. Grant & C. E. Sleeter (Eds.), *Doing multicultural education for achievement and equity* (pp. 10–17). Taylor & Francis.

Grant, C. A., & Sleeter, C. E. (2013). Chapter 3: Race, class, gender, and disability in the classroom. In J. A. Banks & C. A. McGee Banks (Eds.), *Multicultural education: Issues and perspectives* (8th ed., pp. 43–60). Wiley.

Halberstam, J. (1997). Who's afraid of queer theory? In A. Kumar (Ed.), *Class issues: Pedagogy, cultural studies, and the public sphere* (pp. 256–275). New York University Press.

Halberstam, J. (2011). *The queer art of failure.* Duke University Press.

Halperin, D. (2003). The normalization of queer theory. *Journal of Homosexuality, 45*(2–4), 339–343.

He, M. F., & Phillion, J. (2008). Personal~passionate~participatory inquiry. In M. F. He & J. Phillion (Eds.), *Personal~passionate~participatory inquiry into social justice in education* (pp. 1–21). Information Age Publishing.

Holman Jones, S. (2005). Autoethnography: Making the personal political. In N. K. Denzin & Y. S. Lincoln (Eds.), *Handbook of qualitative research* (pp. 763–791). Sage.

Holman Jones, S. (2016). Living bodies of thought: The "critical" in critical autoethnography. *Qualitative Inquiry, 22*(4), 228–237.

hooks, b. (1994). *Teaching to transgress: Education as the practice of freedom.* Routledge.

Howard, G. R. (2006). *We can't teach what we don't know: White teachers, multiracial schools* (2nd ed.). Teachers College Press.

Iannotti, R. (2006). *Health behavior in school-aged children, 2005–2006* [Dataset and codebook]. http://www.icpsr.umich.edu/icpsrweb/ICPSR/studies/28241

Jagose, A. (1996). *Queer theory: An introduction.* New York University Press.

Johnson, D. E., & Lugg, C. A. (2011). Queer theories in education. In S. Tozer, B. Gallegos, & A. Henry (Eds.), *Handbook of social foundations in education* (pp. 233–243). Routledge.

Killermann, S. (2013). *The social justice advocate's handbook: A guide to gender.* Impetus Books.

Kincheloe, J. L., & McLaren, P. (2000). Rethinking critical theory and qualitative research. In N. K. Denzin & Y. S. Lincoln (Eds.), *The handbook of qualitative research* (2nd ed., pp. 279–314). Sage.

King, A. (1993). From sage on the stage to guide on the side. *College Teaching, 41*(1), 30–35. https://doi.org/10.1080/87567555.1993.9926781.

Kissen, R. M. (Ed.). (2002). *Getting ready for Benjamin: Preparing teachers for sexual diversity in the classroom.* Rowman & Littlefield.

Knaier, M. L. (2003, February). *A place where they can be themselves: Issues of gay, lesbian, and bisexual students.* Paper presented at Within Our Grasp: Building Community through Diversity, SUNY Brockport, Brockport, NY.

Knaier, M. L. . (2013, May). *Victims of cyber cullying: A statistical analysis.* Paper presented at Academics IRL: Taking Scholarship Out of the Ivory Tower, Purdue University, West Lafayette, IN.

Knaier, M. L. (2017). A place where they can be themselves: Issues of LGBTQ students [Revisited]. In E. A. Mikulec & P. C. Miller (Eds.), *Queering classrooms: Personal narratives and educational practices to support LGBTQ youth in schools* (pp. 11–25). Information Age.

Knaier, M. L. (2019a, April). *Queer(ing) critical autoethnography: A method for queer multicultural education curriculum development.* Paper presented at the American Educational Research Association Conference, Toronto, Canada.

Knaier, M. L. (2019b). What makes *girls* and *boys* so desirable?: STEM education beyond gender binaries. In W. Letts & S. Fifield (Eds.), *STEM of desire: Queer theories in science education* (pp. 209–221). Koninklijke Brill.

Knaier, M. L. (2020). Our stories *as* curriculum: In S. L. Raye, S. Masta, S. Taylor Cook, & J. Burdick (Eds.) *Ideating pedagogy in troubled times: Approaches to identity, theory, teaching, and research* (pp. 141–156). Information Age Press.

Kosciw, J. G., Greytak, E. A., Zongrone, A. D., Clark, C. M., & Truong, N. L. (2018). The 2017 *National School Climate Survey: The experiences of lesbian, gay, bisexual, transgender, and queer youth in our nation's schools.* GLSEN.

Kozol, J. (1975). Great men and women (tailored for school use). *Learning Magazine, 4*(4), 16–20.

Kozol, J. (1991). *Savage inequalities: Children in America's schools.* Crown

Ladson-Billings, G. (1995, Autumn). Toward a theory of culturally relevant pedagogy. *American Educational Research Journal, 32*(3), 465–491. http://www.jstor.org/stable/1163320

Ladson-Billings, G. (2004). New directions in multicultural education: Complexities, boundaries, and critical race theory. In J. A. Banks & C. A. McGee Banks (Eds.), *Handbook of research on multicultural education* (pp. 50–65). Jossey-Bass.

Ladson-Billings, G. (2014). Culturally relevant pedagogy 2.0: a.k.a. the remix. *Harvard Educational Review, 84*(1), 74–84.

Lekus, I. (2014). Queers of hope, gays of rage. In L. J. Rupp & S. K. Freeman (Eds.), *U.S. lesbian, gay, bisexual, and transgender history* (pp. 224–237). University of Wisconsin Press.

Letts, W. (2002). Revisioning multiculturalism in Teacher education: Isn't it queer? In R. M. Kissen (Ed.), *Getting ready for Benjamin: Preparing teachers for sexual diversity in the classroom* (pp. 119–131). Rowman & Littlefield.

Letts, W., & Fifield, S. (2000). *Sexualities, silence, and science teacher education.* In annual meeting of the American Educational Research Association, New Orleans, LA.

Letts, W. J., & Sears, J. T. (Eds.). (1999). *Queering elementary education: Advancing the dialogue about sexualities and schooling.* Rowman & Littlefield.

Lipkin, A. (2002). The challenges of gay topics in teacher education: Politics, content, and pedagogy. In R. M. Kissen (Ed.), *Getting ready for Benjamin: Preparing teachers for sexual diversity in the classroom* (pp. 13–27). Rowman & Littlefield.

Lorde, A. (1984). *Sister/outsider: Essays and speeches.* Crossing.

Lorde, A. (1988). *A burst of light: Essays by Audre Lorde.* Fireband.

Loutzenheiser, L. W. (2001). "If I teach about these issues they will burn down my house": The possibilities and tensions of queered, antiracist pedagogy. In K. K. Kumashiro (Ed.), *Troubling intersections by race and sexuality: Queer students of color and anti-oppressive education* (pp. 195–214). Rowman & Littlefield.

Luhmann, S. (1998). Queering/querying pedagogy? Or, pedagogy is a pretty queer thing. In W. F. Pinar (Ed.), *Queer theory in education* (pp. 141–155). Routledge.

Luttrell, W. (2008). Responding to the "N-word." In M. Pollock (Ed.), *Everyday antiracism: Getting real about race in school* (pp. 274–278). Basic Books.

Madison, D. S., & Hamera, J. (2006). *Handbook of performance studies.* Sage.

Marcuse, H. (1965). Repressive tolerance (p. 82).In *Berkeley Commune.*

Marcuse, H. (1991a). Philosophy and critical theory. In D. Ingram & J. Simon-Ingram (Eds.), *Critical theory: The essential readings* (pp. 5–19). Paragon House.

Marcuse, H. (1991b). On hedonism. In D. Ingram & J. Simon-Ingram (Eds.), *Critical theory: The essential readings* (pp. 151–175). Paragon House.

Martino, W., & Pallotta-Chiarolli, M. (2003). *So what's a boy?: Addressing issues of masculinity and schooling*. Open University Press.

Mayo, C. (2007, March). Queering foundations: Queer and lesbian, gay, bisexual, and transgender educational research. *Review of Research in Education, 31*, 78–94.

Mayo, C. (2014). *LGBTQ youth & education: Policies & practices*. Teachers College.

Mayo, C. (2016). Chapter 8: Queer lessons: Sexual and gender minorities in multicultural education. In J. A. Banks & C. A. McGee Banks (Eds.), *Multicultural education: Issues and perspectives* (9th ed., pp. 132–148). John Wiley & Sons.

McGarry, M. (1998). *Becoming visible: An illustrated history of lesbian and gay life in twentieth-century America*. Penguin Studio.

McLaren, P. (1994). Chapter 1: White terror and oppositional Agency: Towards a critical multiculturalism. In D. T. Goldberg (Ed.), *Multiculturalism: A critical reader* (pp. 45–74). Blackwell Publishers.

Meyer, E. J. (2007). "But I'm not gay": What straight teachers need to know about queer theory. In N. Rodriguez & W. F. Pinar, W. (Eds.). *Queering straight teachers: Discourse and identity in education* (pp. 15–32). Peter Lang.

Mezirow, J. (2009). *Transformative learning in practice: Insights from community, workplace, and higher education*. Jossey-Bass.

Mikulec, E. A., & Miller, P. C. (Eds.). (2017). *Queering classrooms: Personal narratives and educational practices to support LGBTQ youth in schools*. Information Age.

Miller, sj., & Rodriguez, N. M. (Eds.). (2016). *Educators queering academia: Critical memoirs*. Peter Lang.

Mizzi, R., & Stebbins, A. (2010). Walking a thin line: White, queer (auto)ethnographic entanglements in educational research. *New Horizons in Adult Education & Human Resource Development, 24*(2–4), 19–29.

Mulhern, M., & Martinez, G. (1999). Confronting homophobia in a multicultural education course. In W. J. Letts & J. T. Sears (Eds.), *Queering elementary education: Advancing the dialogue about sexualities and schooling* (pp. 247–256). Rowman & Littlefield.

Murray, O. J. (2015). *Queer inclusion in teacher education: Bridging theory, research, and practice*. Routledge.

Nelson, P. R. (1984). *I would die 4 U*. On Purple Rain (Album). Warner Bros.

Newton, H. (1973). A letter from Huey. In L. Richmond & G. Noguera (Eds.), *The gay liberation book: Writings and photographs on gay (men's) liberation* (pp. 142–145). Ramparts.

Nieto, S. (2003). *What keeps teachers going?* Teachers College.

Nieto, S. (2010). *The light in their eyes: Creating multicultural learning communities*. Teachers College.

Nieto, S. (2012). Chapter 2: Defining multicultural education for school reform. In S. Nieto & P. Bode (Eds.), *Affirming diversity: The sociopolitical context of multicultural education* (6th ed., pp. 40–59). Pearson.

Nieto, S., & Bode, P. (2012). *Affirming diversity: The sociopolitical context of multicultural education* (6th ed.). Pearson.

Nieto, S., & Bode, P. (2013). Chapter 16: School reform and student learning: A multicultural perspective. In J. A. Banks & C.A. McGee Banks (Eds.), *Multicultural education: Issues and perspectives* (8th ed.) (pp. 313–328). Wiley.

Nieto, S., & Bode, P. (2016). Chapter 14: School reform and student learning: A multicultural perspective. In J. A. Banks & C. A. McGee Banks (Eds.), *Multicultural education: Issues and perspectives* (9th ed., pp. 258–274). John Wiley & Sons.

Ngunjiri, F. W., Hernandez, K. C., & Chang, H. (2010). Living autoethnography: Connecting life and research [Editorial]. *Journal of Research Practice, 6*(1), Article E1. http://jrp.icaap.org/index.php/jrp/article/view/241/186

Nussbaum, M. (1997). *Cultivating humanity: A classical defense of reform in liberal education.* Harvard University Press.

Oliva, P. F., & Gordon, W. R. (2013). *Developing the curriculum* (8th ed.). Pearson Education.

Paris, D. (2012). Culturally sustaining pedagogy: A needed change in stance, terminology, and practice. *Educational Researcher, 41*(3), 93–97.

Paris, D., & Alim, H. S. (2014). What are we seeking to sustain through culturally sustaining pedagogy? A loving critique forward. *Harvard Educational Review, 84*(1), 85–100.

Petrow, S., & Chew, S. (2011). *Steven's Petrow's complete gay & lesbian manners: The definitive guide to LGBT life.* Workman Publishing.

Phillion, J. (2002). Becoming a narrative inquirer in a multicultural landscape. *Journal of Curriculum Studies, 34*(5), 535–556.

Phillion, J., & He, M. F. (2004). Using life-based literary narratives in multicultural teacher education. *Multicultural Perspectives, 6*(3), 3–9.

Phillion, J., He, M. F., & Connelly, F. M. (2005). The potential of narrative and experiential approaches in multicultural inquiries. In J. Phillion, M. F. He, & F. M. Connelly (Eds.). *Narrative & experience in multicultural education* (pp. 1–14). Sage.

Phillips, W. (1956, February 24). Negroes pledge to keep boycott. In *New York Times.*

Pillay, D., Naicker, I., & Pithouse-Morgan, K. (Eds.). (2016). *Academic autoethnographies: Inside teaching in higher education.* Sense.

Pillow, W. (2003). Confession, catharsis, or cure? Rethinking the uses of reflexivity as methodological power in qualitative research. *International Journal of Qualitative Studies in Education, 16*(2), 175–196.

Pinar, W. F. (1994a). The Method of "Currere" (1975). *Counterpoints, 2,* 19–27. http://www.jstor.org.ezproxy.lib.purdue.edu/stable/42975620

Pinar, W. F. (1994b). *Autobiography, politics and sexuality: Essays in curriculum theory 1972–1992.* Peter Lang.

Pinar, W. F. (Ed.). (1998). *Queer theory in education.* Lawrence Erlbaum Associates.

Pitt, A. (1995). *Subjects in tension. Engaged resistance in the feminist classroom.* (Unpublished doctoral dissertation.) Ontario institute for the Study of Education. University of Toronto.

Plummer, K. (2011). Critical Humanism and queer theory: Living with the Tensions. In N. K. Denzin & Y. S. Lincoln (Eds.), *The SAGE Handbook of Qualitative Research* (pp. 195–207). Sage.

Pollock, M. (2004). *Colormute: Race talk dilemmas in an American school.* Princeton University Press.

Pollock, M. (Ed.). (2008). *Everyday antiracism: Getting real about race in school*. Basic Books.

Pollard, D. S. (2013). Chapter 8: Understanding and Supporting gender equity in school. In J. A. Banks & C. A. McGee Banks (Eds.), *Multicultural Education: Issues and Perspectives* (8th ed., pp. 145–159). Wiley.

Richardson, L. (2011). Hospice 101. *Qualitative Inquiry, 17*(2), 158–165.

Rodriguez, N. M. (2007). Queer theory and the discourse on queer(ing) heterosexuality: Pedagogical considerations. In N. M. Rodriguez & W. F. Pinar (Eds.), *Queering straight teachers: Discourse and identity in* education (pp. 277–307). Peter Lang.

Rosenberg, T. (2016). Conversations and the cultivation of self-understanding. In D. Pillay, I Naicker, & K. Pithouse-Morgan (Eds.), *Academic autoethnographies: Inside teaching in higher education* (pp. 33–47). Sense.

Rupp, L. J., & Freeman, S. K. (Eds.). (2014). *U.S. lesbian, gay, bisexual, and transgender history*. University of Wisconsin Press.

Sears, J. (1992). Educators, homosexuality, and homosexual students: Are personal feelings related to professional beliefs? In K. Harbeck (Ed.), *Coming out of the classroom closet: Gay and lesbian students, teachers, and curriculum* (pp. 29–79). Haworth Press.

Sears, J. (1999). Teaching queerly: Some elementary propositions. In W. Letts & J. Sears (Eds.), *Queering elementary education: Advancing the dialogue about sexualities and schooling* (pp. 3–14). Rowman & Littlefield.

Sedgwick, E. K. (1990/2008). *Epistemology of the closet*. University of California Press.

Shade, B. J., Kelly, C., & Oberg, M. (1997). *Creating culturally responsive classrooms*. American Psychological Association.

Shafak, E. (2007). *Black Milk*. Penguin Group

Shelley, M. W., & Hindle, M. (2003). *Frankenstein, or, The modern Prometheus* (Rev. ed.). Penguin Books.

Sim, S., & Van Loon, B. (2004). *Introducing critical theory*. Icon Books.

Slattery, P. (2013). *Curriculum development in the postmodern era: Teaching and learning in an age of accountability* (3rd ed.). Routledge.

Sleeter, C. E. (1996). *Multicultural education as social activism*. State University of New York Press.

Snyder, V. L., & Broadway, F. S. (2004). Queering high school biology textbooks. *Journal of Research in Science Teaching, 41*(6), 617–636.

Spry, T. (2011). Performative autoethnography: Critical embodiments and possibilities. In N. K. Denzin & Y. S. Lincoln (Eds.). *The SAGE handbook of qualitative research* (pp. 497–511). Sage.

Stuber, S., Parent, M., & Wilson, O. (Producers), & Russo, A., & Russo, J. (Directors). (2006). *You, me, and Dupree* [Motion picture]. Universal Pictures.

Sullivan, N. (2003). *A critical introduction to queer theory*. University of Edinburgh Press.

Sumara, D., & Davis, B. (1999). Interrupting heteronormativity: Toward a queer curriculum theory. *Curriculum Inquiry, 29*(2), 191–208.

Taibbi, M. (June 2015). Why Baltimore blew up. *Rolling Stone*, 40–47.

Tremmel, R. V. (2014). Industrial capitalism and emergent sexual cultures. In L. J. Rupp & S. K. Freeman (Eds.), *U.S. lesbian, gay, bisexual, and transgender history* (pp. 153–165). University of Wisconsin Press.

Taylor, C. (2002). Beyond empathy: Confronting homophobia in critical education courses. *Journal of Lesbian Studies, 6*(3/4), 219–234.

Tisdell, E. J., & Tolliver, D. E. (2009). Transformative approaches to culturally responsive teaching: Engaging cultural imagination. In J. Mezirow & E. W. Taylor (Eds.). *Transformative learning in practice: Insights from community, workplace, and higher education* (pp. 89–99). Jossey-Bass.

Truth, S. (1851). *Ain't I a woman.* Feminist.com. http://www.feminist.com/resources/artspeech/genwom/sojour.htm

Turner, W. B. (2000). *A genealogy of queer theory.* Temple University Press.

Tyler, R. W. (1949). *Basic principles of curriculum and instruction.* University of Chicago Press.

U.S. Census Bureau. (2010). *U.S. Census Bureau.* http:www.census.gov

Vàsquez, B. (2015). Questions to self: Being a queer Latino educator. In K. Jennings (Ed.), *One teacher in ten in the new millennium: LGBT educators speak out about what's gotten better . . . and what hasn't* (pp. 156–160). Beacon Press.

Warner, M. (Ed.). (1993). *Fear of a queer plant: Queer politics and social theory.* University of Minnesota Press.

Whitlock, R. U. (2010). Getting queer: Teacher education, gender studies, and the cross-disciplinary quest for queer pedagogies. *Issues in Teacher Education, 19*(2), 81–104.

Wilchins, R. (2014). *Queer theory, gender theory: An instant primer.* Magnus Books.

Wilcox, M. (2018). *After life: Ways we think about death.* Orca Book Publishers.

Wittig, M. (1992). *The straight mind and other essays.* Beacon Press.

Wyatt, T J., Oswalt, S. B., White, C., & Peterson, F. L. (2008, Spring). Are tomorrow's teachers ready to deal with diverse students? Teacher candidates' attitudes toward gay men and lesbians. *Teacher Education Quarterly, 35*(2), 171–185.

Zacko-Smith, J., & Smith, G. P. (2010). Recognizing and utilizing queer pedagogy: A call for teacher education to reconsider the knowledge base on sexual orientation for teacher education programs. *Multicultural Education, 18*(1), 2–9.

Zinn, H. (2001). *A people's history of the United States: 1492–present.* HarperCollins.

APPENDIX

# CURRICULUM DRAFT

## Queer Explorations of Identity Awareness

### Michelle L. Knaier

*My Aim*

I want you to realize not only the importance of queer curricula, but the ease with which you may incorporate it into an already established curriculum and/or implement it on your own. I hope you find this curriculum unrestricted, flexible, and critical.

*The Explorers*

The explorations are aimed toward promoting social justice through identity awareness and exploration. The explorers, or performers of this curriculum, may include educators, self-directed learners, parents, community members, or anyone interested in exploring identity and identity awareness as a means of promoting social justice.

*Queer Multicultural Social Justice Education: Curriculum (and Identity) Development Through Performance,* pages 171–181.
Copyright © 2021 by Information Age Publishing
**171**

*Intended Outcomes*

Explorers will:

- Understand the importance of queer(ing) curriculum by recognizing certain hostile presumptions present in our heteronormative society (and within ourselves) and the harm they cause;
- Realize that identity awareness (of self and others) through storytelling is key to contributing to and promoting a more accepting and socially just multicultural society; and
- Develop a multicultural teaching philosophy that recognizes the importance of identity awareness (of self and others) through storytelling as curriculum.

## INTRODUCTION

### What is Queering?

*Queering*, or *to queer*, is to take action against the normative and heteronormative status quo. *Heteronormativity* dictates that being cisgender and heterosexual are the norm while it polices all other gender identities and sexual orientations. Thus, *queer curriculum* provokes critical questioning, critical reflection, and acting toward, the (de)construction of societal norms, identities, and ways of learning.

As a curriculum worker, I queer multicultural social justice teacher education in a way that encourages learners to consider, question, and analyze how gender and sexual orientation—along with other multicultural identities (e.g., socioeconomic status, religion, race/ethnicity, and exceptionality)—interact with, influence, and maintain social power and control. In these explorations, I do so through autoethnographic methods—including storytelling—that encourage you to explore your own identities (as a way of knowing others), to question assumptions about self and others, and to examine how your identities impact your teaching practices.

### What is Queer Multicultural Social Justice Teacher Education?

Queer multicultural social justice teacher education is a critical approach that provides opportunities for and encourages educators to examine and (de)construct identity and its espoused privileges—thus allowing explorers, in part, to investigate ways to dismantle heteronormativity, rethink binary systems of identification, and deconstruct socially constructed identities. To be clear, the practice of analyzing and (de)constructing our identities is a queer approach to learning.

### How May Identity Awareness (of Self and Others) Promote Queer Multicultural Social Justice?

Many multicultural education scholars agree that teachers must know who they are and who their students are—while understanding the changing nature and fluidity of identity—if they are going to be successful (Banks, 2006; Grant & Sleeter, 2011; Nieto & Bode, 2012).

*Queer Explorations of Identity Awareness* is a set of explorations that provide opportunities to develop identity awareness (of self and others) as a means of promoting social justice. These performances encourage critical reflection, storytelling with a purpose (e.g., examining, deconstructing, and eradicating potential hostile presumptions present in our heteronormative society and within ourselves), and practices of identity awareness with a goal of promoting a more accepting, socially just, and multicultural society.

It is my hope that through writing and sharing your stories, you will make personal connections with each other, giving you a stake in what you are learning and how you are learning by (1) exploring identity and identity awareness through autoethnographical methods, (2) connecting personal experiences with the curriculum, and (3) making personal experiences *curricula*.

## ELEMENTS OF THE EXPLORATIONS

**Learning outcomes:** Identity awareness can be achieved through methods like critical dialogue, critical reflection, critical thinking, and critical questioning (Nieto, 2003); therefore, you are encouraged to engage in these critical processes throughout this curriculum. Through these performative autoethnographic methods, you may realize how each exploration provokes identity awareness, and that identity is complicated, fluid, and ever changing. In the end, you should practice identity awareness and may ultimately appreciate that you may never fully know, understand, or define yourself (or others).

**Readings:** Each exploration consists of a reading list that may serve as a guide. These explorations may be paired with other multicultural texts, integrated with an already established curricula, or performed as a stand-alone set of inquiries.

**Prompt(s):** Each exploration consists of one or more prompts for discussions and reflections, along with identity awareness explorations that provoke critical dialogue, reflection, thinking, and questioning.

**Discussion:** Discussions (e.g., large group, small group, partnered, online, internal) may consist of clarifying and defining the prompts and explorations.

**Presentation(s):** Performances include but are not limited to traditional essays, comic strips, short stories, poems, photo essays, auto/photovoice, food essays, videos, drawings, paintings, or other methods through which you want to conduct and communicate your explorations. I encourage you to queer performances and presentations as these performative autoethnographic presentations are representations and reflections of you. Moreover, these presentations are not "finished" products. You need to understand that these explorations will always be works in progress.

**Sharing:** Performances and presentations must be shared with others. It is through these shared interactions that we get to know and learn from each other, where new knowledge is made, and when new perspectives are discovered. I encourage you to share your performances as presentations, written works, or artistic designs.

**Exploration Outline:** You may use this exploration outline as a guide in your explorations and to help narrow your focus. The format of the exploration outline may be queered as you see fit.

1. **Identity.** Describe your identity or identities. *How do I identify?*
2. **Initial questions.** Record any initial questions you plan to explore about your identity or identities. *What are my initial questions?*
3. **Preliminary resources/references.** Record any preliminary resources (e.g., family members, shared stories, recipes, photo collections) or references (e.g., articles, books, music) you intend to use or explore. *Where will I seek information?*
4. **Performance and presentation methods.** Record some method(s) for consideration. *How will I perform and present my exploration?*
5. **Additional questions.** Record any additional questions you asked as you performed the exploration. *What additional questions did I explore?*
6. **Further questions.** Record any questions you want explore in the future. *What are my further (future) questions?*
7. **All resources/references.** List all resources and references (e.g., formal, informal, academic) used during the exploration. *What resources did I use?*
8. **Sharing.** Share your performance with others. *How will I share this exploration?*

**Reaction/reflection responses:** You should critically respond to others' presentations (when applicable), reflect on the exploration and the readings, and address the reflection prompt(s) when offered. The goal here is to be aware of and reflect on your thoughts, vocabulary, feelings, and struggles.

## ADAPTATIONS & SUGGESTIONS

**Learning modalities:** I encourage you to use of a variety of discussion and presentation methods (which supports a broad range of learning methods). Further, elements of queer multicultural social justice education include being flexible and showing care for your needs.

**Adaptations:** This curriculum may be adapted to fit your needs and the resources available (e.g., technology, time).

**Word wall:** A word wall is an interactive teaching and learning tool consisting of a collection of relevant words which may be displayed on a wall, bulletin board, in a virtual space, or in a personal journal. I invite you to create your own word wall, but some possible words include:

| Assumptions | Ethnicity | Race |
|---|---|---|
| Autoethnography | Exceptionality | Reflection(s) |
| Awareness | Gender | Religion |
| Community | Ethnicity | Sexual orientation |
| Creativity | Identity/Identities | Social construct |
| Critical thinking | Identity awareness | Social justice |
| Curriculum | Multicultural education | Socioeconomic status |
| (De)Construct | Queer(ing) | Stories |

## EXPLORATION 1: WHY QUEER CURRICULUM?

**Exploration:** Share a time or times when you were affected by (e.g., a victim of, witnessed, and/or stood up to) hurtful, disrespectful, or violent normative or heteronormative behavior that occurred based on socioeconomic status, religion, gender, sexual orientation, race/ethnicity, and/or exceptionality in a school or learning atmosphere.

**Discussion:** Should include defining *heteronormativity*.

**Presentation:** Consider all options (e.g., a skit, essay, storytelling, graphic art, or comic strip).

**Reflection:** Critically respond to others' presentations (when applicable), reflect on the exploration and the readings, and address the following prompt: 1) How were you affected by telling your story? and, 2) How are you affected by others' stories?

### Readings

*Introduction* section to curriculum.

Chan, M. (2015). My story of self-identity. In K. Jennings (Ed.), *One teacher in ten in the new millennium: LGBT educators speak out about what's gotten better . . . and what hasn't* (pp. 118–120). Beacon Press.

Gilbert, S. E. (2015). There is uncertainty, but there is also hope. In K. Jennings (Ed.), *One teacher in ten in the new millennium: LGBT educators speak out about what's gotten better . . . and what hasn't* (pp. 150–155). Beacon Press.

Knaier, M. L. (2016). A place where they can be themselves: Issues of LGBTQ students [Revisited]. In E. A. Mikulec and P. C. Miller (Eds.), *Queering classrooms: Personal narratives and educational practices to support LGBTQ youth in schools* (pp. 11–25). Information Age.

Letts, W. (2002). Revisioning multiculturalism in Teacher education: Isn't it queer? In R. M. Kissen (Ed.), *Getting ready for Benjamin: Preparing teachers for sexual diversity in the classroom* (pp. 119–131). Rowman & Littlefield.

Vàsquez, B. (2015). Questions to self: Being a queer Latino educator. In K. Jennings (Ed.), *One teacher in ten in the new millennium: LGBT educators speak out about what's gotten better . . . and what hasn't* (pp. 156–160). Beacon Press.

## EXPLORATION 2: HOW DO YOU IDENTIFY?

**Exploration:** Reflect on your identity or identities for each of the multicultural identity categories (e.g., socioeconomic status, religion, gender, sexual orientation, race/ethnicity, and exceptionality). Then explore how each of these are represented in an aspect of your life (e.g., the books you read, the photographs you create, the movies you watch, the social media pages or groups you follow) and put together a presentation (e.g., a collection of quotes, portfolio, collage or word cloud) depicting these representations. (This exploration urges you to think about how you identify and provides a foundation for the following identity awareness explorations. But understand that through the course of these exercises your identities, and/or the language you use to describe yourself, may change.)

**Discussion:** Should include an overview of the multicultural identity categories.

**Presentation:** Consider all options (e.g., a collection of quotes, portfolio, collage or word cloud).

**Reflection:** Critically respond to others' presentations (when applicable), reflect on the exploration and the readings, and address the following prompts: 1) Explain the purpose of multicultural education; 2) Discuss the multicultural identities listed as they pertain to you; 3) What did you learn about yourself?; and, 4) Discuss any difficulties or complexities of choosing a label or labels.

*Readings*

Banks, J. A. (2016). Chapter 1: Multicultural education: Characteristics and goals. In J. A. Banks & C. A. McGee Banks (Eds.), *Multicultural education: Issues and perspectives* (9th ed., pp. 2–23). John Wiley & Sons.

Convertino, C., Levinson, B. A., & González, N. (2016). Chapter 2: Culture, Teaching, and learning. In J. A. Banks & C. A. McGee Banks (Eds.), *Multicultural education: Issues and perspectives* (9th ed., pp. 24–40). John Wiley & Sons.

Nieto, S. (2003). Chapter 2: Teaching as autobiography. In S. Nieto, *What keeps teachers going?* (pp. 22–36). Teachers College.

## EXPLORATION 3: INTERSECTIONALITY WITHIN ACTIVISM AND SUPPORT GROUPS

**Exploration:** Attend a protest, demonstration, march, sign making party, or support group (e.g., a protest related to "the wall," a march for LGBTQ rights, a March for Science, a trans* youth support group), as one who supports or protests—and/or identifies with—the cause or attend with a person who you want to support. Reflect on your experience.

**Discussion:** Should include defining *intersectionality*, determining appropriate events to attend, and understanding that this is not a "tourist" experience but an activist or supportive endeavor.

**Presentation:** Consider all options (e.g., a photo essay, video diary, blog post).

**Reflection:** Critically respond to others' presentations (when applicable), reflect on the exploration and the readings, and address the following prompts: 1) Describe your experience. What event did you attend? Why did you choose this event? Include details of the event and feelings you experienced during or after the event; and, 2) Reflect on other experiences when you had difficulty separating one or more of your identities from your other identities (maybe this occurred while performing Exploration 2). If you did not already address it in your Exploration 2 reflection, discuss any critical awareness or conflict due to intersectionality you experienced when performing Exploration 2 or when attending your chosen event.

*Readings*

Lorde, A. (1988). I am your sister: Black Women organizing across sexualities. In A. Lorde, *A burst of light: Essays by Audre Lorde* (pp. 19–26). Fireband.

Loutzenheiser, L. W. (2001). "If I teach about these issues they will burn down my house": The possibilities and tensions of queered, antiracist pedagogy. In K. K. Kumashiro (Ed.), *Troubling intersections by race and sexuality: Queer students of color and anti-oppressive education* (pp. 195–214). Rowman & Littlefield Publishers.

## EXPLORATION 4: SOCIOECONOMIC STATUS AND THE ARTS

**Exploration:** Explore your past and/or present socioeconomic status identity/ identities in relation to the arts (e.g., writing stories or poetry, drawing or painting, photographing or digital designing, playing a musical instrument or singing, acting or dancing). Explore and reflect on how your socioeconomic status, along with other (multi)cultural beliefs, customs, and/or practices (or other aspects of your life), may have influenced your artistic self. You may conduct this exploration in various ways (e.g., a story, photo essay, poem, video) and from many perspectives (e.g., as an artist, student, parent, art educator, your young self). When appropriate, include samples of artwork and/or performances.

You may use the exploration outline to guide your exploration. There is a lot to explore here, try to narrow your focus. Remember, you are choosing just one of many explorations that you may conduct.

**Discussion:** Clarify the prompt.

**Presentation:** Consider all options (e.g., a story, photo essay, poem, video, dance).

**Reflection:** Critically respond to others' presentations (when applicable), reflect on the exploration and the readings, and address the following prompt: Discuss ways in which you may be empathetic to socioeconomic differences of others.

*Readings*

Lorde, A. (1984). Age, race, class, and sex: Women redefining difference. In A. Lorde, *Sister/outsider: Essays and speeches* (pp. 114–123). Crossing.

Owens, J. (2013). Chapter 8: Not high school as you remember it. In J. Owens, *Confessions of a bad teacher: The shocking truth from the front lines of American public education* (pp. 127–135). Sourcebooks.

Ravitch, D. (2013). Chapter 10: How poverty affects academic achievement. In D. Ravitch, *Reign of error: The hoax of the privatization movement and the danger to America's public school* (pp. 91–98). Alfred A. Knopf.

Sapp, J. (2009). How school taught me I was poor. *Teaching Tolerance, 35,* 52–55.

## EXPLORATION 5: RELIGION AND MORTALITY

**Exploration:** Explore your religious affiliation(s) or religious identity/identities in relation to mortality (e.g., humanity, death). Explore and reflect on how your religion or absence of religion, along with other (multi)cultural beliefs, customs, and/or practices, or other aspects of your life, may have influenced your outlook on mortality. You may conduct this exploration in various ways (e.g., a children's story, scrapbook, memory box) and from many perspectives (e.g., as an educator, parent, daughter).

You may use the exploration outline to guide your exploration. There is a lot to explore here, try to narrow your focus. Remember, you are choosing just one of many explorations that you may conduct.

**Discussion:** Clarify the prompt.

**Presentation:** Consider all options (e.g., a children's story, scrapbook, memory box, photo essay).

**Reflection:** Critically respond to others' presentations (when applicable), reflect on the exploration and the readings, and address the following prompt: Explain any difficulties you had with the exploration.

*Readings*

Brown, L. K., & Brown, M. (2009). *When dinosaurs die: A guide to understanding death.* Little, Brown, and Company.

González, X. (2017). *All around us.* Cinco Puntos Press.

Rowland, J. (2017). *The memory box: A book about grief.* Sparkhouse Family.

Wilcox, M. (2018). *After life: Ways we think about death.* Orca Book Publishers.

## EXPLORATION 6: GENDER AND/OR SEXUAL ORIENTATION AND VIOLENCE AWARENESS AND PREVENTION

**Exploration:** Explore your gender and/or sexual orientation identity/identities in relation to violence awareness and prevention. Explore and reflect on how your gender and/or sexual orientation identity/identities, along with other (multi)cultural beliefs, customs, and/or practices, or other aspects of your life, may have influenced your understanding of, or experience with, violence awareness and prevention. You may conduct this exploration in various ways (e.g., write a letter, create a poster, attend a Transgender Day of Remembrance (TDOR) event or a Safe Space Training) and from many perspectives (e.g., as a victim of violence, member of the #MeToo movement, trans-woman, member of the LGBTQ community, educator).

You may use the exploration outline to guide your exploration. There is a lot to explore here, try to narrow your focus. Remember, you are choosing just one of many explorations that you may conduct.

**Discussion:** Clarify the prompt.

**Presentation:** Consider all options (e.g., write a letter, create a poster, attend a TDOR event).

**Reflection:** Critically respond to others' presentations (when applicable), reflect on the exploration and the readings, and address the following prompt: Explain any difficulties you had with the exploration.

*Readings*

Anonymous. (2018). "A thank you, with apologies." In L. Bean (Ed.), *Written on the body: Letters from trans and non-binary survivors of sexual assault and domestic violence* (pp. 57–59). Jessica Kingsley Publishers.

Anonymous. (2018). To my humble front entrance. In L. Bean (Ed.), *Written on the body: Letters from trans and non-binary survivors of sexual assault and domestic violence* (pp. 100–103). Jessica Kingsley Publishers.

Anonymous. (2018). Dear body. In L. Bean (Ed.), *Written on the body: Letters from trans and non-binary survivors of sexual assault and domestic violence* (pp. 172–175). Jessica Kingsley Publishers.

Freitag, M. B. (2014). Chapter 17: Safety in Unity: One school's story of identity and community. In E. J. Meyer & D. Carlson (Eds.), *Gender and sexualities in education: A reader* (pp. 230–239). Peter Lang.

Knaier, M. L. (2019). What makes girls and boys so desirable?: STEM education beyond gender binaries. In W. Letts & S. Fifield (Eds.), *STEM of Desire: Queer Theories in Science Education* (pp. 209–221). Koninklijke Brill.

## EXPLORATION 7: RACE AND/OR ETHNICITY AND (HI)STORY AND HERITAGE

**Exploration:** Explore your race and/or ethnic identity/identities in relation to (hi)story and/or heritage. Explore and reflect on how your race and/or ethnicity/ethnicities, along with other (multi)cultural beliefs, customs, and/or practices, or other aspects of your life, may have influenced your understanding of (hi)story and/or heritage. You may conduct this exploration in various ways (e.g., a detailed family tree or photo album, story or poem, lesson plan) and from many perspectives (e.g., as part of your chosen family, as a parent, as an educator).

You may use the exploration outline to guide your exploration. There is a lot to explore here, try to narrow your focus. Remember, you are choosing just one of many explorations that you may conduct.

**Discussion:** Clarify the prompt.

**Presentation:** Consider all options (e.g., a detailed family tree or photo album, a story or poem, a lesson plan).

**Reflection:** Critically respond to others' presentations (when applicable), reflect on the exploration and the readings, and address the following prompt: Explain any difficulties you had with the exploration.

### Readings

Hazzard, D. (2018). Queering Black history and getting free. In D. Watson, J. Hagopian, & W. Au (Eds.)., *Teaching for Black lives* (pp. 325–329). Rethinking Schools.

Nicola, M. (2018). Rethinking identity: Afro-Mexican history. In D. Watson, J. Hagopian, & W. Au (Eds.)., *Teaching for Black lives* (pp. 340–347). Rethinking Schools.

Nodding, N., & Brooks, L. (2017). Chapter five: Race. In N. Noddings & L. Brooks, *Teaching controversial issues: The case for critical thinking and moral commitment in the classroom* (pp. 47–62). Teachers College Press.

## EXPLORATION 8: EXCEPTIONALITY AND DIGITAL TECHNOLOGIES

**Exploration:** Explore your exceptionality identity/identities in relation to your use of digital technologies (e.g., video gaming, social media, learning devices). Explore and reflect on how your exceptionality identity/identities, along with other (multi)cultural beliefs, customs, and/or practices, or other aspects of your life, may have influenced your use of digital technologies (e.g., teaching and learning styles, personal and professional communications, mental well-being). You may conduct this exploration in various ways (e.g., a fictional story, photo essay, demonstration of a task using digital technology) and from many perspectives (e.g., educator, learner, worker).

You may use the exploration outline to guide your exploration. There is a lot to explore here, try to narrow your focus. Remember, you are choosing just one of many explorations that you may conduct.

**Discussion:** Clarify the prompt.

**Presentation:** Consider all options (e.g., a fictional story, a photo essay, demonstration of a task using digital technology).

**Reflection:** Critically respond to others' presentations (when applicable), reflect on the exploration and the readings, and address the following prompt: Explain any difficulties you had with the exploration.

*Readings*

Anders, C. J. (2015). Rat catcher's yellows. In D. H. Wilson & J. J. Adams (Eds.), *Press start to play* (pp. 73–88). Vintage Books.

Bacigalupa, C. (2016). Partnering with families through photo collages. *Early Childhood Education, 44*, 317–323.

Doody, K. R. (2015). GrAPPling with how to teach social skills? Try tapping into digital technology. *Journal of Special Education Technology, 30*(2), 122–127.

## EXPLORATION 9: CREATING A QUEER MULTICULTURAL SOCIAL JUSTICE TEACHING PHILOSOPHY

**Exploration:** Create a teaching philosophy reflective of your experiences of performing these explorations.

**Discussion:** Clarify the prompt.

**Presentation:** Consider all options (e.g., a(n) poem, photo essay, autoethnography, philosophical statements).

**Reflection:** Critically reflect on how performing the *Queer explorations of identity awareness* curriculum influenced your teaching philosophy.

*Readings*

Mayo, C. (2016). Chapter 8: Queer lessons: Sexual and gender minorities in multicultural education. In J. A. Banks & C. A. McGee Banks (Eds.), *Multicultural education: Issues and perspectives* (9th ed.) (pp. 132–148). John Wiley & Sons.

Nieto, S., & Bode, P. (2016). Chapter 14: School reform and student learning: A multicultural perspective. In J. A. Banks & C. A. McGee Banks (Eds.), *Multicultural education: Issues and perspectives* (9th ed.) (pp. 258–274). John Wiley & Sons.

## REFERENCES

Banks, J. A. (2006). *Race, Culture, and Education: The selected works of James A. Banks.* Routledge.

Banks, J. A., & McGee Banks, C. A. (Eds.) (2016). *Multicultural education: Issues and perspectives* (9th ed.). Wiley.

Grant, C. A., & Sleeter, C. E. (2011). *Doing multicultural education for achievement and equity* (2nd ed.). Taylor & Francis.

Nieto, S. (2003). *What keeps teachers going?* Teachers College.

Nieto, S., & Bode, P. (2012). *Affirming diversity: The sociopolitical context of multicultural education* (6th ed.). Pearson.

## ABOUT THE AUTHOR

Dr. Michelle L. Knaier advocates for queer multicultural social justice teacher education—a critical approach that breaks down, and may reach beyond, rigid identity labels—by implementing performative methods such as critical autoethnography, which provide learners with opportunities to investigate ways to dismantle heteronormativity, rethink binary systems of identification, and deconstruct socially constructed identities through personal investigation and story-sharing. Moreover, as a former middle and high school science teacher, she often reflects on her experience while incorporating critical theories into her research on queer(ing) curriculum and when developing her teaching practices. Presently, she is a Limited-time Lecturer with the College of Education at Purdue University. Michelle received her PhD in Curriculum Studies from Purdue University. She also is a graduate of SUNY Cortland, holding a Master of Education in Childhood Education, with an emphasis in Educational Technology: and a Bachelor of Science in Education in Elementary and Early Secondary Education, with an emphasis in Biology.

You may contact Michelle about her work and about using her curriculum at mknaier@purdue.edu or mknaier@hotmail.com.

Made in the USA
Columbia, SC
31 August 2021

44623249R10117